Hacking the PSP™

Cool Hacks, Mods, and Customizations for the Sony® PlayStation® Portable

Auri Rahimzadeh

Wiley Publishing, Inc.

D1473248

Hacking the PSP™: Cool Hacks, Mods, and Customizations for the Sony® PlayStation® Portable

Published by
Wiley Publishing, Inc.
10475 Crosspoint Boulevard
Indianapolis, IN 46256
www.wiley.com

ISBN-13: 978-0-471-77887-5
ISBN-10: 0-471-77887-7

Manufactured in the United States of America

10 9 8 7 6 5 4 3 2

1B/SR/RS/QV/IN

For general information on our other products and services or to obtain technical support, please contact our Customer Care Department within the U.S. at (800) 762-2974, outside the U.S. at (317) 572-3993 or fax (317) 572-4002.

Library of Congress Cataloging-in-Publication Data

Rahimzadeh, Auri, 1975–
  Hacking the PSP : cool hacks, mods and customizations for the Sony PlayStation portable / Auri Rahimzadeh.
    p. cm.
  Includes index.
  ISBN-13: 978-0-471-77887-5 (paper/website)
  ISBN-10: 0-471-77887-7 (paper/website)
  1. Computer games—Programming. 2. Sony video games. I. Title.
  QA76.76.C672R34 2005
  794.8'1526—dc22
                        2005032052

About the Author

Auri Rahimzadeh has been tinkering with computers ever since he was six years old and loves all technology. Auri collects computers and has been involved with many computer projects, including teaching computers alongside Steve Wozniak, co-founder of Apple Computer. Auri has written hundreds of articles on various computer technologies; has contributed to many standards including HDTV, DVD, and interactive television; and is the author of *Geek My Ride*, a book on geeking out cars, another ExtremeTech title also published by Wiley. Auri has also contributed to computer education for students across the country and has promoted technology awareness through the Indianapolis Computer Society, where he has served as president for three years. Currently, Auri is a software engineer and spends his free time programming, chatting at Starbucks, and going to Pacers games.

Credits

Executive Editor
Chris Webb

Development Editor
Howard A. Jones

Senior Development Editor
Kevin Kent

Copy Editor
Kathryn Duggan

Editorial Manager
Mary Beth Wakefield

Production Manager
Tim Tate

Vice President and Executive Group Publisher
Richard Swadley

Vice President and Executive Publisher
Joseph B. Wikert

Project Coordinator
Ryan Steffen

Graphics and Production Specialists
Carrie Foster
Lauren Goddard
Denny Hager
Jennifer Heleine
Stephanie D. Jumper
Barbara Moore
Lynsey Osborn
Melanee Prendergast
Janet Seib
Alicia B. South

Quality Control Technicians
Robert Springer
Brian H. Walls

Proofreading
Sossity R. Smith

Indexing
Johnna VanHoose Dinse

Cover Design
Anthony Bunyan

Acknowledgments

To my family—my Mom and Dad, Karen and Fred; my stepparents, Richard and Julie; and my awesome brothers and sister, Noah, Max, and Chloe. Without their support, this book would never have seen the light of day. Without my Mom and Dad, neither would I.

A special thanks goes to my grandparents, Alvin and Irene Goodman and Rabbi and Devorah Rahimzadeh. Rabbi, even though you're gone, you're always in my heart. I've been lucky to have such caring, loving, inspiring grandparents.

Thanks to Richard Doherty, a brilliant engineer, analyst, and friend, whose insight into the PSP's inner workings is incredible and his willingness to help tech edit my book was very much appreciated. Many thanks again to my good friend Steve Wozniak, not only a brilliant technologist but also the man who believed in me and put my technology career into perspective and who continues to help anyone with a passion for technology succeed with their dreams. Steve, you truly are an amazing human being.

To my friends Josh Louden (for being enthusiastic about programming), Dirk Cosemans (for all his engineering assistance), Geoff Smith (for ideas), the rest of the Smith family (Mary, Doug, Brad, and Emily, for their support), the Millers (Laurie, Phil, and Bryon, for their support and a place to stay in California), Jerry Pournelle (for getting me ever more excited about writing books), Andy Marken of Marken Communications (man, you know communications), Peter Glaskowsky (man, you know graphics), and those of you I failed to mention here, you know who you are (and I'm sure you'll let me know, too!).

To Chris Webb, who got me hooked on writing books—thank you so very, very much. To Howard Jones, my development editor—thanks for all of your hard work and a job well done. And of course, to the incredibly dedicated and hardworking team at Wiley—thank you for all your effort and help in this adventure.

To my friend William "Bill" Fulco—you will be missed.

To my friend Anthony "Tony" Rose—the best attorney, ever (and friend). Sorry I forgot to mention you in my first book.

To the hackers and committed software developers who work so hard to make the PSP an awesome device.

And, of course, to my teachers. To quote a phrase: "If you can read this, thank your teacher."

For those of you looking to get into technology or write your own book, I offer you some advice, originally by Benjamin Franklin (or so all my research on the Internet says): "Never confuse motion with action."

As always—GO PACERS! (Think that'll score me some tickets?)

Contents at a Glance

Contents

Introduction

When I first heard about the PSP, I was ecstatic about the possibilities of having such powerful technology on a portable platform. Here was Sony, inventors of the incredible wizardry that went into the Playstation 2, making a portable version that didn't skimp on features, and in fact was actually *in-tune* with the wants and needs of modern gamers *and* computer geeks! Built-in Wi-Fi, full media playback capabilities, expansion using Memory Sticks instead of some weird, expensive format, a USB 2.0 port — it even played games! Wow, talk about a platform waiting not only to be played, but hacked to all get out. I was the first person in line at midnight at a Game Stop in Indianapolis, Indiana. I plopped down the money, ate a few free doughnuts, and went home to see what my new toy could do.

So here we are, months later, and I've learned so much it's hard to fit it all in a book. In that time I've programmed the PSP, figured out new interesting shortcuts on the device, found ways around limitations of the device, and even bought a second PSP along the way so I could have a guinea pig. And here you are, reading this book wanting to find out how to do the same. Well, let's not waste time — read on and see what possibilities the PSP has in store for you.

What Is Hacking?

Hacking is the action of effective (many times creative) solutions to solving difficult types of problems. Years ago, hacking was considered a good skill to have. It's unfortunate that, these days, with all the viruses, trojans, phishing schemes, operating system vulnerabilities, the list goes on, it's considered bad, and can even label you a criminal. Seventh graders want to learn to "hack" so they can get their l33t warez and songs off bittorrents.

Software and hardware engineers tend to fall into the hacker category, as they come up with ways to make systems do things that were never originally intended. Sure, these "hacks" may get around certain limitations purposefully imposed by the original system developer, but more often than not it's to exploit a system's full capabilities. What geek doesn't want to make their system the baddest, fastest, most awe- and envy-inspiring system ever designed?

in this chapter

☑ **What is hacking?**

☑ **What do you need?**

☑ **Will you void the warranty?**

☑ **How to read this book**

In the PSP, Sony has engineered a true marvel of technology. Combining amazingly powerful data and media processing capabilities with a slim, long-life, portable form factor, Sony has literally started the next generation of media on-the-go. Competitors such as Apple, Creative, iRiver and many others are sure to latch onto the ability to have any type of media, anywhere you go. Add into the equation the power of built-in wireless Internet access, and any number of productivity and media applications, coupled with the high-resolution screen, and the PSP truly becomes a one-stop device.

Unfortunately, Sony has limited the capabilities of the PSP by letting only humongous game companies write applications for it, and letting it play only limited (yet omnipresent) music and media formats with no chance for the grass roots developers, now called "hackers," to write powerful applications and build an industry around the PSP. Many companies have done this before, and hackers have always found a way around it. In this book we'll make the PSP do a lot of the stuff we know it can do.

If you haven't "hacked" before, never fear. I am going to hold your hand through the process, explaining every step. Every chapter is organized so a novice can do the projects, but a professional isn't bored (or, at least, that's what I have tried my best to do). Furthermore, if you have any questions, you can go to the official *Hacking the PSP* Web site at www.hackingpsp.com and post a message on the forums, or e-mail me from that very same site, and I will do my best to answer your questions as thoroughly and expediently as possible.

Note   This book has two Web sites associated with it. The first is www.wiley.com/go/ extremetech, which is the publisher's Web site for ExtremeTech titles. There you can find information about this book; about my other book, *Geek My Ride*; and about all the other great ExtremeTech titles. The other Web site, www.hackingpsp.com, is one I maintain for the book myself. You can contact me through that Web site, and I will strive to post new PSP hacks there as they become available.

What You Need for These Hacks

For the majority of these hacks, any PSP will do. There have been many firmware revisions (also called "system software" revisions) for the PSP. The first PSP, released only in Japan, was version 1.0. The U.S. PSP launched with version 1.5. Updates have been released — versions 1.51, 1.52, and 2.0, among others.

The only sections that are truly affected by firmware versions are the programming chapters, and the ability to run "homebrew" applications that you download from the Internet. There have been hundreds, if not thousands of homebrew applications released, ranging from simple console applications to neat games to PDA-like applications to old game system and Linux emulators.

PSP firmware 1.0 allowed you to run these homebrew applications without any modification. PSP firmware 1.5 attempted to lock out homebrew applications (apparently, Sony doesn't want you running software on your PSP from which they get no royalties). Hackers got around this limitation with a few "exploits" that let you run the homebrew software on the U.S. PSPs, which shipped with only firmware 1.5.

Exploit—A routine that exposes a vulnerability in a piece of software to enable other functionality or execute other code that normally wouldn't be allowed to run.

With a firmware update feature built into the PSP, Sony quickly released a "System Software Update" (version 1.51) that was supposed to "increase the security of the PSP operating system." This was code for "we're gonna stop the hackers with this update." The update appeared to have foiled anybody's attempt to launch homebrew applications from then on until some genius hackers were able to take advantage of an exploit in Sony's PSP operating system and downgrade a version 2.0 PSP to version 1.5. Other attempts have been made to re-enable homebrew applications to run on firmware versions 2.01 and beyond, but as of the writing of this book that had not been completed successfully.

It's always a good idea to update your PSP manually instead of using the built-in update feature. This way, you get to keep the EBOOT.PBP, which is the application that updates your PSP. Should you need that EBOOT again, you will have access to it—otherwise you can't "roll back" should you need to. This is a good practice to get into for any hardware platform you are hacking: only update when you *need* to, and *always* have a backup!

Of course, over one million PSPs have been sold with the 1.5 firmware, so chances are your PSP came with that version. (You learn how to check your firmware version in Chapter 19, "Running Homebrew Applications.) You can also find version 1.5 PSPs in stores that sell used equipment, such as GameStop, EB Games, eBay, and many others. If your PSP came with or you have upgraded to firmware 2.0, which includes a host of new features as well as an official Sony Web browser, you can still downgrade that device to 1.5 using the hack in Chapter 16, "Reverting from a 2.0 PSP to a 1.5 PSP."

Either way, you can enjoy all of the hacks in this book, except the programming hacks, with any version of a PSP. Of course, if you want to program the PSP, I recommend getting a version that can run the hacks, because it's a lot of fun (then again, I'm a software developer).

Another item you should have handy is a USB cable to connect your PSP to your computer (these are usually mini-USB to full-size USB cables, available from any computer or electronics store). The only way to get data on your PSP effectively is through the USB port on the top of the device. Of course, you could use a Memory Stick reader connected to your computer, but the USB cable is much, much easier.

I hope you have a lot of fun with this book. It's been great putting all these hacks to the test, and I've spent the money to learn my lessons so you don't have to. The PSP is a great device, not just a toy, and I hope you get the most out of it by reading and doing everything in this book.

Let's get going!

Regarding Your Warranty

There's no nice way to say it: Some of the hacks in this book may void your PSP's warranty. The majority of the hacks will *not* void your warranty. However, taking apart your PSP, running homebrew software, downgrading your firmware — these hacks are taboo per the warranty. Of course, if you don't tell Sony that's what "bricked" your PSP, they'll probably fix or replace your unit anyway. I have done my best to point out any hacks that may cause potential warranty issues, but it should be pretty obvious that if you try to change the inner workings of your device, you're likely voiding the warranty (but hey, that's half the fun, right?).

 Bricked — The action of killing your PSP, making it the equivalent of a $250 brick.

How to Read This Book

I've written this book so you can turn directly to any project and get started. Pick your fancy — if you want to start moving video to your PSP, check out Chapter 10, "Video Hacks." If you want to get started in PSP programming, head on over to Chapter 17, "Programming the PSP: Setting Up the Development Environment." All chapters with projects that require equipment beyond your PSP will give you a shopping list so you have everything before you start.

How This Book Is Organized

Here's an overview of how I've grouped related hacks in this book. Feel free to skip around as much as you like — I've written this book to be flexible so you can start pretty much anywhere. However, with the programming chapters, I suggest you start with Chapter 17, which covers setting up your development environment, just to make sure you cover all the bases (as you should do when learning any programming language).

Keep in mind that new hacks come out all the time. I will do my best to put new hacks up on the official *Hacking the PSP* Web site at www.hackingpsp.com so you can dive even deeper into making your PSP perform ever-cooler feats.

Networking Hacks

This section of the book covers hacking the PSP to enable Web browsing, using instant messaging and RSS applications on your PSP, increasing the speed of your Internet surfing and wireless multiplayer gaming, and more.

Audio Hacks

This section goes over the PSP's powerful audio capabilities, including how to get the best results when moving audio to the PSP, using your PSP like an iPod shuffle, synchronizing your music collection with your PSP, and much more.

Video Hacks

Your PSP is an awesome movie machine. This chapter tells you how to get the most video enjoyment out of your PSP—from UMD-Video discs to movies you put on a Memory Stick. From putting your TiVo and ReplayTV shows on your PSP to tips on conversion and more, you'll find what you want to know about Video and your PSP in this section.

Image Hacks

Share your images, view comic strips, take your documents with you—learn how to leverage the image viewing capabilities of your PSP to maximize fun!

Game Hacks

Use a single UMD cartridge for multiplayer instead of requiring a copy for every PSP, back up and restore your games, change your game backgrounds, and more!

Homebrew Applications and Programming

Don't let the title scare you—even if you've never programmed before you'll get something out of this section. I walk you through how to run the hundreds, if not thousands, of applications freely available for download all over the Internet. I even teach you how to write your own applications, how to share them with your friends, and where to go for more information.

Appendixes

Following the project chapters are the appendixes. Appendix A includes Web sites for learning more about PSP development and getting games and utilities, forum sites and blogs, and third-party hack and add-on manufacturers, as well as how to contact Sony technical support. Appendix B covers what to do when something goes wrong. I've also included a Frequently Asked Questions section so you can quickly find answers to common questions, such as where to find UMD repair tools, how to find replacement LCD screens and motherboards, and even how to save your PSP after you've spilled Red Bull or Bawls on it.

Conventions Used in This Book

As you read through the book, you'll see various icons to alert you to notes of interest, cautions, warnings, tips, and other helpful recommendations. The following are some examples of the various icons used throughout the book.

These icons pertain to items of interest related to the subject at hand. Although you can safely skip these, I recommend that you read them at your leisure.

These are recommendations of best-practice methods, ways to save time or money, and information on the best approaches to this book's projects.

Terms used by hackers that may be new to you are defined when they are first introduced in the text.

These give you valuable information that helps you avoid making serious mistakes in performing various steps. Although Cautions are not as serious as Warnings, you should pay heed to these, so that you don't experience equipment malfunctions or other related frustrations.

Warnings contain important information you should read. The information in warnings will help keep you out of trouble, such as protecting your PSP from damage and warranty concerns, losing data, and possibly even save you from getting arrested.

Overview of the PSP

It's always good to know the specifications of the system you're about to hack. Let's go over what Sony likely has planned for the PSP, what makes it tick, and what makes it so cool.

Sony's PSP Strategy

With the PSP, Sony is not just going for the wanna-play-all-the-time-gimme-awesome-graphics gamer. Instead, their focus is on a great gaming device that can do "everything else" and attracts the young, the teens, the twenty-somethings, and older audiences. Younger audiences will want the games and movies, while older audiences, through a brilliant "buy UMD movies everywhere and play media anywhere" strategy, will buy the unit as a portable movie player and media device. When the Playstation 3 comes out, Sony will integrate the media capabilities of the PSP with Playstation 3's media center focus and extend the "media anywhere" gaming and media solution. Coupled with the wireless Internet capabilities, Sony could potentially deliver home media stored on a Playstation 3 (or other Sony devices) to the PSP anywhere you can get Wi-Fi access. Pretty cool, huh?

Full Technical Specifications of the PSP

Here are the fairly official technical specifications of Sony's flagship handheld:

- **Size:** 170 mm (6.7 in) in length, 74 mm (2.9 in) in width, and 23 mm (0.9 in) in depth, weighs 280g / .62 lbs (Source: Wikipedia)

- **Processor:** 32-bit MIPS "R4000" 4KE or 24KE, dual-core. Primary core is for standard system functions, including hardware-based data decryption. Second core, called the "Virtual Mobile Engine," is for graphics processing, including native H.264 decoding.

    - Speed: 1-333 MHz (although Sony has made mention to a cap of 222 MHz to conserve battery life)

Note Programmers can get around the 222 MHz barrier in code.

    - Runs on 0.8 to 1.2 volts

    - Designed using a 90-nanometer process

- **Graphics:** Runs at 166 MHz, reconfigurable to handle particular processing tasks.

    - 2 megabytes video memory

    - Supports a maximum of 33 million polygons/second, although the effective polygon performance is likely much lower (many critics don't like the "max" polygons rating because it excludes the use of effects like lighting, fog, and so forth)

    - 664 million pixels/second maximum fill rate

    - 512-bit interface

    - Supports 16-bit and 32-bit color modes (32,768 colors and 16.77 million colors)

- **Audio:** Supports Stereo sound, Dolby Headphone sound. Supports playback of WAV, ATRAC and MP3 (MPEG-1 Audio Layer 3) audio in Firmware 1.0 and 1.5, and adds AAC (MPEG-4) audio in Firmware 2.0.

- **Display:** 4.3" (diagonal) 480 × 272 Widescreen display, 16:9 aspect ratio, just like widescreen DVDs and HDTV

- **RAM:** 32MB of RAM. 4MB of DRAM; half (2MB) is connected to the main core, and the other 2MB is for media processing functions.

- **Storage: The PSP has the following storage capabilities:**

    - Sony Memory Stick Duo slot takes only Memory Stick Duo media (although Chapter 3, "Quickies," covers using standard Memory Stick media, which is usually cheaper).

    - UMD discs support up to 1.8GBeach and basically any type of data. Official formats include UMD-Game, UMD-Video, and UMD-Music. This appears to be based on Sony's MiniDisc format.

    - USB 2.0 port supports data transfers up to 480 megabits/second.

    - Supports sharing of files on inserted Memory Stick with a USB-capable computer.

- **Power:** Includes 1800 mAh Lithium Ion (LIon) battery, provides 4–6 hours of battery life (Sony offers an official 220 mAh battery as well, and third parties such as Datel have batteries providing 3600 mAh).

    - A/C charger included with package yields 2000 mAh

    - Capable of charging using power provided via a computer's USB 2.0 port

- **Networking:** Built-in 802.11b (11 megabits/second max throughput) wireless supports both ad hoc (computer-to-computer) and infrastructure (device-to-access point) modes.

    - IrDA (Infrared Data Association) line-of-sight communications

    - IR Remote (SIRCS compliant), although no "official" remote control software was available at the time this book went to press

    - Potential to use USB port for other networking devices, should they ever be released

- **Navigation system:** Uses Sony's XMB, or *Cross Media Bar*, interface, used in some Sony TVs and their PSX product. (I call this the "PSP Navigator" in this book.)

- **Region coding:** Supports region coding of games, music, movies, and photos on UMD discs, similar to how DVDs do the same thing to prevent media use in other regions of the world.

Video Capabilities

Everything considered, the PSP's graphic capabilities are roughly the equivalent of the PS2. But how can that be? Well, the PSP's 480 × 272 maximum resolution is quite a bit less than a PS2's 1280 × 1024, but its rendering capabilities for the 480 × 272 resolution match what the PS2 can do at 1280 × 1024. So what does this mean to you? It means PS2 games should easily be ported to the PSP, and the graphics should be similar if not identical. Take a look at Table 2-1.

Table 2-1   The PSP's graphics capabilities compared to modern-day consoles and handhelds

Game system	Max # of polygons/sec.	Max resolution	Max colors	Video memory (VRAM)	Main Memory (RAM)
PSP	~33,000,000 (likely much less with lights, fog, and so forth)	480 × 272	16.77 million	2MB	32MB
PS2	~75,000,000 (likely only ~13,000,000 with lights, fog, and so forth, according to Wikipedia)	1280 × 1024	16.77 million	4MB	32MB
Xbox	~116,500,000 (likely much less with lights, fog, and so forth)	1920 × 1080	16.77 million	Up to 64MB (shared with main memory using shared-memory architecture)	64MB

Continued

Table 2-1 *(continued)*

Game system	Max # of polygons/sec.	Max resolution	Max colors	Video memory (VRAM)	Main Memory (RAM)
Game Boy DS	~120,000 (likely much less with lights, fog, and so forth)	256 × 192	262,144	656KB	4MB
Game Boy Advance	Not applicable, no 3D acceleration	240 × 160	511 colors on screen at once out of 32,768 colors (16-bit)	96KB	256KB

Battery Life

Compared to other portable gaming systems, the PSP is not only more powerful, it's also more power hungry. Indeed, with a 333 MHz processor, ultra-bright widescreen color display, wireless networking, and an optical UMD drive to run, the battery is working overtime to make sure you stay entertained for hours on end. Thankfully, Sony has included a rechargeable 1800 mAh Lithium Ion battery to help out — normal alkaline batteries wouldn't survive the load for long and would be darn expensive to replace all the time.

On a full charge, you will get (and independent organizations have confirmed this) up to six hours of battery life when playing video games, and up to four hours for movies. This is assuming you're running the screen at half intensity and half volume with wireless off. I tend to run with the brightness and volume all the way up, so take about 10 percent off that figure if you play the same way. To see how other portable game systems, such as Nintendo's Game Boy stack up in the battery-life arena, see Table 2-2.

Table 2-2   Approximate battery life of modern (2005) game systems

System	Approx. battery life
Game Boy Advance	15 hours
Game Boy Color	10 hours
Game Boy DS	6–10 hours
PSP	6 hours

Networking Capabilities

Excluding games on PDAs and cell phones, the PSP is the only mass-market game system ever shipped with robust networking capabilities: 802.11b wireless, IrDA, and a Web browser (in firmware 2.0 and above). The PSP can also update itself over the Internet, making it the first mass-market handheld product with a network update function, similar to Microsoft's Windows Update feature and Apple's Software Update function.

PSP Firmware Versions and Why They Matter

The PSP has a "flashable" firmware, meaning it can be updated with bug fixes, and upgraded with new capabilities. This enables Sony to support new technologies as they emerge, address vulnerabilities in the PSP software (such as Web browser and buffer overrun vulnerabilities), and keep the product competitive as the market evolves. Unfortunately for us hackers, Sony removed the ability to program the PSP on our own starting with the 1.51 "update," which featured "security updates" — just another way of saying "we don't want software developers." Of course, you don't have to update to run most games on your 1.0 or 1.5 firmware PSP, and there are utilities, such as the WAB Version Changer (available from the official *Hacking the PSP* Web site) to get around such issues. Chapter 16, "Reverting from a 2.0 PSP to a 1.5 PSP," discusses how to downgrade a firmware 2.0 PSP (not 2.01 or higher) back to version 1.5.

If you are not going to program the PSP, the upgrades from Sony can be quite a boon. With firmware update 2.0, officially named System Software 2.0, Sony added a Web browser, enhanced wireless network access (supporting additional encryption technologies such as WPA and PSK), and support for MPEG-4, or AAC, audio files. These new features greatly enhanced the PSP's already impressive media capabilities. If you want to program a 1.5 PSP and still have these capabilities, I suggest acquiring two PSPs (if your wallet stretches that far), or running the hack in Chapter 16.

Note New hacks come out all the time. If a solution for running homebrew apps on firmware 2.01 and higher emerges, I will post it on the official *Hacking the PSP* Web site at www. hackingpsp.com.

Tip Always keep your update EBOOT.PBP files so you can use them again later if necessary. Chapters 16 and 19 explain EBOOT.PBP files and their use in more detail.

Table 2-3 shows the features enabled by the various Sony firmware updates since version 1.0.

Table 2-3 PSP firmware feature sets

Firmware version	Capabilities
1.0	Original Japanese release.
1.5	Original U.S. release. Added copy protection, disabling the native ability to run homebrew applications. The KXploit, covered in Chapter 19, "Running Homebrew Applications," handles running these applications on this firmware. A notable change in the U.S. version: the X and O button functionality was reversed (O goes back and X is select, whereas it was the opposite in Japan).
1.51	Added "security updates," which simply disabled the KXploit's ability to run. No games required the 1.51 update. If you have a game that requires 1.51, and you have 1.5, you can use the WAB Version Changer to trick the PSP into thinking it's running 1.51.
1.52	Added "security updates" as well as UMD Music support. No games appeared to require the 1.52 update. If you have a game that requires 1.52, and you have 1.5, you can use the WAB Version Changer to trick the PSP into thinking it's running 1.52.
2.0	Added a Web browser, MPEG-4 audio support and additional image format (TIFF, GIF, PNG and BMP/Bitmap) support. New video playback capabilities were added, including a "Go To" format and 4:3 "Full Frame" video playback mode. Personalizaiton features were added, including the ability to change the color of the background and to add a wallpaper, or background image. Also provided additional "security updates" and some new operating-system functionality. Some games check for the existance 2.0 firmware. At the time of this book's publication, a hack was not readily available to reliably run homebrew applications on firmware 2.0. More information about this massive update is available on Sony's Web site.

UMD, the "Universal" Media Disc

UMD, or Universal Media Disc, is the official distributed media format for the PSP. You can use Memory Stick Duo media (and standard Memory Sticks as well, which is discussed in the next chapter); however, most PSP games utilize UMD discs, which for the time being cannot be copied (although it is possible to "dump" their contents to the Memory Stick using certain utilities this book does not discuss).

UMDs are optical discs that can hold up to 1.8GB of any type of data, just like a DVD or CD. The "official" UMD formats are UMD Game, UMD Music, and UMD Video. In addition to game distribution houses, Sony has licensed a number of movie studios (such as Universal, Paramount, and New Line Home Cinema) to release UMD Video titles. Sony has also discussed submitting the format for standardization, but this seems unlikely for the near future, as control over the recorders would become an issue due to piracy.

Piracy is likely the reason for the proprietary UMD format, plus the fact that it appears to be based on the HiMD MiniDisc media format, a product Sony failed to bring to successful mass-market penetration many years ago. Hackers have already figured out a way to dump the data from a UMD to a CD or DVD, but Sony attempted to stop this type of copyright infringement in firmware update 1.51.

Here are the specifications for the UMD media format (source: Wikipedia, `http://en.wikipedia.org/wiki/Universal_Media_Disc`):

- ECMA (an international standards body) standard number ECMA-365: Data Interchange on 60 mm Read-Only ODC (optical disc cartridge). More information on the standard can be found at `http://www.ecma-international.org/publications/standards/Ecma-365.htm`.

- Capacity: 1.8 GB (UMD)

- Dimensions: Approx. 65 mm (W) × 64 mm (D) × 4.2 mm (H)

- Diameter: 60 mm

- Maximum capacity: 1.80GB (single-sided, dual layer)

- Laser wavelength: 660 nm (red laser)

- Encryption: AES 128-bit (decryption of which is built into the PSP's hardware)

- Conforms to ISO-9660 file format, the same as CDs and DVDs.

- A good site to discuss the UMD format is UMD Talk, `http://www.umdtalk.co.uk`.

Summary

In this chapter we went over what makes the PSP tick, and why it's so darn cool in so many ways. Now that you (hopefully) appreciate the fundamentals of the system, let's get to hacking!

Quickies

Just to whet your appetite, let's get started with these simple, yet incredibly useful, hacks.

Using Non-Duo Memory Sticks

Don't want to shell out all that extra cash for a Memory Stick Duo when the full size Memory Sticks are on sale all the time? Here's your answer: retrofit an adapter to work with your PSP. This hack works for both standard full-size Memory Sticks and full-size Memory Stick Pros.

Note In a funny sort of way, you can also stick your Memory Stick Duo into the full-size Memory Stick adapter included with most Duos and use your Memory Stick Duo in this adapter. Fairly worthless, but a funny trick.

There is another path, my young Jedi — there are adapters for sale on the Internet that do the same thing. Go to the PSP-Hardware Web site at `http://psp-hardware.com` to buy one if you don't want to build it yourself.

I must give credit where credit is due. The first person to report this was "ZMcNulty" on the PSP Vault Web site at `http://psp-vault.com`.

Here's what you need to do this hack:

- Expansys Memory Stick Expansion Jacket ($30 from `http://www.expansys-usa.com/product.asp?code=P800_MSEXP`)
- Memory Sticks you want to use
- A Dremel with a sanding bit (bit usually comes with the Dremel; see Figure 3-1)

FIGURE 3-1: Dremel sanding bit

Note The PSP appears to be limited to using Memory Sticks (including Memory Stick Duo) up to 2GB. Anything beyond that it may not support, so verify that the Memory Stick you purchase is compatible with your PSP before you spend good money on something you can't use.

Step 1: Sand Down the Duo Connector So It Fits Properly in the PSP

The Expansys jacket has two main components:

- The adapter that holds the standard Memory Stick
- The ribbon cable that has the Memory Stick Duo connector for use in your PSP

Right now you need to work with the ribbon cable and its adapter. Unfortunately, the adapter has a small piece of metal that prevents it from fitting in the PSP's Memory Stick Duo slot, so you need to dremel it down a bit. Using a sanding bit on a Dremel (it is round and looks like sandpaper and usually comes with the dremel), you need to remove the metal near the slanted ridge, as shown in Figure 3-2. Just do a little at a time, and then it should fit fairly snugly in your PSP. You should even be able to close the PSP's protective door, shown in Figure 3-3.

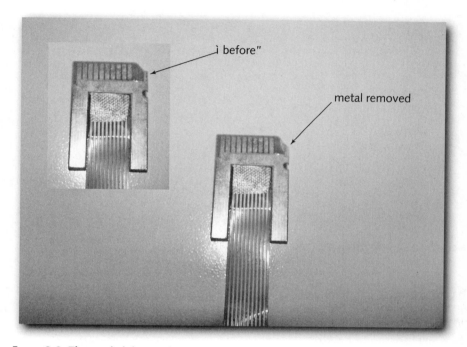

FIGURE 3-2: The sanded down adapter

FIGURE 3-3: The adapter in the PSP's Memory Stick Duo slot

Step 2: Attach the Adapter Ribbon Wire to the Memory Stick Adapter Case

Now you have to attach the ribbon cable to the standard Memory Stick adapter casing. The ribbon cable connects to the adapter's circuit board using a ribbon cable holder. This is easier than it looks. Just follow these steps:

1. Gently pull the black tabs on the ribbon cable connector out about 4 millimeters (basically, as far as they'll come out with some gentle rocking).

2. Insert the ribbon cable with the metal connectors up, with slight pressure to get the ribbon all the way into the connector.

3. Move the tabs back into place to secure the cable.

You can see the result in Figure 3-4.

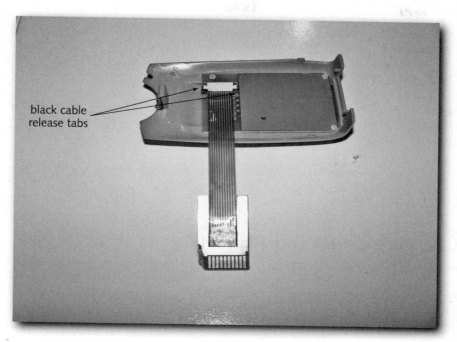

black cable
release tabs

FIGURE 3-4: The ribbon cable properly connected

Step 3: Use the Memory Stick

Now you should be able to insert any Memory Stick into your adapter case and it should work fine. You can also retrofit the case as you see fit, because most of the plastic and circuit board isn't necessary, so cutting down the board isn't a bad idea if you know what you're doing.

Viewing eBooks on Your PSP

Even though there is no "official" eBook reader for the PSP, you can still attempt to transfer text files, word documents, PDFs, eBooks, and more to the PSP just by "printing" them out as images. There are a few different approaches to this, of course:

- Use the PSP's image viewer to view the pages of your book using an image builder such as PaperlessPrinter or JPEGBook. The benefit to this approach is you can use it anywhere, because all you need is a Memory Stick with your "book" on it. The drawback is the books are huge.

- Hack the Web browser in Wipeout Pure to show your book as HTML, with graphics and everything. Hacking Wipeout's Web browser is explained in Chapter 6, "The Web on Your PSP." The benefit here is you can view the book with its graphics without using a lot of space on a Memory Stick, because you can just serve the individual chapters, pages, or whatever sections of the book you like with your Web server.

Note

With the hardware RSA decryption and its fast processor and highly readable display, the PSP is well prepared for a developer to write an eBook reader for it. Time will tell.

Tip

You can use the Paperless Printer and JPEGBook products to convert any document into a file viewable on your PSP, not just eBooks.

Converting eBooks with PaperlessPrinter or JPEGBook

You can use either the PaperlessPrinter or JPEGBook program to convert text documents to images for viewing on your PSP. However, JPEGBook supports only text documents, so if you want to convert any other type of document, you'll have to use PaperlessPrinter. If you have a Mac, you're pretty much stuck with JPEGBook (available from http://www.fumi2kick.com/jpegbook/).

Here's what you need:

- PaperlessPrinter (free, download it from http://www.rarefind.com/paperlessprinter/downloads.html).

- An eBook or other similar document that allows printing. (Some eBooks, PDFs, and even Microsoft Office documents don't allow printing because of security concerns. Of course, there may be applications out there that remove such flags, but who knows.)

- A Memory Stick capable of holding the converted pages. Assume 15k per page at high quality, and 4k per page at low quality.

Step 1: Transfer the eBook

Now that you have what you need, transfer the eBook you want to print.

Step 2: Install PaperlessPrinter

This step is fairly self-explanatory. Download the software, and then install it. PaperlessPrinter shows up as an available printer in any print dialog box, so you use it like any other printer, except its output isn't on paper. Its files represent pages of your document.

Step 3: Open the eBook or Document in Its Appropriate Reader

Open your eBook or document in its appropriate reader. This usually involves just double-clicking it as you normally would.

Step 4: Configure PaperlessPrinter to Print the Document

Once the program has opened, go to its File menu and select Page Setup (or Printer Setup, or a similar printer configuration option). When the setup box comes up, select the PaperlessPrinter icon or list item (see Figure 3-5), and click Properties. When the Preferences window comes up, click the Settings tab, and then set the Page Size to Custom, and 3.5 × 11 inches, as shown in Figure 3-6.

FIGURE 3-5: The PaperlessPrinter icon in the Page Setup box

FIGURE 3-6: Setting the custom paper size

Note In Microsoft Office applications, the process is a bit different. Instead of going to Page Setup, you select Print, select the PaperlessPrinter in the Print dialog box, click Properties, and then select Close instead of Print, as shown in Figure 3-7.

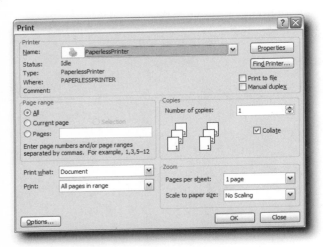

FIGURE 3-7: The Print box in Microsoft Office with the Close option

Step 5: Print the Document

Now that everything's configured, select File, then Print, and make sure Paperless Printer is still selected (it should be).

When you click Print, you are given a list of the formats you can save your document in (see Figure 3-8). Select JPEG and click OK. Then slide the quality to 40 percent (which should be good enough for easy reading, but you can always adjust this to your tastes), and make sure you save everything in gray scale unless you really need color.

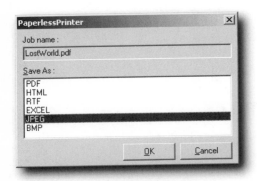

FIGURE 3-8: The image format selection dialog box

When the Save dialog box appears, save the resulting documents in a folder with the name of the eBook or document you are transferring (see Figure 3-9). There may be a lot of images, so it's important you keep them organized. Printing can take about one minute for every 100 pages (or less on faster systems), so be prepared to wait.

FIGURE 3-9: The image tuning settings dialog box

Step 6: Copy the Images to Your Memory Stick

Connect your PSP via USB and copy the entire directory of images you created with PaperlessPrinter from your PC to the PSP \ PHOTO directory on your PSP. Do *not* copy the files individually — copy the entire folder by dragging it onto your PSP, as shown in Figure 3-10. The reason you want to transfer the directory all at once is the files are timestamped, and the PSP shows files in timestamp order, not filename order — so you don't want your pages to be out of whack!

Step 7: View the eBook

Now that the images are on your PSP, fire it up, select Photo in Navigator and read your book (see Figure 3-11).

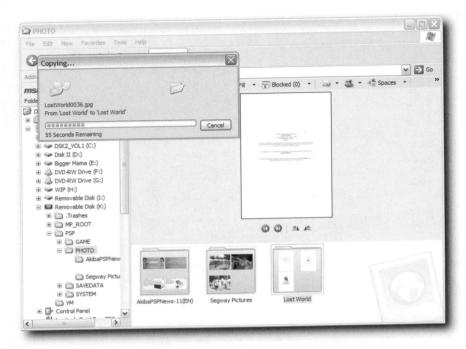

FIGURE 3-10: Copy the converted eBook to your PSP

FIGURE 3-11: Viewing the eBook on your PSP

The PSP as a Storage Device

Armed with a Memory Stick and a PSP with an appropriate USB cable, the PSP can be used to save any sort of data file, ultimately becoming a very large "thumb" drive. The PSP ships with USB 2.0, so transferring your movies will happen at speeds (up to) 440 Mbps (megabits per second), and your capacity is only limited by the Memory Stick you have. If you don't want to carry a bunch of thumb drives, just take your PSP with you and a decent size Memory Stick Duo and you can play games and transfer files, without carrying any extra equipment.

Here's what you need:

- A Memory Stick in your PSP's Memory Stick slot
- A USB to mini-USB cable (about $10 from any computer store; see Figure 3-12)
- A computer (Mac, PC, and Linux should work fine; no drivers required)

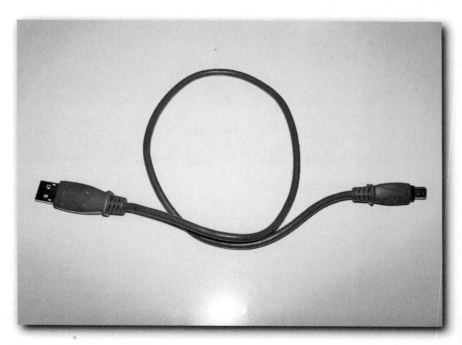

FIGURE 3-12: A mini-USB to full-size USB cable

Follow these steps to turn on the USB data transfer function:

1. Plug the mini-USB end of your USB cable into your PSP (see Figure 3-13) and the other end into your computer.

FIGURE 3-13: The USB port on the PSP

2. Go to Settings in Navigator.
3. Select USB Connection and press .

Your drive appears on your computer desktop.

 Don't delete any of the folders that exist on your memory card that you didn't create yourself. Removing those can erase your saved game data, among other settings the PSP needs on that Memory Stick.

Syncing the PSP with Your Computer

A number of utilities have emerged that automatically sync your PSP's saved game data, music, music, photos, movies, and even Web site bookmarks. These products include iPSP, PSPWare, PSP Sync, PSP Video 9, Browser 2 PSP (I wrote that one), and a number of others. iPSP and PSPWare are the most popular "all around syncing" utilities, while PSP Video 9 is the most popular video conversion and sync product (plus it's free). I cover these products in detail in Chapter 10, "Video Hacks," and Chapter 23, "Synchronization and Utility Software."

You don't have to use a program to move data from your PC to your PSP or vice versa. Using the PSP's built-in USB connection capability, you can back up your games, transfer music, images, and video back and forth, and even transfer your Web bookmarks. Of course, it's a little more difficult because you have to do all the manual work, and the utilities I discuss do a lot of the work for you automatically, but it's fairly simple if you don't want to install additional software on your machine.

Should you decide to do everything manually, Table 3-1 points out the locations to put different types of media on your PSP's Memory Stick, and where you can find certain PSP data.

Table 3-1   PSP media locations

Media type	Location
Video	MP_ROOT \ 100MNV01
Audio	PSP \ MUSIC
Photos	PSP \ PHOTO
Games	PSP \ GAME
Saved games	PSP \ SAVEDATA
Browser data	PSP \ SYSTEM \ BROWSER
Shared data (usually the default location for Web browser downloads)	PSP \ SHARED

Changing the PSP's Background Color and Wallpaper Image

You know that background color for Navigator screens that seems to magically change every once in a while? Well, the truth is it's keyed on the PSP's date settings. To change your background color, simply change the date on your PSP, like this:

1. Go to Settings.

2. Go to Date and Time Settings.

3. Change the month in the date (see Table 3-2 for a list of colors).

Table 3-2 Month colors on the PSP

Month	Background color
January	Silver
February	Light Gold
March	Lime Green
April	Pink
May	Green
June	Periwinkle Blue
July	Sky Blue
August	Pure Blue + Sky Blue (it's mixed)
September	Purple
October	Gold
November	Bronze
December	Red

New Background Features in Firmware 2.0

With Firmware 2.0 (a.k.a. System Update 2.0), Sony introduced the ability to change the background color to any of the colors mentioned in Table 3-2, although it's possible that future firmware versions may let you choose *any* color. You can even set a photo to be your background, or wallpaper, image if you have images on your Memory Stick.

To change your background color, open the PSP Navigator and select Settings, then Theme Settings, then Theme, and set your background color by pressing X on the color of your choice. If you change the setting back to Original, it will go back to the monthly color changing scheme.

Changing Your Wallpaper

To set your wallpaper image, open the PSP Navigator, select Photo, and then select the image you want as your wallpaper (background image) by pressing X on the selected image. When the image is displayed, press TRIANGLE, and select the icon for "Set as Wallpaper" and press X. Select Yes when your PSP asks you if you want it to set the image as the wallpaper. Then press O when it says "Save completed" and your wallpaper is set.

To disable your wallpaper, open the PSP Navigator and select Settings, then Theme Settings, and then Wallpaper. Change the option from Use to Do Not Use to turn off your wallpaper. You can set it to Use to turn it back on again. After turning off your wallpaper, your background color reappears.

Warning If you want to do homebrew software development on your PSP, do *not* upgrade to firmware 1.51 or later, or you'll lose the ability to code for your PSP.

Saving Xbox Games on Your PSP

This is a funny hack, considering how Sony and Microsoft are bitter rivals in the game console market. Using the PSP's USB connectivity, and the Xbox's ability to recognize USB storage devices, you can use the Memory Stick in your PSP as a game-saving tool.

Don't worry; even though this hack formats your Memory Stick, it won't affect your PSP's internals at all. You're not risking your PSP by plugging it into an Xbox.

Here's what you need:

- Microsoft Phantasy Star Online Keyboard Adapter or Xbox Controller USB Adapter (see Figures 3-14 and 3-15), which are available on eBay

FIGURE 3-14: The Phantasy Star Online Keyboard Adapter

FIGURE 3-15: The Xbox Controller USB Adapter

- A Memory Stick you don't care about, like the 32MB one that shipped with the PSP Value Pack (it will be erased by this operation, but you can still use it again by formatting it on the PSP)

- An appropriate USB cable (mini-USB to full-size USB)

- An Xbox and games you want to save data for

You may also need a USB gender-bender, taking the PSP connector from male to female, which is shown in Figure 3-16. This depends on what the adapter's USB connection looks like. Most likely you won't need it, but if you do you can pick it up at any CompUSA, Fry's, Best Buy, or other computer store.

Tip The Phantasy Star Online Keyboard Adapter has been discontinued by Microsoft. However, if you cannot find one online, you can still get a USB adapter that plugs into the front of your Xbox. The only drawback to this is you have to sacrifice a controller port, so no 4-player games if you want to save on the PSP. The Phantasy Star Online Keyboard Adapter, on the other hand, plugs into any Xbox controller. You're likely not saving 4-player games on your PSP, of course, so this shouldn't be a problem. When you're done with the save, simply unplug the PSP. When you need it again, just plug it back in.

FIGURE 3-16: A USB gender-bender

Warning Using the PSP as an Xbox game saving device makes the Memory Stick unusable in the PSP. To use the Memory Stick in your PSP again, you have to format it with the PSP's format utility.

Step 1: Get to the Save Game Point in an Xbox Game

The first step is to find an Xbox game and get to the point where it will let you save a game. I chose Halo, but you can choose whatever you want. You actually don't *have* to have a game in there — you can just use the Xbox's configuration menu's storage devices (which are also called *Memory Units* on the Xbox) section.

Step 2: Plug Your PSP into the Xbox USB Adapter

Now that you're ready to save your game, plug your PSP into the Xbox USB adapter using the adapter and the USB cable, as shown in Figure 3-17.

Note Microsoft's Xbox runs a modified version of the Windows 2000 operating system, and the Xbox's controller ports are all USB-based, so that's why this hack works.

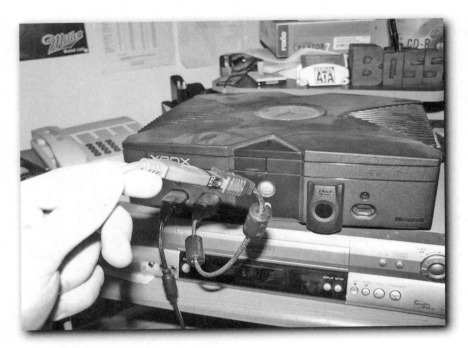

FIGURE 3-17: Connecting the Xbox adapter

Step 3: Put Your PSP in USB Connection Mode

Place your PSP in USB Connection Mode by using the PSP Navigator to open Settings, then USB Connection. Your Xbox should detect the PSP as a memory card and display an error message, as shown in Figure 3-18.

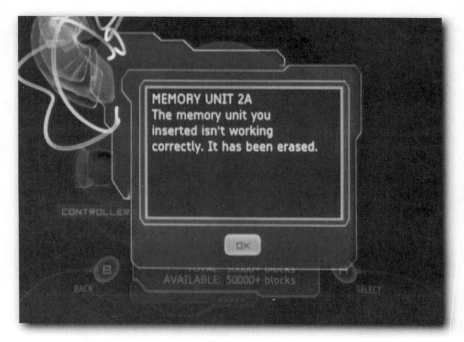

FIGURE 3-18: The Xbox informing you it has formatted your Memory Stick for use

Step 4: Save

Press A on your Xbox controller to continue and you see your hard disk and the new Memory Stick, ready for game saving action! Figure 3-19 shows you what this should look like. Now, simply save your game and you're all set. This is quite convenient if you want to take game saves between your friends' houses and don't want to plunk down the money for the Xbox Memory Units.

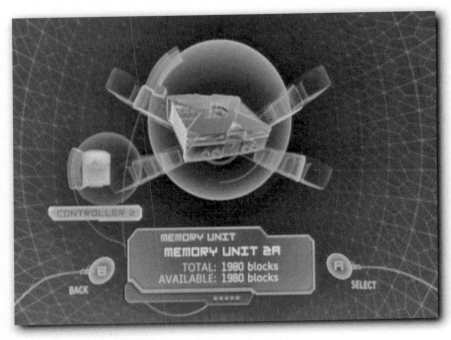

FIGURE 3-19: The PSP shows up as a storage device on the Xbox

Preventing Screen Glare

One of my pet peeves about the PSP is it is hardly usable outside in the daytime. If the sun is shining, you just can't see the screen. Of course, this shouldn't be a problem, because the PSP sports a "fully transparent" display, but apparently it's poorly implemented. The backlight helps to cancel the sunlight a little bit, but it's still hard to play. So what do you do?

What you need are a PSP case to block the sun and a protective screen cover to prevent glare off the PSP's very, very shiny display. Luckily, for under $30 you can resolve the issue.

Pick up a Logitech PlayGear Pocket (see Figure 3-20) case and the Pelican screen guards (see Figure 3-21). The Pelican screen guards serve two purposes. One, they greatly reduce glare. Two, they protect your PSP's screen from unsightly scratches.

FIGURE 3-20: The Logitech PlayGear Pocket

FIGURE 3-21: Pelican screen guards

Summary

In this chapter you did a lot of hacks. From using non-Duo Memory Sticks to customizing your PSP's background color and wallpaper image, to viewing eBooks, to even saving Xbox games, you can see how the PSP's capabilities go far beyond just gaming. Now that you've whetted your hacking appetite, let's move on to some more involved hacks.

Taking Apart Your PSP

Taking apart your PSP is a fragile, not infallible process. The parts are stamped on or connected to the motherboard by machines, and then never touched again. This means loose solder, poorly connected or cheap wires, and irreplaceable parts may be damaged even if you do nothing wrong, so be prepared to forfeit your $250 investment! Of course, while I always encourage exploration, you can still safely read this whole chapter without taking a screwdriver to your PSP.

Warning Opening your PSP is strictly verboten in the manual, and thus voids your warranty.

You don't have to take your PSP all the way apart. Once you get the screen removed is where the really delicate parts come into play. However, if you ever need to replace the screen or degunk keys, you can do so without ever going beyond the screen removal step, giving you the ability to repair your PSP's screen and buttons by yourself, and send it back to Sony if you need to go deeper than the screen (it's cheaper to send the PSP to Sony for hardware repair than to risk voiding the warranty).

Getting Replacement Parts

Sometimes sending your unit back to Sony is not an option. For example, you may be out of warranty, or you don't want your unit to be swapped for a new, non-programmable version. If you need to find a new motherboard, a new LCD screen, or possibly even a new optical drive unit, there are a number of places selling parts a la carte. Look in Appendix A, "Additional Resources," for a list of hardware distributors so you can get the parts you need.

Opening Up Your PSP and Removing Parts

The following hack tells you, step-by-step, how to open up and remove the main parts of your PSP. To put your PSP back together, just perform these steps in reverse order.

What You Need

You'll need a number of items for this venture:

- A precision flat-blade screwdriver with a thin shaft and preferably with a magnetic tip ($20 in a set at Fry's, CompUSA, or any hardware store, as shown in Figure 4-1)

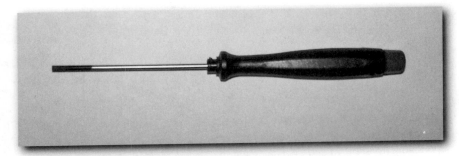

FIGURE 4-1: The precision flat-blade screwdriver with a thin shaft

- A precision Philips head screwdriver also with a thin shaft and preferably with a magnetic tip ($20 in the same set the previous screwdriver would come with at Fry's, CompUSA, or any hardware store, as shown in Figure 4-2)

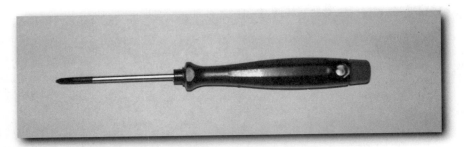

FIGURE 4-2: The precision Philips head screwdriver with a thin shaft

■ Electrostatic wrist strap to prevent against shock ($5 from Fry's or CompUSA, as shown in Figure 4-3)

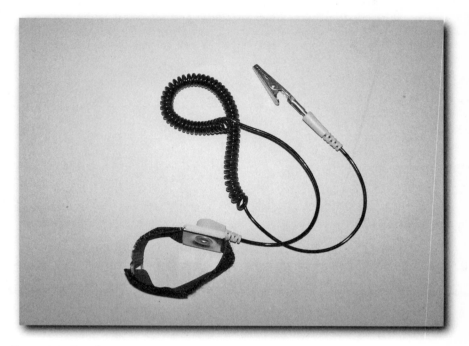

FIGURE 4-3: The electrostatic wrist strap

■ An electronics mat or a white towel (dark towels make it easy to lose screws and small parts) in a non-dry environment (where there's likely very little static) to protect the screen from scratches as you take the unit apart

■ A flat surface to keep the mat or towel and loose screws on

■ Copies of the PSP diagrams in this chapter to place your screws on so you know where to put them back when you're done

■ A lack of cats or dogs in the room (because they not only are static magnets, they love to knock screws and the like off the table)

Step 1: Prepare the PSP

Be very careful working with your PSP. Just like a medical operation, you need to take precautions. The first step is to place the PSP face down on the electrostatic mat or white towel (only if there's no static), and to put on your static wrist strap and ground it appropriately. Using the mat or towel prevents scratches to the PSP's plastic screen cover.

Remove any Memory Stick and UMD game cartridge you have loaded, and remove the battery from your PSP.

Figure 4-4 is a diagram of the locations of the screws on the backplane and battery compartment. Print this diagram and when you remove a screw, place it on the diagram on a flat surface far enough from where you're working (and away from pets) so you don't bump into it. Using a little bit of two-sided tape can help as well, keeping the screws in place, but that's generally overkill as long as you're careful.

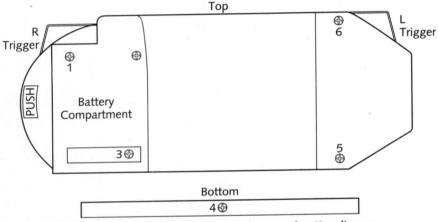

FIGURE 4-4: PSP backplane and battery compartment screw location diagram

Step 2: Remove the Back Plane

The PSP's back plane (the side with the word PSP in a circle) is your doorway to the insides of your PSP. You're going to need to remove the battery cover to complete this step. Note that some of the screws are covered by a sticker, which you will have to move out of the way or remove altogether to access. However, removing that sticker likely voids your warranty, so be prepared.

You need to remove eight screws with your Philips head screwdriver. The screw holes have a very narrow radius, so this is where the thin shaft of the screwdriver and the magnetic tip come into play. Make sure you don't strip the screw heads.

The first seven screws are located in easily accessible positions. However, the last screw is under the sticker mentioned earlier, as shown in Figure 4-5.

last screw

FIGURE 4-5: The last screw hides under a warranty-voiding sticker

Once you've removed all the screws (don't leave them loose in their sockets), gently separate the backplane from the cover. At this point the clear Left and Right triggers (marked as L and R) may come out— that's okay, because they rely on the case being together to stay where they are. You can safely leave them off and just slide them back into place when you put your PSP back together (you'll see the grooves they slide into).

Put the faceplate away in a safe location, face-up, so you don't scratch the plastic, and put the PSP face-up in front of you, as shown in Figure 4-6. You should now see the guts of your PSP, including the screen, the bottom button bar, what that slick analog stick looks like underneath, and your arrow and shape button contacts.

Note

If you have to put the L and R buttons back in when putting your PSP back together, make sure they move like they did before. When they are properly in place, they will move like they're supposed to (like triggers). You know you've got it wrong if they don't have any spring action when you press them—in that case, just reseat them and make sure they're in the proper grooves on your PSP.

FIGURE 4-6: The first layer of PSP guts

Step 3: Remove the Metal Button Bar

Now that you've removed the faceplate and can see the guts of your system, it's time to remove the screen. In order to do this you're first going to have to remove the metal button bar on the bottom of the device, as shown in Figure 4-7.

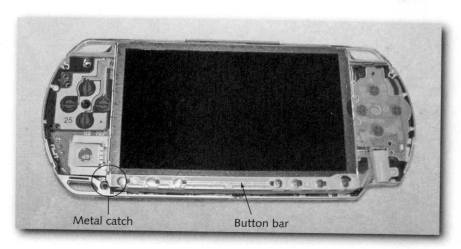

FIGURE 4-7: The metal button bar

To remove the metal button bar, simply pry a little on the metal catch to left of the bar and very gently lift it out at an angle. It is connected to the PSP's mainboard by a circuit strip connector. You need to very carefully move the circuit strip connector up with the flat-blade screwdriver so you can pull the circuit strip out of its holder (the tan tab). Remember which side was up when you pull the circuit strip out or the button bar won't work when you put it back in.

Step 4: Remove the Screen

Now that you've removed the button bar, you can remove the screen. This part's a little tricky because you don't want to crack the screen or bend any metal. Patience and gentleness are virtues during this entire process—your PSP is at stake here!

On the bottom-left corner of the screen is a metal piece in between the analog stick controller board and the display, making up part of the metal border of the screen. Wedge the thin flat-blade screwdriver into that crevice and the metal wedge should pop up and out a little bit. Do the same on the top-left, and now you should be able to carefully wiggle the screen out. Be very careful; do not bend the display or pry too hard or you may crack the LCD panel or irreparably bend the metal—hence the reason for the very thin precision flat-blade screwdriver. Figure 4-8 shows the crevice for the screwdriver. and Figure 4-9 shows the display partially removed.

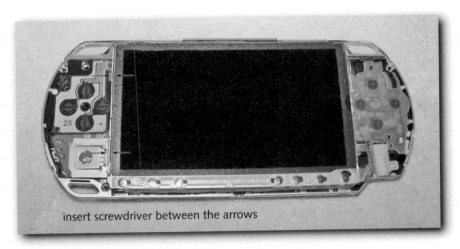

insert screwdriver between the arrows

FIGURE 4-8: Flat-blade screwdriver insertion location for removing the display

FIGURE 4-9: The screen partially removed

To remove the screen completely, you have to remove more circuit strips (and pay attention to which angle you had to open their catches and which way the circuit strip goes in). The long connector on the left lifts from the bottom, while the shorter one on the right lifts from the top (see Figure 4-10).

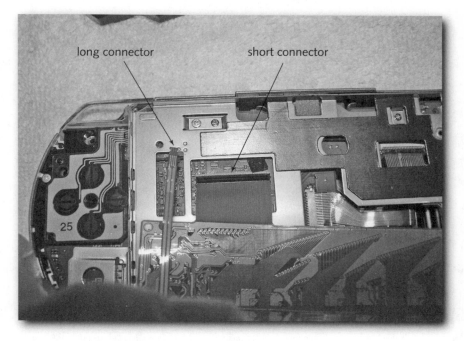

FIGURE 4-10: The display circuit strips connected to the mainboard

Once you have removed the screen, place it face-down on a towel to prevent scratching. Preferably, you should put it somewhere it won't fall onto a hard surface.

Step 5: Remove the Metal Screen Holder

Now that you removed the display, you need to remove the metal display holder so you can access the PSP's mainboard. To do this, you need to remove the nine remaining screws with the precision Philips-head screwdriver. After you have removed each screw, place it in the appropriate position on your copy of the screw location diagram. In addition to the screws, the metal screen holder is held in place by the release switch for the UMD drive. Gently slide it to the right to release its grip on the metal, then all you have to do is gently lift out the display holder, shown in Figure 4-11.

FIGURE 4-11: The metal screen holder with the nine screws removed

Step 6: Carefully Remove the Circuit Strips

Now that you've removed the screen holder, you need to get to the mainboard. You need to remove the circuit strip connecting the UMD drive to the mainboard (as shown in Figure 4-12). Be *very careful*, as the first time I did this the solder was weak the circuit strip holder actually came off the mainboard! Then remove the power plug at the top left, but not the small ones on the bottom of the board, while continuing to be careful not to break any wires or solder.

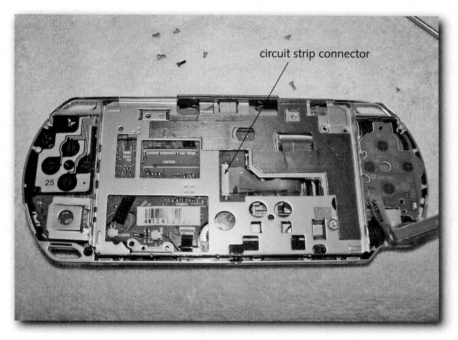

circuit strip connector

FIGURE **4-12: The circuit strip connector for the UMD drive on the mainboard**

Once you disconnect the cables, you may still have one more step to complete depending on how your PSP was made. You may see the black wireless antenna cable running alongside the top of your PSP (see Figure 4-13). Gently remove this from the groove it runs through on the top left of the mainboard so you can successfully remove the mainboard.

antenna

FIGURE 4-13: The PSP's wireless antenna

Step 7: Remove the Mainboard

Now that the cables are out of the way, gently lift up the mainboard and put it aside, as shown in Figure 4-14. If you take a look at the mainboard, you'll see the ARM-based processor Sony uses, their graphics chip and USB controller, as well as many other items.

Figure 4-14: The mainboard successfully removed

Step 8: Remove the Wi-Fi Shielding Plate

All this work and you're still not at the Wi-Fi interface yet! (I sure wish Sony had made this easier.) To get to the final piece, the Wi-Fi card, you need to remove the shielding plate by using your precision Philips-head to remove the three remaining screens holding it in place, as shown in Figure 4-15.

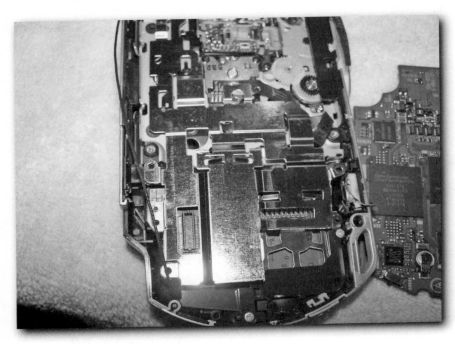

FIGURE 4-15: The screws holding the Wi-Fi card in place

Step 9: Remove the Wi-Fi + Memory Stick Board

Now here's the final piece: the Wi-Fi communications board, which also houses the Memory Stick interface, as shown in Figure 4-16. You can remove this piece if you like and see an entirely gutted PSP, or just start putting things back together (good thing you have those screw diagrams!) or fidgeting around. Note that the Wi-Fi board has a socket connector, making upgrading or replacing the antenna fairly easy (well, besides the PSP disassembly step), also highlighted in Figure 4-16. Appendix A has a link to an online project to add an external wireless antenna. If you've come so far that you're at the Wi-Fi + Memory Stick board, feel free to try that project. I did not discuss it in detail in this book because most people may not take apart their PSP so fully (there's usually no reason other than for exploratory purposes).

FIGURE **4-16:** The PSP's Wi-Fi board, Memory Stick interface, and antenna socket connector

Summary

In this chapter you took apart your PSP and hopefully put it back together again. Knowing how the PSP ticks on the inside is important for any hardware hacks you may want to attempt, including fixing your PSP yourself when sending it to Sony is not an option.

Getting Online: Configuring Your PSP for Networking

T he PSP is the first portable game system with built-in wireless networking capabilities for gaming with many people (instead of just one-to-one like many handhelds) and a full TCP stack for access to the Internet. The PSP is the only handheld game system ever made that enables more than two players to play a game, just like regular console systems! Although there are no commercial Web browsers or other Internet applications available yet, we will be going over how to get around that little issue in Chapter 6, "The Web on Your PSP." In this chapter, we'll go over how to get the wireless access configured properly and how to extend your wireless range so you can play with friends from far away and browse the Net from a little further down the street.

Note While the PSP has wireless out the wazoo with its 802.11b and infrared transceiver, a notable missing wireless topology is Bluetooth. Bluetooth could have enabled many wireless keyboards and mice to work with the system, which would have been nice. Of course, Sony could have something up its sleeve.

Configuring Wireless Internet Access

Setting up the PSP to get on the Internet via Wi-Fi is fairly easy. Let's go through those steps now.

Turning Wireless On and Off

To enable and disable the built-in wireless of your PSP, simply flip the switch on its left side. Up enables wireless and down disables it. This doesn't turn wireless on, however. Games and applications selectively turn the wireless feature on and off, so you can safely leave the switch up and it will only actually be "on" when an application needs it.

Tip   You can tell if your wireless is being used when the wireless access light is flickering (see Figure 5-1).

FIGURE 5-1: The wireless access light on the PSP

Set Up a Networking Profile

The PSP's networking capabilities are very similar to a Macintosh's, where you can set up different network profiles for use in different locations. This will be very helpful in Chapter 6, "The Web on Your PSP," which presents a profile for regular use, and then one specifically for your "hacked" network.

To set up a network profile, go to the PSP Navigator, select Settings, and then select Network Settings (see Figure 5-2). You are given two options, both of which pertain only to wireless networking — Ad Hoc Mode and Infrastructure Mode (see Figure 5-3). If you're not familiar with the difference between the two, read the sidebar "Wireless Modes in Focus: Ad Hoc and Infrastructure." Ad Hoc Mode is generally used when playing head-to-head with multiple PSPs in close proximity (10–20 feet), as it doesn't require a base station. Infrastructure is useful when there are multiple people in different rooms and you use a central base station to connect.

Wireless Modes in Focus: Ad Hoc and Infrastructure

There are two types of connections in wireless networks: *Ad Hoc* and *Infrastructure*. In Ad Hoc networks, there is no central access point—all devices communicate with each other directly instead of having an access point to run all communications through. With an Ad Hoc network, there is no guarantee that all devices can see each other, because their "vision" is limited to whatever devices they can receive receptions for (or "hear").

Infrastructure networks, on the other hand, are the most common type of wireless network connection. Utilizing a central base station, called a *wireless access point*, all devices connect to the access point, then relay all their interdevice communications through the single device. Each device connects to the base station based on its SSID, or *service-station ID*, which is the name you see when you try to "join" a wireless network. Most home networks have infrastructure networks to connect out to the Internet and to communicate wirelessly with both wireless and wired devices.

Most of the time you are involved with multiplayer games you will be using Ad Hoc networks. However, when you're browsing the Internet on your PSP you will usually be using an Infrastructure connection.

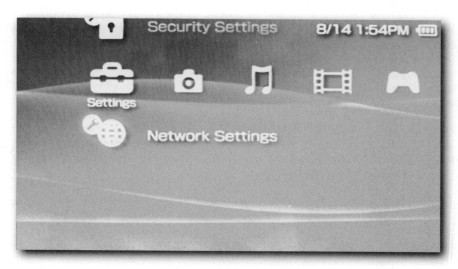

FIGURE 5-2: The Network Settings option in the PSP Navigator

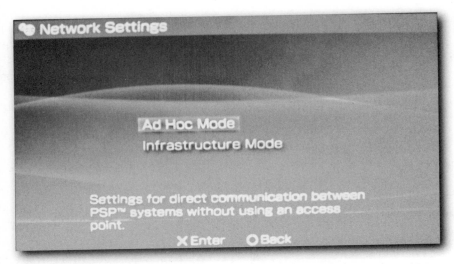

FIGURE 5-3: The wireless network mode selector under the PSP Network Settings option

Note

It's actually a good thing that most PSP games limit wireless play to eight players. As wireless networks get more and more crowded, the devices' transmissions adversely affect the overall available bandwidth and you could lose data and therefore have poor gameplay. Remember, when you're on an 11 Mbps wireless network, you're *sharing* that bandwidth with everybody else, so the more you do on the network, the less bandwidth that's available for others. This is especially true if you're trying to play a PSP game with eight people while someone's downloading a huge file and printing a large document over your wireless network—there's a good possibility of losing packets and having issues with gaming.

Let's go through configuration of both network types. Some games may actually require one type over another—the back of the box says "Wi-Fi Compatible (Ad Hoc/Infrastructure)," as shown in Figure 5-4. Some games may not support wireless play at all and won't have the Wi-Fi Compatible logo on their box at all.

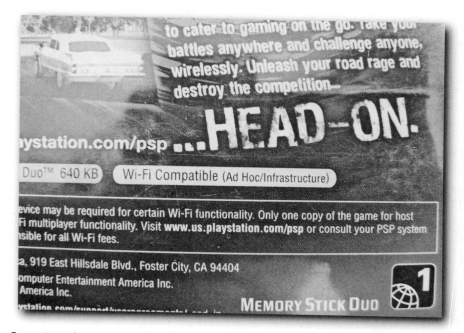

FIGURE 5-4: The required networking configuration modes listed on a PSP game case

Creating an Ad-Hoc Wireless Profile

If you're just going to do some quick gaming with friends, you all need to have the same network name, or *SSID*, so you can all connect with each other. Once everyone has the same profile, you can all connect and play your games together.

Note

The PSP doesn't actually let you set your SSID in Ad Hoc Mode, so it just defaults to a generic name beginning with PSP, followed by a number of different characters. This can vary depending on the game you're playing, too, as some games will set a different SSID to differentiate the PSP hosting the game from the other PSPs in the vicinity (which may be hosting games, too). Unfortunately, this means anyone with a PSP and the same game could potentially join in your game (if your game supports uninvited joins), so feel free to be paranoid and check to see who's around you before you start a wireless match.

Warning

If you switch to Ad Hoc Mode, you will have to switch back to Infrastructure Mode at the Network Setting menu before you can use your PSP in infrastructure mode again.

Follow these steps to set up an Ad Hoc network:

1. Use the PSP Navigator to select Settings and then Network Settings. Select the Ad Hoc Mode option and press ⊗

2. Set the channel to Automatic and press ⊗.

3. Press ⊗ to save the settings.

Creating an Infrastructure Wireless Profile

If you're at home and want to connect to other PSPs on your existing wireless home network (i.e., you don't want to set up a separate PSP network, which would be called an Ad Hoc network, described earlier), you need to set up an Infrastructure profile.

 Warning If you switch to Infrastructure Mode, you have to switch back to Ad Hoc Mode at the Network Settings menu before you can use your PSP in Ad Hoc Mode again.

Follow these steps to set up an Infrastructure network:

1. Use the PSP Navigator to select Settings and then Network Settings. Select the Infrastructure Mode option and press ▷.

2. Select New Connection and press ▷.

3. Enter a name for the connection (see the PSP manual for instructions on how to enter text), and then press ▷.

4. Enter the SSID of the base station you will be using (this would likely be the same one your computers use to connect to the Internet). If you don't know the SSID, use the arrows to move down to Scan and press ⊗ to choose a list of available base stations from a list.

 Note By default, many base stations broadcast the SSID so other systems can detect them and use them. However, if you or the network administrator for the wireless network has disabled SSID broadcasting, you will likely be forced to enter the SSID. Use a program like NetStumbler (search on Google for it) to detect wireless networks in the area and you can get around this problem (but you'll have to have a wireless-enabled PC to run the application).

5. If your network has a WEP network key, move down with the arrow pad and enter your WEP key, or leave it as None. Then press ▷.

6. If you have a DHCP server (most wireless networks do), select Easy mode. If you want to enter a custom IP address, gateway address, and/or DNS server address, select Custom. Then press 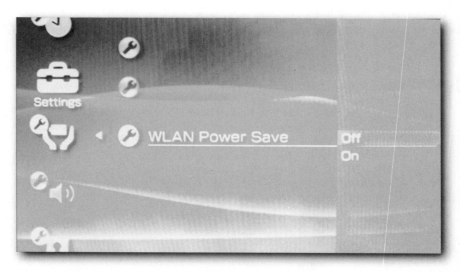.

7. Press ◀ ▷ to save your settings.

8. You can optionally test your settings here as well. Your new connection will appear in the list of available networks to use next time you are in a game that supports infrastructure mode.

Speeding Up Wireless Internet Access

To save battery life, the PSP defaults to a "wireless power saving" mode, which lowers the transmit and receive speed of the built-in wireless. To improve wireless performance, especially for Internet access, you should turn that mode off. Of course, it will eat more battery power, but play around with it and see what you think.

You may actually *need* to disable the wireless power saving mode, as some wireless access points and devices aren't compatible with the power saving feature of the PSP, so knowing how to do this may help you when you can't connect in certain places.

Follow these steps to disable wireless power saving mode:

1. Use the PSP Navigator to select Settings, and then Power Settings.

2. Select the WLAN Power Save option and press ⊗ to select it (see Figure 5-5).

3. Set the option to Off and press ⊗ again.

FIGURE 5-5: Disabling WLAN Power Save mode

Why Is It Called 802.11?

Many people wonder what the heck the 802.11a, b, and g stand for. The IEEE (Institute of Electrical and Electronics Engineers), the same people who brought your IEEE-1394 (also called *FireWire, iLink*, and so forth) is an established standards body that has defined many technologies via its internal open working groups (WGs). 802.11 is named this due to its IEEE working group being group 802.11. IEEE Project 802 is also called the LAN/MAN Standards Committee, or LMSC, and the 802.11 working group handles wireless LANs. Tens of millions of IEEE 802.11 devices have been deployed worldwide and are interoperable.

IEEE 802.11 has many flavors. The most widespread today is 802.11b (named after IEEE 802.11 working group B), which operates in the unlicensed ISM (Industrial, Scientific, and Medical) band at approximately 2.45 GHz, and can transmit up to 11 Mbps. Newly available 802.11 flavors include 802.11a and 802.11g. 802.11a and g support speeds up to 54 Mbps (in the standard, proprietary solutions claim faster speeds), and operate in the ISM band, as well as the newly unlicensed U-NII (Unlicensed National Information Infrastructure) band, at 5.2 and 5.8 GHz.

Even though 802.11 is a standard, its availability is restricted in different regions of the world because of varying regulations. Generally, 802.11b in the United States has 13 broadcast channels available for use (3 optimal ones because they are non-overlapping), and 802.11a in the United States supports 140 channels, with 12 non-overlapping optimal channels. However, in France and Spain, the various channels available to 802.11b and g users are severely limited (1 non-overlapping channel), while there are actually *more* channels available in Japan (13 channels, 3 non-overlapping). Take note: Even though 802.11a provides so many optimal channels, the international legalization of its 5.2 GHz frequency use has not been standardized, so outside-U.S. deployments may run into broadcast legal issues. Another note: The 5.2 GHz U-NII spectrum is also used by microwave landing systems to help planes land in bad weather.

Summary

This chapter showed you how to configure your PSP to get online using the built-in 802.11 Wi-Fi capabilities so important to extreme multi-player gaming. You also learned how to boost the performance of your network connection by turning off the wireless power saving mode. The chapter also described the differences between the various 802.11 flavors available today. All of what you've learned comes into play not only in your games, but in the next few chapters, as you delve into using your PSP on the Internet.

The Web
on Your PSP

A few months after the PSP was released in the US (March 2005), Sony released a Web browser for the PSP in Japan. About a month after this, Sony released a U.S. version. The Web browser was part of a larger set of features in an update called System Update 2.0, which updated the PSP's firmware to version 2.0. Along with the Web browser, the update provided for playback of the AAC (MPEG-4) audio format and more personalization features including wallpapers and themes. Photo sharing was also introduced.

The most anticipated feature was the Web browser, of course. Much to the chagrin of homebrew software developers, the required update would disable their ability to write and run homebrew applications on their PSPs. However, there's a hack where homebrew developers can still get access to a Web browser by hacking one of Sony's own products (as described in "Wipeout Pure: A Cool Game with a Fantastic Feature," later in this chapter).

Sony's Official Web Browser

Sony's "official" Web browser has a number of features found on regular Web browsers, sans keyboard support of course. The browser supports automatic scaling of pages to fit the PSP's already high-resolution screen, Javascript (to an extent), bookmarks (called Favorites in Internet Explorer), saving files, submitting forms, and even proxy connections (for those on corporate networks). The browser does not yet support Macromedia Flash or Java applets, but rumor has it Flash support is in the works.

---

in this chapter

☑ Browsing the Web on your PSP

☑ Moving your PC's bookmarks to your PSP

☑ Saving files using Sony's Web browser

☑ Spoofing

If you don't have System Update 2.0 on your PSP, and you don't want to run homebrew applications, you can update using your PSP's built-in wireless Internet access, or download the update from Sony's site at `http://playstation.sony.com/psp`. However, if you want to continue to run homebrew applications, read Chapter 16, "Reverting from a 2.0 PSP to a 1.5 PSP," to learn how to trick your PSP into thinking it's running firmware 1.51, 1.52, and 2.0, so you can run newer applications that require newer firmware versions.

You also can downgrade a firmware 2.0 (not 2.01 or higher) PSP to firmware 1.5, as discussed in Chapter 16. While at the time this book was written there was no hack for firmware versions 2.01 and beyond, there's a good chance one will appear. If a solution presents itself, I will post it to the official *Hacking the PSP* Web site at www.hackingpsp.com.

Scrolling Web Pages in Sony's Web Browser

While viewing a page, hold down SQUARE and use the round analog stick to scroll the page. To scroll a page at a time, hold down SQUARE and use the direction arrows (up, down, left, and right).

Sometimes you have to wait for the page to load completely before these navigation controls work. You can tell a page is loading when the "loading swirl" is swirling in the corner of the screen, and that it's finished loading when the swirl disappears or stops moving.

Tabbed Browsing in Sony's Web Browser

Sony's Web browser supports *tabbed browsing*, which means you can have multiple Web sites open at once, each in their own "tab," just like Firefox, Opera, and Internet Explorer 7 (due out in 2006). To open a page in a new tab, go to the Web browser's menu by pressing (△), and then go to the File icon (the leftmost icon) and press (✕). Select Open Link in a Different Tab and press (✕).

To switch tabs, hold down SQUARE and the Left and Right trigger buttons to switch between tabs while viewing a page.

You can tell you're in a different tab based on the wide color bar at the top of the screen when you're selecting tabs, as shown in Figure 6-1.

To open a link on a page in a new tab, hold (✕) down until it opens in a new tab.

Tabs

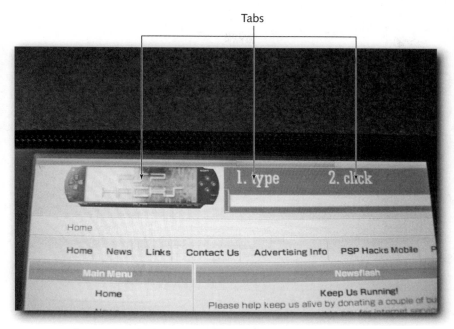

FIGURE 6-1: Tabs are identified as a multi-colored bar

Quick Overview of Buttons and Menu Options

This section describes the officially supported button commands and menu contents for quick reference.

Buttons

Table 6-1 lists the PSP buttons and describes how they work.

Table 6-1	Buttons and their functions
Command	**Function**
Left trigger	Go back one page (if available)
Right trigger	Go forward one page (if available)

Continued

Table 6-1 *(continued)*

Command	Function
△	Display/Hide browser menu
○	Close browser; also takes you back from the browser menu to the Web page you were viewing
✕	Enter/Open links on pages
Hold ✕ on link	Open link in new tab
Arrow buttons	Scroll page (most of the time, otherwise use the next two options)
SQUARE + analog stick	Scroll page
SQUARE + arrow buttons	Scroll page
SQUARE + left trigger	Previous tab (if available)
SQUARE + right trigger	Next tab (if available)

Menus

Tables 6-2 through 6-5 describe the PSP menus and their options, starting from the leftmost menu to the rightmost.

Table 6-2 File menu and options

Menu option	Description
Address Entry	Use this option to enter a Web address (URL) to navigate to.
Open Link In Different Tab	Opens the selected link in a new tab.
Save Link Target	Saves the current link's target on your PSP, such as a music file download link.
Save Image	Saves the selected image to the PSP's PHOTO directory. A checkered outline around an image indicates that it is the image to be saved.
Page Information	Displays the title and URL of the page currently loaded into the browser.
Display Certificate	Displays the details of a Web site's SSL certificate, if available. This option is only available on https:// Web sites, not http://.
Close Page	Closes the current page so you can load a new one in that tab.
Close Internet Browser	Quits the browser.

The following buttons are available on this menu:

- **Left**: Goes back one page; functionally equivalent to pressing the left trigger while viewing a page.

- **Right**: Goes forward one page; functionally equivalent to pressing the right trigger while viewing a page.

- **Refresh**: Reloads the current page; functionally equivalent to pressing Control-R or F5 in Firefox and Internet Explorer.

- **Home**: Takes you to your home page, as defined under Tools → Settings → Home Page Settings.

Table 6-3   Bookmark menu options

Menu option	Description
My Bookmarks	Takes you to your personal bookmarks.
PSP™	Takes you to the official Sony PSP Web page for support, news, and downloads.

The following buttons are available on this menu:

- **History**: Shows you the last few pages you have visited; functionally equivalent to the History function in Firefox and Internet Explorer, except it's not sorted by Date and Time.

    Press (△) on an item in history to open a menu that gives you the option to Delete All history items, Delete only the selected history item, Open the selected history item, or get Information on the selected history item.

Table 6-4   View Menu and options

Menu option	Description
Text Size	Enables you to change the text size between Large, Normal, and Small. The default is Normal.
Encoding	Enables you to change the character encoding on the page. Most of the time this won't matter, but if you have trouble reading data on the page or entering text into form fields, adjust this option.
Display Mode	Enables you to choose how the PSP browser renders pages.

Continued

Table 6-4 *(continued)*

Menu option	Description
Normal renders pages as they were intended, with no scaling, so you will have to scroll often with this option.	
Just-Fit adjusts the page content to fit within the PSP's screen width. Some items may not scale well and may be hard to read.	
Smart-Fit works like Just-Fit, but reorders the items on the page so they are still readable, although the page won't necessarily look "normal" in some circumstances.	

Table 6-5   Tool menu and options

Menu option	Description
Settings	Enables you to set your home page and default view settings, setup a proxy server connection if one is required, configure cookie settings, and configure cache settings.
View Settings lets you control whether images are loaded, whether animations are displayed, and whether Javascript is enabled.	
Delete Cookies	Deletes your stored cookies.
Delete Cache	Removes all your cache files. Cache is used to speed up Web browsing by keeping common files saved locally so they don't have to be retrieved over the Internet.
Delete Authentication Information	Deletes your saved usernames and passwords.
Delete Input History	Deletes the entries saved for auto-completed form fields (although the auto-complete feature doesn't work very well).
Display Connection Status	Displays network connection status, including the name of the connection you're using, wireless signal strength, SSID of the wireless connection, BSSID (the MAC address of the wireless base station you're connecting to), the base station channel number, the wireless security protocol being used, and your PSP's IP address).

On this menu, the **Help** button provides limited help on how to use the PSP browser.

Resolving Out of Memory Errors

To resolve most "out of memory" errors, you need to increase your cache. To change your cache size, press Ⓐ to get to the Web browser menu, and then move to the toolbox icon and press Ⓧ. Select Settings and press Ⓧ Select Cache Settings and press Ⓧ. Press Ⓧ on the cache size (it defaults to 512K), and use your arrow keys to increase it to 2048, as shown in Figure 6-2. Press Ⓧ again, and then select *OK* and press Ⓧ to save your new cache settings.

 Tip Keep in mind that your PSP doesn't have a lot of RAM (between 4MB and 32MB depending on the model), so some very complex pages may not load. If a page doesn't load, it does *not* mean your PSP is broken.

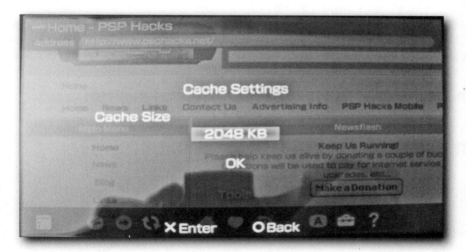

FIGURE 6-2: Increasing the cache size

Viruses and the PSP

It goes without saying that eventually there will likely be a virus written to affect the PSP. The most obvious route to infection is the PSP's Web browser. To this effect, it is important that you exercise the same caution when browsing with your PSP as you do on a regular computer. Some warez and black-hat hacking sites, as well as other unsavory sites, may try to exploit your PSP and "own" it — so please be careful.

Web Sites Formatted for the PSP

There are Web sites specifically formatted for the screen size and capabilities of the PSP. If you can't find a PSP-formatted Web site, try a mobile version of the Web site to save page load time. The PSP's Web browser is perfectly capable of viewing most any site on the Internet.

Sony's Official PSP Web Site

Sony has an official PSP Web site that is bookmarked by default. Well, actually, you can't delete the bookmark — you can either go to your own bookmarks or to Sony's PSP site. Sony's official PSP Web site is located at http://www.ps-portable.net. You can access the official PSP Web site by going to the bookmarks menu and selecting PSP instead of My Bookmarks.

The PSP Web site has a host of neat things to do, from downloading game extras, to getting trailers for upcoming UMD movies to downloading images, photos, screen shots, and more. You can get the latest news from Sony on the PSP and buy gear for your PSP. Of course, this site will likely expand to offer you much more in the future, such as downloadable music, new games, and more, for a fee.

Using the My Account feature on Sony's site requires registration on the PSP Underground site. While you can do this on your PSP, it's a lot faster on a computer with a keyboard, and then you can just log in on your PSP and save your login information on it by selecting Remember Me on the login page.

Downloading Files with Sony's Web Browser

Sony's Web browser can also download music, video, and image files directly onto the Memory Stick inserted into your PSP for viewing in its various media viewing applications. It can also download any other type of file, which you can access via USB mode on your PSP or by placing your Memory Stick into a media card reader after it's been downloaded.

To download a file, simply find the link to the file you want to download and highlight it. Then go to the Web browser menu by pressing (△), and then select the File menu (the left-most icon) and press (✕). Select Save Link Target and press (✕). You can change the file-name to whatever you want, and set the destination. Table 6-6 shows the locations on the Memory Stick to save different types of media items so they show up in the appropriate PSP application.

If you want to save an image on the screen, highlight and follow the same steps, except choose Save Image instead of Save Link Target.

Table 6-6	PSP media locations
Media type	Save in
Image	PSP \ PHOTO
Music	PSP \ MUSIC
Video	PSP \ MP_ROOT \ MNV001

Importing Favorites from Internet Explorer into Your PSP's Web Browser Using BROWSER 2 PSP

It can be tedious to enter all your favorites using the PSP's on-screen keyboard. Luckily there's an easier way to get your bookmarks onto the PSP. Using BROWSER 2 PSP, you can export your Internet Explorer favorites to a text file, and then add them to your PSP's bookmarks.

Step 1: Organize Your Favorites

You may have a lot of favorites already saved in Internet Explorer. You likely don't want them all on your PSP. Use the Organize Favorites option under the Favorites menu to organize the bookmarks you want on your PSP into a folder. I created a folder named PSP Links and placed all my PSP favorites in there, as shown in Figure 6-3.

Tip

If you do not know how to use the Organize Favorites feature of Internet Explorer, go to Tools, then Help, and click Contents and Index. Click Search and type **organize favorites** and click List Topics. Finally, click the topic Organize Your Favorite Pages into Folders.

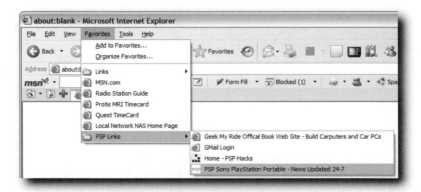

FIGURE 6-3: Favorites organized in folders in Internet Explorer

Step 2: Export Your Internet Explorer Favorites

Now that your favorites are organized, you need to export them to a special HTML file so you can put that information in the PSP.

In Internet Explorer, select the File menu, and then select Import and Export. The Import/Export Wizard appears. Click Next to start the wizard, and then click Export Favorites as the action to perform, as shown in Figure 6-4.

FIGURE 6-4: Internet Explorer's Import/Export Wizard

Click the folder containing your PSP favorites and click Next, as shown in Figure 6-5.

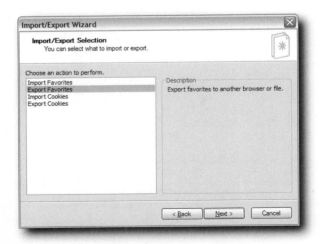

FIGURE 6-5: Selecting the PSP favorites folder

Now choose a location to save the bookmarks file by clicking the Browse button under Export to a File or Address. I suggest saving it on your desktop or in your My Documents folder so it's easy to find (you can throw it away when you're done with all this). Name the file "bookmarks. html" (without the quotes, and all lowercase). Click Next when you're done, then Finish, and Internet Explorer tells you it has successfully exported your favorites.

Step 3: Launch BROWSER 2 PSP

When BROWSER 2 PSP loads, click Load Favorites and select the Favorites file you just exported. BROWSER 2 PSP brings the bookmarks into the grid on the left so you can edit the URLs or title text prior to moving the datafile to your PSP.

Using the datagrid to edit your bookmarks is very similar to using Microsoft Excel. You can select a row and press the Delete key (not Backspace) to remove an item. You also can add an item by scrolling to the bottom of the grid and pressing the Down Arrow and filling in all the spaces. The columns are pretty obviously named. Cut (Control-X), Copy (Control-C), and Paste (Control-V) commands work as well. Figure 6-6 shows BROWSER 2 PSP in action.

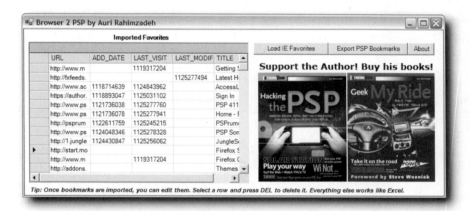

FIGURE 6-6: BROWSER 2 PSP in action

Step 4: Copy Bookmarks Over to PSP

Now that you have a bookmarks file, you can copy it over to your PSP and use it on your PSP's Web browser. Now you just have to get it on there.

Connect a USB cable to your PSP and your computer and put your PSP in USB Connection mode.

Click the Export PSP Bookmarks button in BROWSER 2 PSP. When the Save File dialog box appears, navigate to your PSP, the PSP folder, SYSTEM, and then BROWSER.

If there is already a Bookmarks.html file in the BROWSER folder, I suggest backing it up to your computer, just in case your new Bookmarks file doesn't work. Simply click Cancel if you need to do that, and then come back to this step.

Now simply click OK and BROWSER 2 PSP will export the files to your PSP. If your computer asks you if you want to replace the file, say yes. Finally, exit USB connection mode on your PSP and connect to the Internet, and you'll see your bookmarks.

Wipeout Pure: A Cool Game with a Fantastic Feature

They say most hacks are elegantly simple. They are so much sweeter when you can use a company's own products to perform the hack. Such is the case with Web browsing on the PSP, where Sony's own game— Wipeout Pure— has a fairly decent Web browser (well, enough to read blogs and the RSS feeds and lots of other stuff which we'll get to in other chapters). Using tried and true DNS and Web server spoofing techniques, you can intercept Sony's game's calls to Sony's Web servers and point all those requests to your own, hacked server. Of course, you should only do this on your local network, as Sony's legal hounds would probably tear into your flesh with ferocious persistence, but this hack will work outside of your own network if you believe you have legal-bullet-proof powers.

 Note   While this hack will work on any PSP, it is generally intended to provide a Web browser to those who do not use a 2.0 PSP (such as software developers or those who want to run homebrew applications). Either way, by reading this section you should learn quite a bit about the art of spoofing.

Here's what you'll need:

- A Web server (otherwise known as an HTTP Daemon, which you'll download in a moment)
- A DNS server (otherwise known as a Name Daemon, which you'll download soon, too)
- A PC or Mac that can run both of the previous applications (called the "host PC")
- Wipeout Pure PSP game
- 802.11b-compatible wireless base station (or the host PC with an 802.11b-compatible wireless card and configured as a wireless base station)

What we're about to do is trick the game Wipeout Pure. Wipeout uses its own Web browser to access Sony's Web site to download extra content. What you're going to do is redirect it to a different site (your Web server) by spoofing Sony's Web site's IP address (via your DNS server) so you can surf the Internet through that same browser and do whatever you want online (for the most part).

Get a Web Server

There are many options if you don't already have a Web server. If you have Windows, your best choice is MooPS, a free Web server and DNS server preconfigured for use in this hack. You can download MooPS from `http://seamonkey420.tech-recipes.com/psp/Wipeout_moops.html`.

If you have Windows 2000 or XP Professional and are already running IIS, you can still use IIS as the Web server — you'll just use MooPS for the DNS configuration.

If you have a Mac or are running Linux, there's already a free Web server included with your system — Apache. Let's go over how to install each one.

Note If you're on a Mac or you already have a PC Web server, you can skip this step. Macintoshes since Mac OS 8 have had a service called Personal Web Sharing. Windows XP Pro and Windows 2000 machines have IIS built-in.

Warning Before setting up any sort of server, especially if you will make it public, make sure you have the latest security patches. The last thing you need is for it to get owned by a hacker.

Warning Before installing any server product, make sure your machine is behind a firewall and is not allowing any external traffic. Before you allow other people (even you) access to services you provide, make sure your system is fully updated before and after you install server software. In Windows you do this via Windows Update, and on the Mac it's through Software Update. Linux and other operating systems have various update paths. Also make sure any third-party server software is fully up-to-date, as the built-in update mechanisms in operating systems only update the operating system components, not applications.

Installing MooPS

Download MooPS from the site mentioned earlier and double-click the installer to run it. You should be welcomed by the MooPS Setup Wizard, which walks you through the fairly straightforward installation (see Figure 6-7).

FIGURE 6-7: The MooPS Setup Wizard

Next, select the installation directory for MooPS. I suggest the default location of your Program Files directory, which is usually the C:\Program Files directory and is entered by default. Then click Next and then Next again and MooPS is installed. When MooPS has installed, click Close to exit the installer.

Locking Down IIS

If you are running IIS instead of MooPS on Windows, you should lock down your IIS configuration (because security is always key, even in closed networks). If you have not done so already, you should install and run the IIS Lockdown Tool, available for free from Microsoft at `http://www.microsoft.com/downloads/details.aspx?displaylang=en&FamilyID=DDE9EFC0-BB30-47EB-9A61-FD755D23CDEC`. If that URL doesn't work, simply go to Microsoft's Web site (`http://microsoft.com`) and search for IIS Lockdown Tool.

Download the IIS Lockdown Tool and run it using the Dynamic Web Server (ASP Enabled) profile (just follow the prompts — it's pretty self explanatory), as shown in Figure 6-8. Make sure the box for Install URLScan Filter on the Server is checked (this prevents certain types of hack attempts).

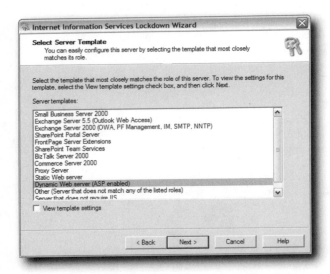

FIGURE 6-8: Selecting the lockdown profile in the IIS Lockdown Tool

Once the IIS Lockdown Tool has completed its run, put the program away in a location you'll remember so you can undo its changes later if you need to. To undo the IIS Lockdown Tool's changes, simply run the application again and it automatically knows it's installed and gives you options to remove its changes.

Enabling Personal Web Sharing (Macintosh)

Macintoshes have a Web server installed, but not enabled, by default. To enable your Web server, first make sure you run Apple's Software Update to make sure your patches are up to date, and then do the following:

1. Open System Preferences.

2. Click Sharing.

Enabling Apache (Linux)

Because every flavor (distribution) of Linux is configured differently, check your distro's documentation as to how to install and configure Apache. This book does not cover the configuration of Apache in Linux or Unix, but there are many fine books that do.

Tip

See the "Setting Up a Web Server" chapter of any edition of *Red Hat Fedora and Enterprise Bible* (Wiley) for advice on configuring Apache.

Download the DNS Server

Now that we have the Web service part out of the way, let's get the DNS server squared away.

If You Have Windows

Use MooPS. It has a DNS server built in that is pre-configured for use in this hack.

If You Have Mac OS X or Linux

On Mac OS X and Linux, you can simply install Berkeley Internet Name Daemon, or BIND for short. Refer to the BIND documentation on how to download and install BIND.

BIND for Mac OS X can be downloaded from `http://www.versiontracker.com/dyn/moreinfo/macosx/658`.

BIND for Linux is usually included with the distro, so check your install.

If You Have Mac OS 9

If you're running Mac OS 9, get your hands on MacDNS, a very simple DNS server that will do just fine for hacking DNS.

Configure the DNS Server

Now that you've installed the Web server, it's time to configure it.

Finding Your Network Address Information

To do this hack, you need to know the IP address, gateway address, and subnet mask of the machine hosting your newly setup Web and DNS server. Here's how to find this information if you don't already know it:

- If the server is running Windows, this can be found by going to Start, then Run, and then typing **cmd**. When the command prompt comes up, type **ipconfig**, and note the IP address of your computer. If you have both Ethernet and wireless on your computer, use the IP address of the wireless interface, as shown in Figure 6-9.

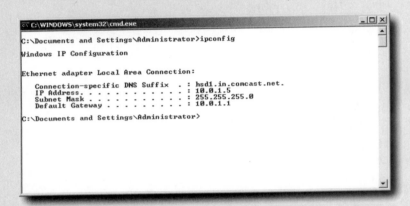

Figure 6-9: The IP address and gateway address from the ipconfig command

- If the server is running on Mac OS X, go to the Apple menu, then System Preferences. Click Networking and note the IP address and gateway address listed.

- If you're running Linux, open a terminal window and type **ifconfig** and note the IP address and gateway address.

Write down the IP address, gateway address, and subnet mask so you can set up the PSP to properly talk to your network at home.

If You're Using MooPS

Follow these steps:

1. Select Launch MooPS from the Start → All Programs → MooPS menu. After a few moments, the MooPS status window appears, as shown in Figure 6-10.

2. From the Options menu, select Server Settings.

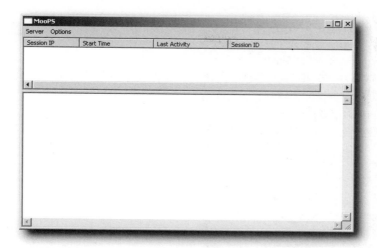

FIGURE 6-10: The MooPS status window when you first launch MooPS

3. When the MooPS – Server Settings window appears, enter the following:

 ▪ Your computer's IP address into the Redirect IP Address field.

 ▪ Change the drop-down selection under IP Address from (Any) to your computer's IP address.

 ▪ Your router's IP address (the gateway address) into the IP Address field under DNS Client.

 ▪ Change the IP address under *Web Server* from *(Any)* to your computer's IP address.

See Figure 6-11 for what my settings looked like. Click OK when you are done.

Note If you don't change the IP addresses in the drop-down lists that say (Any), MooPS will likely crash when you attempt to use it.

Note If you don't know your IP address and router address settings, read the sidebar "Finding Your Network Address Information."

4. Now that your server is configured you need to start it. From the Server menu, select Start. MooPS should then start its services and tell you everything's okay, as shown in Figure 6-12.

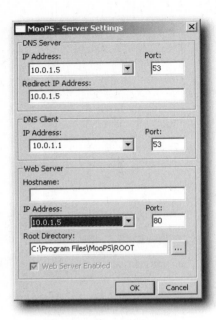

FIGURE 6-11: MooPS settings window

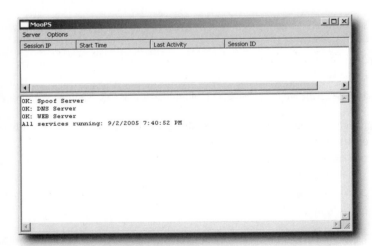

FIGURE 6-12: MooPS successfully started.

If You're Already Using Microsoft's IIS to Host Your Own Web Site

Follow these steps:

1. Follow the instructions for MooPS, but in the Server Settings window set the server port number to 33333 so it doesn't conflict with IIS, which runs on port 80 (the standard port for Web and HTTP traffic).

2. Open the Control Panel and then click Administrative Tools.

3. Select Internet Information Services. This opens the Internet Information Services MMC (Microsoft Management Console) plug-in, as shown in Figure 6-13.

4. Click the plus sign next to the computer icon, then click the plus sign next to Web Sites, and you'll see Default Web Site.

5. Right-click Default Web Site and select Properties.

6. Under the Web Site tab, make sure IP Address is set to All Unassigned and that TCP Port is set to 80.

7. Click the Documents tab and make sure Default.htm is in the list of documents, as shown in Figure 6-14.

8. Click the Home Directory tab and make a note of where your Web site's documents are stored (see Figure 6-15). You can change the directory, too, but the default location of `c:\inetpub\wwwroot` is usually just fine.

9. All right, you're good to go with IIS. In the next section, you configure the DNS server.

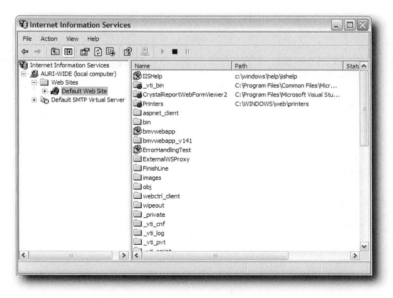

FIGURE 6-13: Internet Information Services MMC plug-in

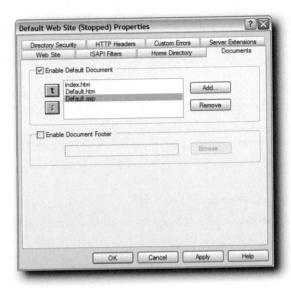

FIGURE 6-14: IIS Documents tab

FIGURE 6-15: IIS Home Directory tab

If You're Using Mac OS X's Built-In Web Server

Follow these steps:

1. Open System Preferences from the Apple menu.

2. Select Sharing.

3. Under Personal Web Server, click the On check box, as shown in Figure 6-16, and then click Start.

4. Close the System Preferences window.

 Note Your Web site documents are *not* stored under your home directory. Your Web site documents go into a global Web document folder. To access this directory in Finder, select Computer from the Go menu, then open the Library folder, then the WebServer folder, and then the Documents folder, as shown in Figure 6-17. In the terminal, you can also type **cd /Library/WebServer/ Documents**. This location may be different depending on the version of Mac OS X you are running. If the directory isn't right for your version, load Help and search for Personal Web Sharing.

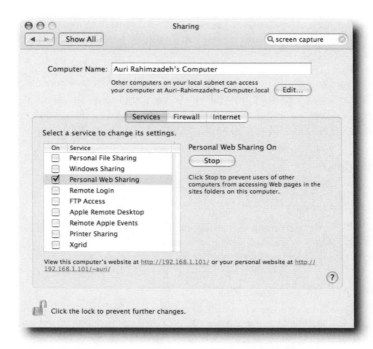

FIGURE 6-16: The Personal Web Server option in Mac OS X

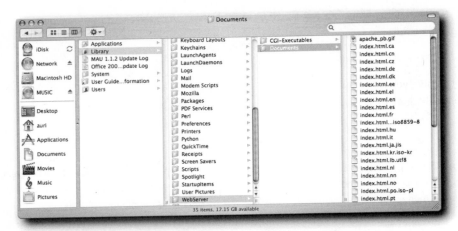

FIGURE 6-17: The Web server documents folder for Web documents in Mac OS X

Configure the DNS Server

Here is the big key to this hack. As I mentioned earlier, you need to trick Wipeout Pure into loading your Web page instead of the one it expects. You do this by spoofing the location of the server that the game looks for. Once it finds your page, the sky's the limit.

Note

It's probably not a good idea to make your DNS server publicly available. Not only may the traffic get unmanageable, but Sony's legal team may call you telling you to cease and desist. If you leave this on your local network, or at least undisclosed to all the hack boards out there, you should be safe, but there are no guarantees if you open your hack up to the public.

If You're Using Windows

Follow these steps:

1. Make sure MooPS is running.

2. Configure MooPS' Server Settings menu as directed in the previous section, "If You're Using MooPS." If you're using a Web server other than MooPS, set the MooPS Port under Web Server to 33333 so it doesn't conflict with your Web server.

If You're Using BIND on Unix or Mac OS X

In the case of BIND, you will be creating a zone file to spoof Sony's Web site, `ingame.scea.com`. I will assume that if you have a BIND instance running, you already know how to configure BIND, so we won't go over it here. There are many fine books on setting up BIND, so hop onto Amazon.com or go to your local bookstore and you'll find some excellent guides.

Tip See the "Making Servers Public with DNS" chapter of any edition of *Red Hat Fedora and Enterprise Bible* (Wiley) for advice on setting up BIND.

Note Make sure you aren't using any other DNS server software on the same machine or BIND will likely not work at all.

Tip If you decide to hack other games' DNS settings, this project is a good starter on how to do it. If you want to see what sites other games are looking up, simply look at the query log in BIND as you make requests with those games. Then you'll know what you need to spoof.

Note You can leave out the comments, which are denoted by a semicolon and some following text. Comments are very useful in documenting zone files, however. I have included some constructive comments to help you understand what's going on in the zone file.

The zone file for BIND should have the following contents:

```
; scea.com zone file
$TTL 86400
@    IN    SOA    scea.com       hacked.scea.com     (
                  2005070942    ; serial number YYYYMMDDNN
                  28800    ; refresh interval
                  7200     ; retry interval
                  86400    ; expire timeout
                  86400    ; min. time to live (ttl)
                  )

; spoofed entries to point traffic to our local server instead of
out on the Internet
  NS    192.168.2.1    ; says where the name server is (us, haha)
  A    192.168.2.1    ; points the root to this IP address
Ingame   A    192.168.2.1  ; resolves ingame.scea.com to our local
server
Webcluster   A    192.168.2.1   ; resolved webcluster.scea.com to
our local server
```

Next you need to update your named.conf file and add the scea.com zone, as shown in the following code. Enter the text at the end of the file's contents and then save the file. Like the zone file, be sure to use the tab key, not multiple spaces, when adding the entry.

```
zone "scea.com"    {
    type master;
    file "scea.zone";
};
```

Create the Wipeout Directory

The Wipeout Web browser looks for documents to be stored in a folder called "wipeout," so you need to create that folder. In your Web server's documents folder, create a folder named **wipeout**. Figure 6-18 shows the folder created in the `c:\inetpub\wwwroot` folder that Microsoft's IIS Web server generally uses. For MooPS you will simply place your files in `c:\Program Files\MooPS\ROOT`, where `c:\Program Files\MooPS\` is where you installed MooPS — no wipeout directory is necessary.

FIGURE 6-18: Creating the wipeout folder

Build Your Portal Web Page

If you're already familiar with building HTML pages, go ahead and build your own page; otherwise, you can build your page from the following code, which gives you a few "quick links" to use, as well as the option to enter any URL you want and go there:

```
<html>
<head>
<title>Hello My Name Is PSP Portal</title>
</head>
<body bgcolor="white">
<h3 align="center">PSP Portal</h3>
<p align="center">Quick Links:<br>
<a href="http://www.google.com">Google</a>    
```

```
<a href="http://www.hackingpsp.com">Hacking
PSP</a>   
<a href="http://www.psphacks.net">More Hacking PSP</a></p>
</body>
</html>
```

Keep in mind that the Wipeout Pure Web browser is fairly limited, so Java and Flash apps won't run (yet), frames don't work, and you're limited in the graphics support, but otherwise you're pretty open on everything else. JavaScript is limited as well, but experiment to see what works.

Tip You can do more advanced things if you use dynamic pages, such as ASP, ASP.NET, JSP, ColdFusion, and so forth. Tasks like telling you if you have mail, displaying photos or RSS feeds, and more, can be done with server-side code if you know how to do it.

Once you have created your portal page, save it as the default filename you set up in your Web server. For MooPS the default is index.html, for IIS it is default.htm, and for Abyss Web server it's index.htm. If you're using a different Web server, refer to its documentation on how to set the default page.

Set up a Networking Profile for Your Hack

Once you have the servers set up and a portal page to navigate to, it's time to set up the PSP to use your hack.

Step 1: Get Server Address Information

The first thing you need is the IP address, gateway address, and subnet mask of the machine hosting your newly setup Web and DNS server. If you don't know these, read the sidebar titled "Finding Your Network Address Information."

Step 2: Create the PSP Connection Profile

Now that you have the needed information, you're ready to create the connection profile. Before you begin, enable wireless on your PSP by sliding the switch on the left side to the up position. Then follow these steps:

1. Turn on your PSP and navigate to the Settings menu. Go to the Network Settings menu and press ⊗.

2. Select Infrastructure Mode and press ⊗.

3. Under Select a Connection to Edit, select New Connection and press ⊗.

4. Press ⊗ to change the connection name. Give the profile a meaningful name, like Hacked PSP. Then press ⬆.

The connection name cannot be longer than 15 characters.

5. Under WLAN Settings, enter your wireless network's SSID (also known as the base station or wireless network's name), or move down to Scan to find your wireless network with an easy interface. Then press to continue to the next step.

6. Under Address Settings, select Custom and press [▷].

7. Under IP Address Setting, select Automatic, unless you are going to assign your PSP a specific IP address (you don't have to, but if that's your thing, go for it). Then press [▷].

8. Under DNS Settings, select Manual, then press [×].

9. Next to Primary DNS, enter the IP address of the server you wrote down earlier by using the up and down arrows on each number field in the list, as shown in Figure 6-19. Then press [×].

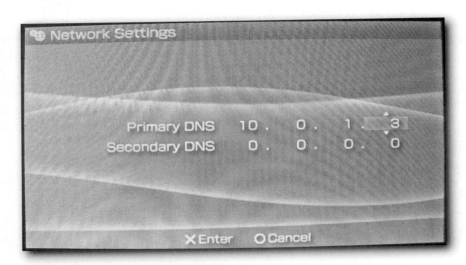

FIGURE 6-19: Setting the DNS server IP address

10. Under Proxy Server, select Do Not Use. Then press [▷].

11. Now you should be at the Setting List. This recaps all the settings you just made. Confirm the settings and press ◁▷ to continue.

12. Press ⊗ to save your new connection profile, just like the screen says.

13. After your settings are saved, your PSP should display "Save completed." You can now go back to the Navigator, or you can test your connection. I suggest testing your connection, just to make sure all is good.

14. Once you've tested the connection, go back to the Select a Connection to Edit screen, which should now list the newly created connection profile, as shown in Figure 6-20.

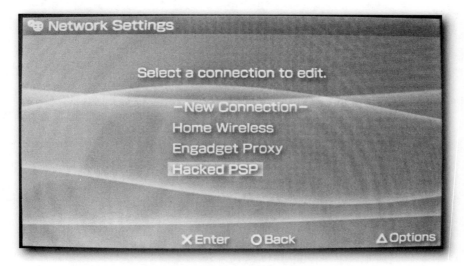

FIGURE 6-20: Your newly created connection profile in the connection list

Launch Wipeout Pure

It's time to put your hack to the test:

1. Make sure your Web and DNS servers are up and running.

2. Make sure your PSP's wireless switch is set to on (flipped to the up position).

3. Launch Wipeout Pure and select the Download option from the main menu, as shown in Figure 6-21.

4. Here's where the magic happens: Select the hacked network connection you created earlier in this chapter, similar to Figure 6-22.

FIGURE 6-21: The Download option in Wipeout Pure

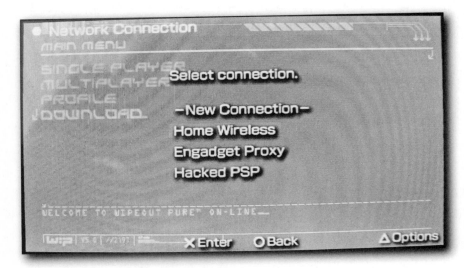

FIGURE 6-22: Select the hacking network profile

Surf!

That's it! Your portal page should appear, as shown in Figure 6-23.

Note If you're using MooPS, the first screen you see is a blue MooPS splash screen. Simply press to continue past this screen.

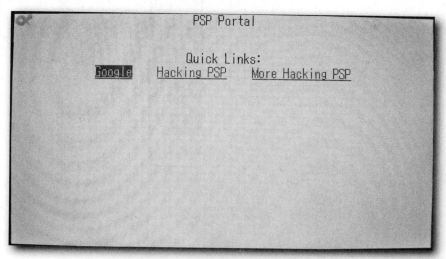

FIGURE 6-23: Your portal running on your PSP

What If It Doesn't Work?

Should the hack not work, try the following to see if you can find your answer. If you can't, post a message at the official *Hacking the PSP* Web site, www.hackingpsp.com.

- **Make sure your servers are running and properly configured:** Make sure your servers are running by opening their respective control panels and checking that they are started. Also, if you are running Windows 2000 or XP, go to Control Panels, then Administrative Tools, then Services, and make sure the word Started appears next to the service's name. In Mac OS X and Linux, open a terminal window and type **top** and see if your server's process is listed. You can also try **ps -al** in the terminal window to see all running processes.

- **Make sure your wireless network is running:** Sometimes your wireless network may not be enabled. Make sure your router has it enabled. A telltale sign that you are connected is your ability to surf the Web on your server. If you can do that, your network connection shouldn't be the problem.

- **Double-check your firewall settings:** As I mentioned earlier, you need to open TCP port 80 (for HTTP/Web traffic) and TCP Port 53 (for DNS traffic) in your firewall software. If you don't have firewall software, this shouldn't be a problem. However, if you do, you will have to check the software's advanced settings to make sure the proper ports have been opened so your PSP can make successful network requests.

Summary

In this chapter you learned how to get on the Web with your PSP, how to hack your pre–firmware 2.0 PSP to surf, and how to get your bookmarks on your PSP to save you a ton of time when going to your favorite sites on the road. As you can see, the PSP is an excellent Web surfing tool, so go play with your new toy's awesome Web-enabled features!

Online Hacks

Just like media, the PSP is no slouch when it comes to Internet access. While Sony's grand scheme right now only includes Wi-Fi Internet access through their own Web browser (or the Wipeout Pure browser hack as described in Chapter 6, "The Web on Your PSP"), Sony's big picture is likely to have content downloaded to your PSP from anywhere, including movies, music, games, and more. As of the writing of this book, Sony already had a television show download service available in Japan.

In this chapter, we will go over applications you can run in Sony's official PSP Web browser or the Wipeout Pure Web browser hack (oddly enough, a browser also created by Sony) and get your Internet news, IRC, instant messaging, and Webmail fixes on the road.

Tip

Many of these hacks work well on cell phones, too. This is especially true if your cell phone has a good size screen and a keyboard, like Treo, RIM BlackBerry, Windows Mobile, and Pocket PC phones.

Note

None of the Web browsers running on the PSP support saving form field entries. If your Webmail server doesn't support saving your login information in a cookie, be prepared to enter your username and password using the PSP's on-screen keyboard. If you do have an option to save your login information (like the option shown in Figure 7-1), it will be stored on your PSP's Memory Stick, so protect the cookie from other people if it has your password stored in it.

It should go without saying that every hack here will require the use of an Internet connection and a Web browser on your PSP. The Internet connection can be any WiFi infrastructure connection that gets you out to the Internet (via a wireless access point you define in your PSP's Network Settings) — *ad hoc connections will not work for any of these hacks*. The Web browser you use can be the hacked Wipeout Pure browser or the official Sony PSP Web browser that shipped with firmware version 2.0 and later versions.

FIGURE 7-1: The "store log-in information" check box on a Web mail server can be very handy

Sites Optimized for Mobile Devices

Many Web sites have versions of their content optimized for mobile devices. These optimized pages lack the extranneous graphics and scripts and just show the images and text you need, ideal for a device like the PSP, which doesn't have a lot of RAM or screen real estate to display all the images, ads, and so forth on pages. If you can find a mobile version of the site you want to browse, use it — you'll find browsing the site is much more responsive, and you'll spend less of your PSP's processor and battery life rendering pages because you can leave the wireless power-saving option on.

AOL Instant Messenger

Even thought America Online is not likely to release a PSP Instant Messenger version of AOL soon, you don't have to be without your buddy list. Using your PSP's Web browser you can log on to WebAIM at www.webaim.net, type your username and password, and access your buddy list, send and receive instant messages, and more (see Figure 7-2 for a look at WebAIM in action in a regular PC browser). WebAIM even has a login page made especially for PSPs, with an on-screen keyboard to save you time entering your username and password — just head over to http://dev.webaim.net/psplogin.jsp.

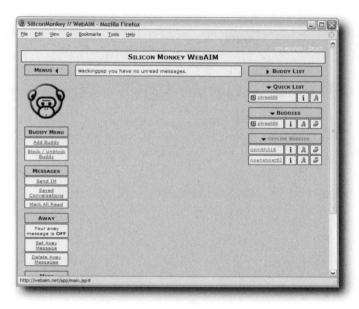

FIGURE 7-2: WebAIM in action in Firefox

Figure 7-3 shows WebAIM in action on my PSP using Sony's Web browser, which is enabled in the Firmware 2.0 update. Of course, you can still use the Wipeout Pure Web browser hack from Chapter 6, "The Web on Your PSP," so you don't have to upgrade to Firmware 2.0 and lose the ability to program your PSP and run homebrew applications.

FIGURE 7-3: WebAIM in action on the PSP

WebAIM's free servers are often pretty crowded, so getting one can take a while. I opted to pay for their premium service, which guarantees me access any time of the day, for around $4 per month or a scant $17 for six months.

Accessing Most of the Messenger Services for Free

Instead of using WebAIM, you can also use the free service Meebo, available www.meebo.com. Meebo lets you access your AOL Instant Messenger (AIM), MSN Messenger, Yahoo Messenger, and Jabber (Google Talk uses Jabber) accounts from a single interface. Try it out on your PSP.

Note   Microsoft also has a Web version of their MSN Messenger product at `http://webmessenger.msn.com`.

Viewing RSS Feeds

Bloglines is a free service for using RSS (Really Simple Syndication) feeds using practically any Web browser instead of a dedicated RSS Reader application. To register on Bloglines, you will have to use the full Bloglines interface. Once you're done registering, you can use the faster, simpler interface called Bloglines Mobile, which is ideal for the PSP because it gets rid of all the ads and other unnecessary items on the page.

Note   After you create your account on Bloglines, make sure you check the message at the e-mail address you gave them and confirm your account. You won't be able to use their service until you do. If you want to read the activation e-mail on your PSP, read the "Accessing E-mail and Webmail" section later in this chapter and just take care of everything on your PSP.

After you've confirmed your Bloglines account, log in to BlogLines and start adding the RSS feeds you want to subscribe to. The first time you log in to Bloglines, you are presented with a number of different and popular feeds in case you don't know any off the top of your head. Figure 7-4 shows where I added popular feeds like Engadget, Boing Boing, Dilbert, and Wired News, among others, so I could get started reading some good content.

It is much easier and faster to configure your Bloglines feeds and account settings with a regular computer and keyboard rather than the PSP's on-screen keyboard. You can still subscribe to more RSS feeds while browsing on your PSP, but it's a lot easier with a keyboard and mouse.

After you have subscribed to some feeds, they will appear on the left side of the screen for you to click and browse, as shown in Figure 7-5. From that same list, you can add, edit, and remove RSS feeds.

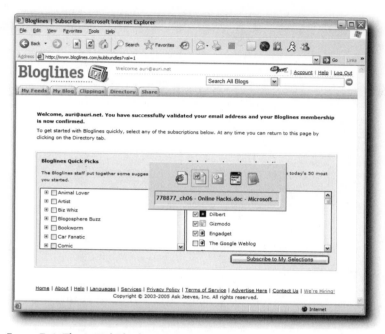

FIGURE 7-4: The initial Bloglines setup screen

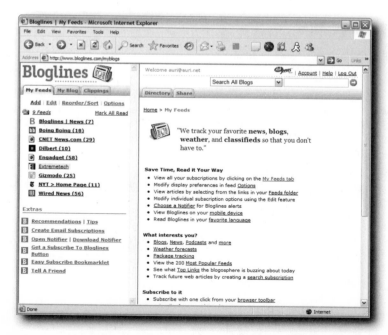

FIGURE 7-5: The RSS feeds showing up in the Bloglines feed navigator (top left)

Clicking a feed displays the latest headlines or content items in that feed, as shown in Figure 7-6. In this case, I clicked the ExtremeTech feed. Clicking an item's title then shows you that item's content.

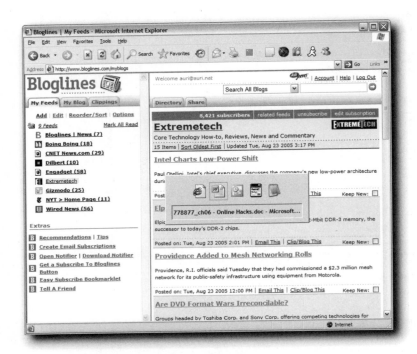

FIGURE 7-6: The ExtremeTech RSS feed's headlines

Up until now, you've been using a desktop computer's browser to configure Bloglines, getting your feeds and whatnot. The pretty browser interface you have on a PC doesn't mesh incredibly well with the PSP's limited resolution. As I mentioned earlier, Bloglines has a special version of their site for mobile devices, including the PSP, which is stripped down and only shows you the content you need, without all the extra goop.

To access your feeds on your PSP, log in to the Bloglines Mobile site at `http://bloglines .com/mobile`. Once you're there you can enter your username and password and access your feeds, as shown in Figure 7-7.

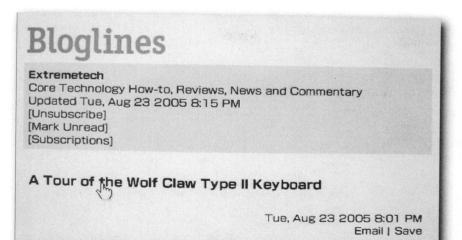

FIGURE 7-7: Your RSS feeds on the PSP

Accessing E-mail and Webmail

The number one use for the Internet is accessing e-mail. The PSP does not ship with a mail client, and rightly so — it would have to store its messages on the Memory Stick, which is expensive storage, and there's no keyboard. However, the PSP is an ideal reader for many types of media, including e-mail, so all you need is a Web browser, the right Web site to retrieve your e-mail, and a Wi-Fi connection.

Note If your Web mail server requires a certain port to be used, such as `http://mail .servername.com:8383`, you have to enter the http:// as well as the :8383. If you don't enter the http://, the PSP's Web browsers will usually time out (this is a bug in Sony's software, it's not your server).

If you already have Web mail access, go ahead and use that. Most Web mail programs should work fine with any of the PSP Web browsers (including Microsoft Exchange Webmail). However, if you don't already have Webmail access, you don't have to go get your own server or kidnap a hacker. Simply point your browser to `https://mail2web.com/`. Mail2Web is a free service that enables you to enter your e-mail address and password and send and receive mail from anywhere with just your PSP and an Internet connection.

Tip If you want to use your cell phone with Mail2Web, go to `http://mail2web.com/wap`.

Figure 7-8 shows Mail2Web in action in the PSP Web browser accessing my own auri@hackingpsp.com e-mail.

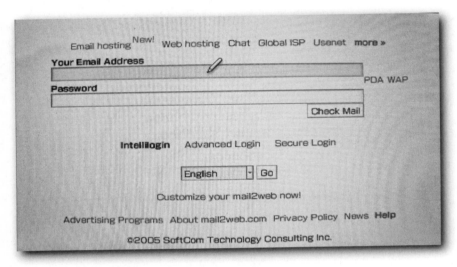

FIGURE 7-8: Accessing e-mail on the PSP with Mail2Web

Sony PSP Web Browser Tips

Here are a few tips to save you a lot of time when using the official Sony PSP Web browser that shipped starting with PSP Firmware 2.0:

- Use the Bookmark feature, which is the same as Internet Explorer's Favorites feature. It saves you a lot of typing. To access the bookmarks feature, press (△) to access the Web browser menu, and then go to the picture of the heart and press (✕). Press (✕) on Bookmarks. To add a bookmark, navigate to the page you want to bookmark, and then go to your bookmarks and select Add to Bookmarks.

Note If you use the bookmarks feature of Sony's Web browser, a Memory Stick must be inserted for the PSP to save the bookmarks file.

- When you need to scroll around a page, hold down (□) and then use the analog (round) stick to scroll the page up, down, left. and right.

- If you often visit the same site first, such as your Webmail, RSS feeds, search engine, and so forth, make it your default home page. To set your default home page, press (△) to open the Web browser menu, and then scroll over to the toolbox icon, and press (×). Select Settings and press (×). Then select Home Page Settings and press (×). Enter the home page you would like to use, and then press (×) to save it. Now whenever you press (×) on the Home icon in the PSP menu, you are taken to the Web site you just entered.

- If you have to use a proxy server on your network, press (△) to open the Web browser menu, and then scroll over to the toolbox icon and press (×). Select Settings and press (×). Then select Proxy Server Settings and press (×). Enter your proxy information and you should be able to browse the Web. Unfortunately, Sony's Web browser doesn't support profiles, so if you switch networks, you will have to remove and re-enter proxy information as needed.

Summary

In this chapter you learned how to get more out of the Internet with your PSP. From instant messaging to reading your e-mail on-the-go to getting your news fix wherever you want it, the PSP is a powerful platform to do it all. The hacks in this chapter took advantage of the PSP's Web browsing capabilties. In the future there may be applications written for the PSP that are specifically designed to provide all these services, just like when you install software on your computer.

Offline Hacks

There's a lot of Web content you likely want to take with you, from Web pages with map directions to news articles and blogs. This chapter covers how to pack it all with you wherever you go, with viewing tips and transfer tips. As an added bonus, you'll see how to bring Microsoft PowerPoint presentations with you when you're on-the-go.

A number of discussions have been posted on the Web about why Sony's Web browser (released in the version 2.0 firmware) doesn't allow viewing of standard HTML files, and it's unfortunate you can't use the one in Wipeout Pure when you're offline. This may be fixed in a future release so you can just package up HTML files, and maybe someday even PDFs, and take them with you without these hacks. Until then it's a g33k's market.

Viewing Saved Web Pages on Your PSP

Sometimes you may want to take Web pages with you to view offline. PCs make this very easy, but the PSP really doesn't. It sure would be nice to take Dilbert comics with you on trips, read gaming news articles on the bus to school, and so on and so forth. Fortunately, it's pretty easy to get around this lack of built-in capability.

Here's what you need:

- Web browser (see Chapter 6, "The Web on Your PSP")
- full-size to mini-USB cable
- Paperless Printer (see Chapter 3, "Quickies")
- HTML files you want to view

Step 1: Find Web Content

Obviously the first step is to find the Web content you want to save. Navigate to your favorite news Web site and get the news articles you want on the screen. You can repeat these steps for every Web page you want to move to your PSP. (Tabbed browsing in Mozilla and Firefox work great for queuing up lots of news you want to move to your PSP.)

Step 2: Print Your Web Pages Using Paperless Printer

Select the Print command in your browser, select Paperless Printer as the printer, and then click the Print button. Use the following settings when Paperless Printer asks you what format to save the files in (as shown in Figure 8-1):

1. Under Save, set the filename to the name of the news article.

2. Also under Save, click Browse and set the directory you want to save the exported Web site to by first creating a directory specifically for the Web site you are visiting (such as *New York Times*, *Engadget*, HackingPSP.com, and so forth) so you can easily navigate to it on your PSP, and then clicking OK, as shown in Figure 8-1.

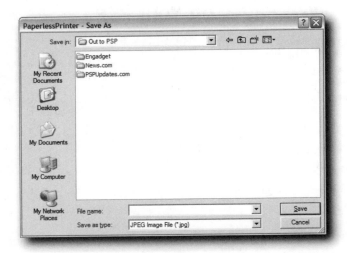

FIGURE 8-1: Creating multiple directories to store content from different sources

3. Under Quality, set the Quality level to 70, as shown in Figure 8-2.

4. Click OK to save the new settings.

By saving the files in a folder named Directions, you can easily separate your map directions from other sets of slides and photos you have on your PSP.

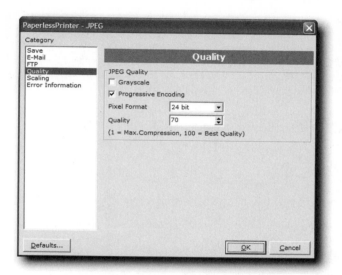

Figure 8-2: The appropriate settings for "images" for viewing on your PSP

Step 3: Copy the Files to Your PSP

Connect your PSP to your computer using the USB cable. Use Navigator to go to Settings, then up to USB Connection and press ⊗. Your PSP appears on your computer. Open the PSP folder, and then open the PHOTO folder. If the PHOTO folder isn't there, just create a folder named PHOTO (all capital letters) and copy the folder containing your Web page export into your new PHOTO folder. See Figure 8-3 for a view from Windows Explorer.

Step 4: Take It with You

Use Navigator on your PSP to navigate to Photos, then the Engadget folder, and press ⊗, as shown in Figure 8-4. Use the right and left triggers to move forward and backward through your web pages, and the analog stick to scroll up and down.

FIGURE 8-3: The Web page content copied to your PSP

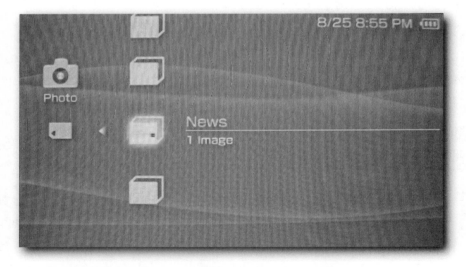

FIGURE 8-4: The Web page for easy on-the-go viewing on your PSP

The Web pages will likely appear scaled, which is hard to read, but never fear! Press ◯, select View Mode, and press ◯. Press ◯ to back out of the options menu. The page is now displayed in a much larger scale, as shown in Figure 8-5. Use your analog stick (the small round one on the bottom left of your PSP) to scroll up and down through the exported Web page image. There may be a slight delay (approximately two seconds) after scrolling before the data comes into focus.

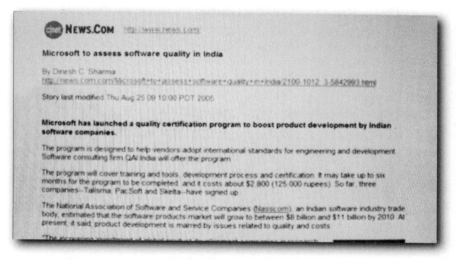

FIGURE 8-5: A viewable Web page on your PSP

There you have it! Your Web pages, to-go, on your PSP!

Taking Maps with You

It can be really hard to read scribbled notes, or have to waste ink and paper whenever you need directions somewhere. Why not let your PSP share the load? With this hack, we'll cover how to take your online maps with you.

Here's what you need:

- Maps you want to take with you (free from any number of Web sites)
- A full-size to mini-USB cable
- Paperless Printer

Note Before doing this hack, make sure you install Paperless Printer, as discussed in Chapter 3.

Step 1: Find the Map and Directions

Obviously the first step is to find the map you need. Navigate to your favorite mapping Web site, get the directions on the screen, and click the link for Printer Friendly format (most sites have this — it removes most of the clutter from the screen).

Step 2: Print the Directions Using Paperless Printer

Once you have the directions, go to your browser's File menu and select Page Setup (or Printer Setup, or a similar printer configuration option). When the setup box comes up, select the PaperlessPrinter icon, and click Preferences. When the Preferences window comes up, click the Settings tab, and then set the Paper Size to Custom and 3.5 × 11 inches.

Now that your printer is set up, "print" the directions by selecting the Print command in your browser. Use the following settings, when Paperless Printer asks you what format to save the files in:

1. Under Save, set the filename to Directions.

2. Under Quality, set the Quality level to 70 (see Figure 8-6).

3. Click OK to save the new settings.

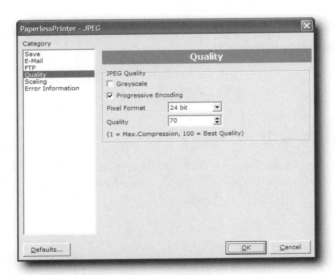

FIGURE 8-6: The appropriate Quality settings for viewing "images" on your PSP

By saving the files in a folder named Directions, you can easily separate your directions from other sets of slides and/or photos you have on your PSP.

Step 3: Copy the Files to Your PSP

Connect your PSP to your computer using the USB cable. Then use Navigator to go to Settings. Go to USB Connection and press ⊗. Your PSP appears on your computer. Open the PSP folder, and then open the PHOTO folder. If the PHOTO folder isn't there, just create a folder named PHOTO (all capital letters), and copy the folder containing your exported map images into your new PHOTO folder. See Figure 8-7 for the view from Windows Explorer.

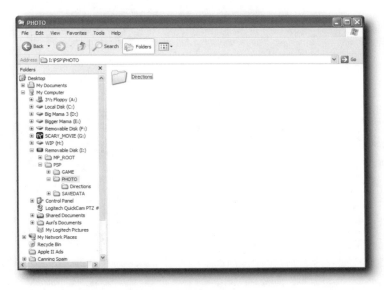

FIGURE 8-7: The directions copied to your PSP

Step 4: View the Directions on Your PSP

Use Navigator on your PSP to navigate to Photos, then the Directions folder, and press ⊗, as shown in Figure 8-8. Use the right and left triggers to move forward and backward through your directions, as you can see in Figure 8-9.

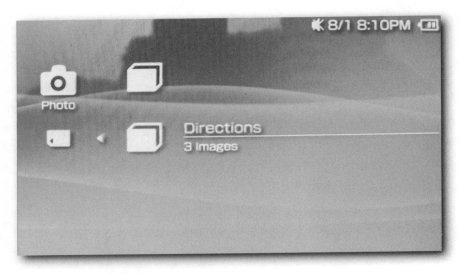

FIGURE 8-8: Selecting the Directions folder

Directions	Distance
1: Start out going SOUTHEAST on CAMERON RIDGE DR.	<0.1 miles
2: Turn LEFT.	<0.1 miles
3: Turn LEFT onto N GRAY RD.	0.2 miles
4: Turn RIGHT onto E 96TH ST.	1.2 miles
5: Turn LEFT onto ALLISONVILLE RD / ALLISONVILLE AVE. Continue to follow ALLISONVILLE RD.	3.3 miles
6: Turn RIGHT onto ORCHARD BLVD.	0.2 miles
7: Turn RIGHT onto HEADY LN.	<0.1 miles
8: Turn RIGHT onto NORTHWOOD DR.	0.1 miles
9: Turn LEFT onto MEADOW LN.	0.1 miles

FIGURE 8-9: The directions ready for viewing on your PSP

There you have it! Directions on your PSP!

Caution Please don't drive and look at the directions. Pull over to the side of the road and review your directions, or view your directions at a stoplight. I don't want you to get into a car accident!

Tip If your images didn't scale to the right size, press Ⓐ and select View Mode to stretch the image. Then use your analog thumbstick to scroll up and down on the picture in full high-resolution detail. Note there may be a slight delay before the high-resolution version of the image appears after scrolling — just wait a couple seconds after letting go of the thumbstick and your image will come back into focus.

Converting PowerPoint Presentations

One of the most popular presentation packages is Microsoft PowerPoint. However, keeping these presentations with you on a laptop you have to lug around can be quite a nuisance. Fortunately, with the PSP being the media machine it is, you can take your PowerPoint presentations with you on your super lightweight PSP. And should Sony release a video-out solution for the PSP, you'll be able to just hook your PSP up to a projector instead of a laptop. Talk about entertainment value!

Here's what you need:

- A PowerPoint presentation to convert
- A full-size to mini-USB cable
- Microsoft PowerPoint

Note When you're copying image files to your PSP, make sure you copy them in order. The PSP does not create slide shows based on a filename. It instead uses the creation date of the file. So if you drag images out of order, they'll display out of order on your PSP. (Hopefully a future firmware update will nix this limitation.)

Step 1: Export the Images

Open the PowerPoint presentation in PowerPoint. For this hack example, I opened a presentation of mine called "Canning Spam." Once the presentation is loaded, select Save As from the File menu. In the Save As dialog box, change the Type to JPEG File Interchange Format, as shown in Figure 8-10. In the filename box, use the name of your presentation. Then navigate to where you want to save the files and click Save. All of the individual frames of the presentation are saved, individually numbered, in a folder with the same name as your presentation.

FIGURE 8-10: Selecting JPEG as the export format in the Save As dialog box

Step 2: Copy Images to PSP

Connect your PSP to your computer using the USB cable. Then use Navigator to go to Settings. Go to USB Connection and press ⊗. Your PSP appears on your computer. Open the PSP folder, and then open the PHOTO folder. If the PHOTO folder isn't there, just create a folder named PHOTO (all capital letters), and copy the folder containing your slides into your new PHOTO folder. See Figure 8-11 for a view from Windows Explorer.

Step 3: View Your Presentation

Now that you've got your files on your PSP, turn on your PSP and go to the Navigator. Then select Photo, and then your presentation, as shown in Figure 8-12. Select the first slide and press X, and you can start your presentation on your PSP.

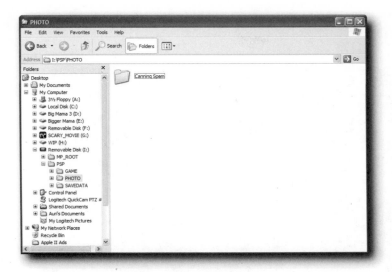

FIGURE 8-11: Copying the slide folder to the PSP

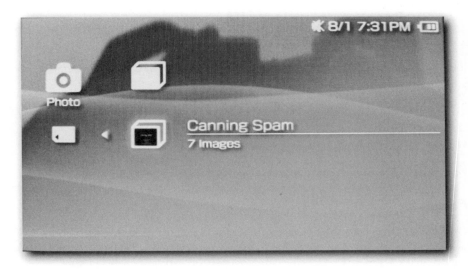

FIGURE 8-12: Selecting your presentation on the PSP

Use the right and left triggers to move forward and backward through your presentation (Figure 8-13).

FIGURE 8-13: The presentation slides on your PSP

Tip   If the image isn't scaling to the size of your display, press (△) while looking at an image, and press X on View Mode to stretch the image.

What If You Want the Animations?

Unfortunately, exporting slides as images removes the animations. So what do you do if you want to keep the presentation with its animations intact? Lucky for you, there are software solutions out there to solve that problem.

This may be a first — the Mac version of a Microsoft product actually has a feature the PC version doesn't have. All of Microsoft's OS X versions of Office (Office X, Office 2002, and Office 2004) have a feature to export any PowerPoint presentation to a Quicktime movie. Once the movie has been created, you can convert that movie file to MPEG-4 format using PSP Video 9 (www.pspvideo9.com) or iPSP (http://ipsp.kaisakura.com/) and view it on your PSP, using the Pause command (the (△) key) on your PSP to pause between slides.

If you have a PC, all is not lost. There is a commercial product, PowerVideoMaker Professional (http://www.presentersoft.com), that for under $150 will convert your PowerPoint presentations to practically any movie or picture format you want. Of course, animations aren't usually what make the presentation, so it may be more cost-effective to stick with the individual image files.

See Chapter 10, "Video Hacks," for much more detail about converting video for viewing on your PSP.

Summary

This chapter covered a number of useful offline hacks. The techniques you learned in this chapter can be applied to many different types of documents, as well as give you the ability to bring your valuable information with you without lugging around a laptop or lots of paper. It's always good to experiment; so if you find newer, better techniques, please post them on the official *Hacking the PSP* Web site at www.hackingpsp.com.

Game Hacks

Sometimes you may want to take a break from hacking your PSP and actually play a game. In this chapter I show you how to get the most out of your PSP for playing games, its original raison d'être.

Play Multiplayer Games with Only One Game UMD

Wireless multi-player gaming is one of the flagstone features of the PSP. Unfortunately, multi-player gaming requires one copy of the game for each PSP joining in. This is good for game developers, but bad for poor college and high school students. PSP games can be expensive, running $40–$50 for new releases, and usually nothing less than $20 for an older title unless it's pre-owned. Luckily for us, the PSP has so much memory that many games often load much of what they need into RAM when they load a level, so they don't need the UMD disc when a level is being played. Using this assertion, it's possible to use a single game UMD to play a multi-player game.

Now, be warned: this hack doesn't work with all games. It won't damage your PSP, however. I've compiled a list of known compatible and incompatible games. It doesn't hurt to experiment, so try other games, too, and let me know which ones work and which ones don't. I'll keep a forum open on the official *Hacking the PSP* Web site for discussing this hack.

Known compatible games are:

- Ridge Racer
- Tony Hawk's Underground 2 Remix (the game we'll use as an example)
- Twisted Metal (needs to be set up so anyone can join at any time)

Known incompatible games are:

- Hot Shots Golf Open Tee
- Wipeout Pure

Here's what you need for this hack:

- Two or more PSPs (two players would be good, too)
- One compatible game (see the preceding list)

Running the Hack

This example uses Tony Hawk's Underground 2 Remix. Other games may vary, but for the most part these instructions will work. If you have questions about particular games, post the question to the *Hacking the PSP* web site at www.hackingpsp.com and I'll answer it for you.

Before running this hack, make sure the Wi-Fi switch is toggled to the up (on) position on both PSPs.

Step 1: Create the Mutliplayer Game on System 1

Follow these steps:

1. Select WiFi Play, then your skater, and then select Ready.

2. Accept your settings, or change them if you want.

3. Select Host Game, then confirm your settings and select Ready. In this case, the game being hosted is named Shaba.

Underground loads and lands System 1 in Free Skate mode (see Figure 9-1). Just let it sit at that screen. When all is done, you can press ⊗ to start playing—but only after you've completed all these steps.

FIGURE 9-1: Free Skate mode starts on System 1

Step 2: Eject the UMD Disc from System 1

Now that System 1 is in Free Skate mode, eject the UMD Disc from System 1. System 1 asks you if you want to quit the game, as shown in Figure 9-2. Select No, and press ⊗. Take the UMD disc and put it into System 2.

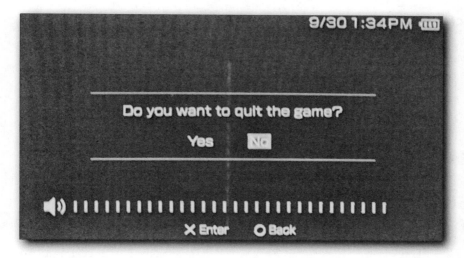

FIGURE 9-2: Don't quit the game on System 1

Step 3: Load and Join the Game with System 2

With the UMD disc in System 2, turn on System 2 and load the game. Go through the same steps as System 1, stopping just short of hosting a game. You should see the game that was started (in this case, it is named Shaba) on the right. Instead of selecting Host Game, choose Join Game. Figure 9-3 shows the two systems — System 1 is on top.

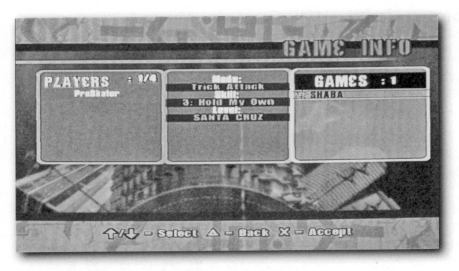

FIGURE 9-3: Joining the game with System 2 while System 1 waits

Step 4: Swap the UMD Back to System 1

Once System 2 flashes Joining Game on the display, wait ten seconds and then take the disc out of System 2 and put it back in System 1. You should see that it is waiting for the other player that has joined the game, but it will be frozen for a moment. After another 15 seconds or so it should come back up, with System 1's character skating on the screen.

Tip

If more than two players intend to use a single cartridge, you can repeat steps 2–4 for each player.

Step 5: Make One Last Swap to System 2, then Play

Once System 1's player starts skating, put the UMD back into System 2 and the game should start loading the level and place you in Skate Mode on System 2 as well. Now that both PSPs are playing, you're set! The level's in memory, so you shouldn't need to insert the disc again. However, if you change levels, you'll have to go through the same quick swap. See Figure 9-4.

FIGURE 9-4: Both of you can play now

Note If you put your PSP to sleep or turn it off, you will lose the connection to the multi-player game and will have to do the process all over again. This applies even if you have a copy of the game for each PSP.

The PSP's Saved Data Utility

Unlike any other portable game console, the PSP has a central management utility for all of the games saved on the Memory Stick. This utility is called the Saved Data Utility and is available under the GAME menu.

Using the Saved Data Utility, you can do the following:

- Copy saved games from one Memory Stick to another. It does not yet support transferring games over wireless to another PSP.

- See saved game data for game profiles you have saved, such as points, extra lives, and so forth. This differs based on the game you're playing. You also can see when you last updated the data, and how much space the item takes up on the Memory Stick. Many games create multiple items for each profile you create, such as different golfers in Hot Shots Open Tee, or different racers in Wipeout Pure.

- Delete saved games, in case you need to start over with a game, or for some reason the saved game becomes corrupted (a good reason to back up your games, discussed later in this chapter).

All of these options are available when you open the Saved Data Utility and then press ⓐ on any saved game. Each game has its own preview icon, as shown in Figure 9-5. After you select a game, the screen changes to reflect the game that created it.

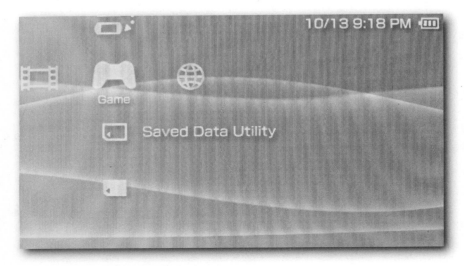

FIGURE 9-5: The Saved Data Utility

Unfortunately, you cannot launch the game from the saved game, even if it's in the drive.

Backing Up Games

All saved game data is stored on the Memory Stick in the SAVEDATA folder under the PSP folder, as shown in Figure 9-6. Game data is not stored in the PSP's internal storage, although this may change at some point in the future. The Web browser is an exception.

Note You may see some extra files in the SAVEDATA folder, such as .DS_Store, Thumbs.db, or Finder.dat — these aren't PSP files, they're actually files created by the Windows and Mac OS file systems. The extra files will not affect your saved games.

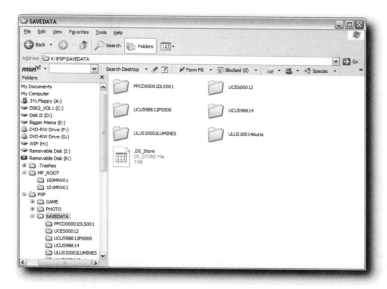

FIGURE 9-6: The SAVEDATA folder

As you also can see in Figure 9-6, the names of the folders are not very legible. Lumines is one of the lone exceptions. So what can you do to find out what folder is which?

Note Don't rename the folders or your saved games won't appear on the PSP.

To find out which folder belongs to what game, turn on Thumbnail view in Windows XP or Windows 2000, and all images will show their respective preview image. From here you can usually tell what game the folder represents, as shown in Figure 9-7. Sometimes you'll see generic icons, because the game or application may have no preview icons, but most of the time that won't happen.

Note On Macintoshes running OS X 10.4 "Tiger" and earlier, folders don't automatically change themselves to reflect their contents. However, if you open the folder, and view the folder by Icon (which is the default), you'll see the image previews.

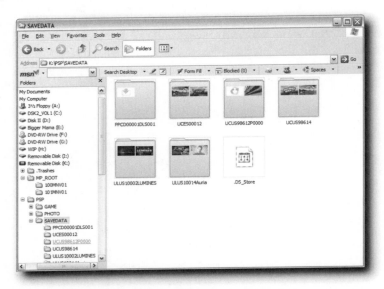

FIGURE 9-7: Thumbnail view reveals what games each folder represents

Tip If you want to use the icon for your game, look at the PNG files in the game save directory for your game and open it up in an editor or viewer.

To backup your games, simply copy the SAVEDATA folder or the individual game saved data folder to your computer. That's it — nothing special about it. Keep the folder name the same. If you want to keep things organized, create a folder for the game with a proper title, and then drop the entire folder into that properly named folder.

There are programs that backup and restore games for you automatically, such as PSPWare and iPSP. You can find the download locations for these applications in Appendix A, "Additional Resources."

Changing the Saved Game Background Image

You can change the background image used for saved games by creating your own graphic and saving it in PNG (Portable Network Graphics) format. To do this, you'll need an image editor that can save in PNG format, such as Photoshop Elements, Photostudio, The Gimp, and GraphicConverter, among others. Then, all you have to do is find the PNG image used for the background image (you can see which image this is in Thumbnail view), which is usually named PIC1.PNG.

To become more famous, I decided to swap Tony Hawk's mug for my own, and add some cheesy graphics to impress my friends. The original saved game image is shown in Figure 9-8.

FIGURE **9-8: Tony Hawk's mug is about to be remixed**

Here's what you need for this hack:

- Your PSP in USB Connection Mode so you can copy the new PNG file to it
- A PNG image you want to use to replace the game's background image

The following are the specifications for the replacement PNG image file you create:

- Image resolution must be 480 × 272 pixels (width × height).
- Resolution dots per inch shouldn't be more than 72 dpi. This will likely be the default in your editing application.
- Don't save the image in interlaced mode.

Tip This same technique applies to the icon files used in the Saved Data Utility's game list. Instead of 480 × 272 pixels, you would use 144 × 80.

Step 1: Back Up the Original Background Image and Copy the New Image

Connect your PSP to your PC or Mac using USB Connection Mode (Settings → USB Connection). Open the PSP folder, then the SAVEDATA folder, and finally the saved data folder you want to replace the background image in.

Now, rename the file PIC1.PNG to PIC1_OLD.PNG, just in case this hack doesn't work. Then, copy your new PNG file to the folder, and make sure it is named PIC1.PNG.

Your folder should look similar to Figure 9-9. Obviously your replacement image will look different from mine.

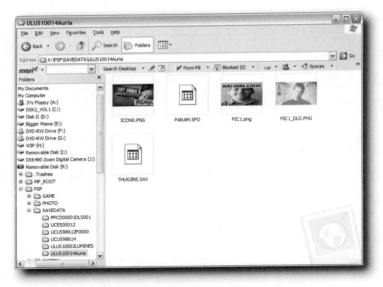

FIGURE 9-9: The folder with the old and new background images in place

Step 2: View the Image

Now that you've got all the files in place, disconnect your USB cable and open up the Saved Data Utility. Select your game and you should see the new background image.

Figure 9-10 shows my modified background image for Tony Hawks Underground 2 Remix.

FIGURE 9-10: The camera always makes you look big

Tip

Sometimes your custom background and icon images may be replaced with the original ones from the game. This is likely to happen when you save your game again. Make sure you have a backup of your custom images so you can keep using them (just copy them over again).

Restoring Game Backups

Restoring backups can be very handy if you have "point in time" backups, popular on many PC games but sorely missing on the PSP. In case you want to venture ahead when you are in a good position, it is a good idea to save your game to your computer. Should you die and lose everything in the game, you can always restore to where you left off, knowing what's ahead and how to avoid it.

Restoring game backups is basically the opposite of backing up. Instead of copying the folder to your computer, you'll copy it from your computer to your PSP.

When restoring games, it is important that you keep the folder name the same and copy over *all* of the files in your backup folder, in case one relies on another.

As I stated earlier, there are programs that will backup and restore games for you automatically, such as PSPWare and iPSP. You can find the download locations for these applications in Appendix A.

Summary

In this chapter you learned how to play a multi-player game with one disc, how to hack your background image to make it yours, how to backup and restore your games, and how to use the PSP Saved Data Utility. The PSP has incredible gaming capabilities, as you know because that's probably why you bought it. Knowing how to use its built-in tools is essential to getting the most out of the machine.

Video Hacks

As I've said over and over, the PSP is a media *machine*. There's almost nothing it can't do. Indeed, when it comes to video it is no slouch— that sleek, sexy screen, the stereo sound, and the high resolution (for a gaming system)— the system beckons to be playing or played.

Play Almost Anything— But There's a Catch

The problem with the PSP is Sony's never-ending arrogance when it comes to format support. Unless a homebrew application comes out that plays other video types, the PSP is limited to playing Sony's own UMD movie discs and MPEG-4 video on Memory Sticks. While that's not a terribly bad thing (MPEG-4 is a great format for small-format, mobile video), the time spent (and audio/video quality lost) converting other formats (called *transcoding*) is annoying, even if you have a fast machine. Plus, if you have a hefty pocketbook, you can buy many popular movies on UMD (although those discs get annoying to carry around).

Less Data Means More Video

The PSP's display is only 480 pixels wide by 272 pixels high—quite a bit larger than most analog TV screens (about 350×250 pixels) but smaller than a DVD's resolution, which runs about 720×480. This is quite a benefit to you, as a Memory Stick can hold many more movies at a high quality (which in this case means full PSP resolution) than if they were just large movies the PSP had to scale down.

UMD: The Not-So-Universal Universal Media Disc

UMD discs, like DVDs, are capable of holding about 1.8GB of any type of data. All commercial games for the PSP are shipped on "Game" UMDs, and all commercial movies for the PSP are shipped on "Movie" UMDs, called UMD-Video.

While many game manufacturers have signed up for PSP game releases, Sony, Paramount, and Universal Studios, among others, are also gearing up (and have already released) UMD-Video titles. Only Warner Home Video had not signed itself up for UMD-Video titles for the PSP (Warner has a competing format called Mini-FVD) at the time this book went to press. UMD-Video titles for the PSP tend to be released on the same date as DVD titles and are usually priced at the same or lower cost for the UMD-Video versions.

UMD-Video, like DVD-Video, uses the MPEG (Motion Picture Experts Group, www.mpeg .org) format for recording video. DVD-Video uses MPEG-2, while UMD-Video is encoded in MPEG-4, a superior quality and higher data efficiency format. The PSP's chipset supports native decoding. The hardware-based decoding saves battery life and guarantees performance of video playback. Also similar to DVDs, the UMD format can be dual-layer, where the laser shifts its focus to read the two layers of the disc. Dual-layer DVDs support up to 9.0GB of data storage, while the UMD supports approximately 1.8GB.

Out-of-the-Box Limitations on Media Format Compatibility

Unfortunately, while the PSP is a powerful media machine, Sony severely limited its support of media playback formats. Also, the PSP video navigator only plays back MPEG-4 video files, requiring potentially lengthy conversions of video (and no utility is provided with the PSP, which is somewhat annoying). Of course, we're going to hack our way around all these limitations, but hopefully Sony will release an update that enables new format playback capabilities *and* doesn't impede our ability to run our hacks.

Getting Videos on Your PSP

Before you get into converting video, it's a good idea to know where things are stored on the Memory Sticks you'll be using for storing your video, audio, and so forth. When you insert a Memory Stick into your PSP and browse it with the PSP navigator, it looks for certain folders to exist, and then enumerates its list of media files from what's in those folders. Table 10-1 shows the folders it looks for different types of media in. These folders are where you will be placing your audio and video files (or where the programs you use will place their converted files).

Table 10-1   Media locations on the Memory Stick

Media type	Location
Video	MP_ROOT \ 100MNV01
Audio	PSP \ MUSIC
Photos	PSP \ PHOTO
Games	PSP \ GAME
Saved Games	PSP \ SAVEDATA

These folders are not created by default when you format a Memory Stick, so if they're not there when you insert your Memory Stick or connect your PSP in host mode, you will have to create them. Note that when you are using your PSP in host mode, you *start out* in the MPROOT directory, so you only have to create the sublevel folders if they don't already exist. The PSP does support subfolders in the individual media directories, so if you want to sort your videos by genre (Comedy, Music Video, and so forth), or your audio by artist, you can do so just by creating new folders. Keep them under 32 characters, though, or you may not be able to see the entire folder name (or the PSP will shorten it for you).

Tip The directories used on the PSP for media are the same as those used on many of Sony's CLIÉ PDAs and digital cameras. This enables plug-and-play media viewing on the PSP from any other Sony device. Once you have the media on the PSP, you can also delete the files and get information about them (resolution, date picture taken, size, and so forth), making the PSP a makeshift media-content management device.

If you plan on placing full-length movies or a number of television shows on your PSP, make sure you have a Memory Stick big enough to hold your content. A 1GB Memory Stick ran between $80 and $120 at the time of this book's writing, and is sure to be cheaper by the time it is published. The largest Memory Stick available at the time was 2GB, but that may be higher by the time this book has gone to press. To get an idea for how large videos are, use the Profile Picker feature in PSP Video 9, which estimates the size of a video file based on which encoding profile has been selected.

Converting and Transferring Video to Your PSP

The first step to getting video on your PC is to convert it to the PSP's native MPEG-4 format. Once it's converted, you can easily transfer it to the PSP via USB host mode or directly to a Memory Stick via a Memory Stick reader.

Here's what you need:

- A PC or Macintosh
- A video conversion program (discussed later)
- A USB cable for transferring video between your computer and PSP
- A Memory Stick to hold the video on (at least the size of your movie — a 1GB Memory Stick is fine for holding many videos)

Depending upon whether or not you have a Macintosh running Mac OS X or a PC running Windows, your first step will be different.

Windows Step 1: Download and Configure PSP Video 9

PSP Video 9 is a free utility that translates practically any video format to the PSP's MPEG-4 video format. PSP Video 9 is highly configurable, and will even transfer converted videos to your PSP when it's done. Best of all, it's free. You can download PSP Video 9 at `http://www.pspvideo9.com/`.

Mac Step 1: Download iPSP Media Manager

iPSP is a powerful media management utility that runs on both PCs and Macs and was written specifically to take advantage of the PSP's unique media capabilities. It not only converts video, it can automatically convert and transfer photos and audio from your PC or Mac to your PSP. iPSP also backs up your saved games, just in case your Memory Stick gets lost or stolen. On a Macintosh, it even integrates with iTunes and iPhoto. iPSP isn't free, but it's cheap at only $20. Figure 10-1 shows iPSP in action.

FIGURE 10-1: The iPSP media management utility

Tip Know a Web site with a bunch of video already formatted for the PSP? Download iPSP Movie Loader (available for Mac and PC, `http://pspmovies.kaisakura.com/`) and it will automatically transfer the video to your PSP once the movie is downloaded.

Note PSP Video 9 is a great product and deserves your support. If you use the program, donate some money to the author using the convenient Click Here to Donate link right inside the program (just click the About button and you'll see it). Supporting authors who write great software ensures they can afford to write more great software for you to enjoy.

Other Video Conversion Programs

In addition to PSP Video 9 and iPSP, there are many other video conversion programs to choose from, including the following:

- **3GP** (www.nurs.or.jp/~calcium/3gpp/, **Free**): The first program to be released that automatically reformatted video to the PSP's video format (MPEG-4 audio and video at the appropriate resolutions). 3GP's interface is in Japanese, but its use is still pretty straightforward.

- **iPSP** (http://pspmovies.kaisakura.com/ipsp.php, **$20**): Automatically converts and transfers video, audio, and images from a PC or Mac to your PSP. Also backs up your saved games to your computer, and integrates with Apple's iLife applications (iTunes and iPhoto).

- **Kinoma Video Producer** (www.kinoma.com, **$30**)

- **Ulead VideoStudio** (www.ulead.com, **$50**)

- **Apple's QuickTime Pro** (www.apple.com/quicktime, **$30**): Apple's QuickTime is a free download that enables you to play a multitude of different media types. By paying a small fee, you can upgrade to QuickTime Pro, which enables the authoring capabilities of the program. While it's fairly easy to export video from native formats, as well as RealPlayer and Macromedia Flash, QuickTime is unable to export Windows Media formatted video to MPEG-4, which is where the PSP Video 9 program excels (and it's free to boot).

You can often find many more video conversion programs on CNet's Download.com Web site at www.download.com.

Step 2: Find the Video to Convert

Regardless if you have a PC running Windows or a Mac, step 2 and the following steps are the same.

The obvious next step to getting video on your PSP is to find video you want to play. Technically you can play any video on your PSP that you can play on your computer, because PSP Video 9 converts the majority of formats from whatever they're encoded in (MPEG, DiVX, and so forth) to the PSP's format, which is MPEG-4. Keep in mind that the rule "Garbage in, Garbage out" applies here, so if you have a poor quality video to begin with, it won't look any better on the PSP.

Tip   Make sure movies play on your PC before you transfer them to the PSP. If you download video from the Internet, you will need to make sure you have the right CODEC installed on your machine in order to play it back. CODECs that don't usually ship with computers include DiVX, Real, QuickTime, and Sorenson Video, among many others.

New Term **CODEC**—Stands for COmpressor/DECompressor, the algorithm for audio or video, often shipped in the form of a plug-in that encodes and decodes media in a certain format. Popular video CODECs include DiVX, Windows Media Video (WMV), RealVideo, and MPEG. Popular audio CODECs include MP-3 (which stands for MPEG-1 Audio Layer 3), RealAudio, Windows Media Audio (WMA), Qualcomm, and AIFF. There are many, many CODECs available on the market for many uses, such as cell phones (Qualcomm TruVoice), mobile audio (MP-3), mobile video (MPEG-4), high-definition television broadcasts (MPEG-2), home theatre (Dolby Digital, DTS) and more. CODEC is often spelled without capital letters—*codec*.

Step 3: Convert the Video

Once you have found the video file you want to convert, simply click Convert in PSP Video 9 and it will do the rest. Figure 10-2 shows PSP Video 9 converting an episode of "Family Guy" that I transferred from my ReplayTV (more on that later in this chapter).

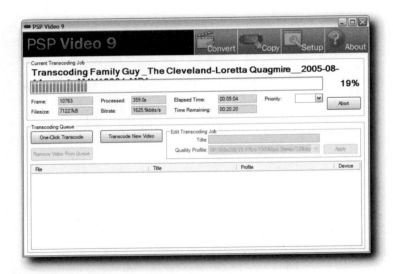

FIGURE 10-2: PSP Video 9 converting a video

If you are converting a large video (greater than 10 minutes) or converting multiple videos, go do something else while they convert. There's usually a 2:1 to 4:1 time conversion ratio, so if you have a fast (2.4 GHz or greater) machine, you may convert an hour-long video in 15–30 minutes. Slower machines may be closer to 1:1. The CODEC the original video is in, as well as the amount of memory you have, also affects your conversion rate (some formats require more resources to decompress than others). PSP Video 9 displays an estimate of how long the conversion will take and how quickly it is processing data.

Tip If the video you want on the PSP is already in MPEG-4 format, there may be no need to convert it. Try transferring it to the PSP first and see if it plays. Why wait when you don't have to?

Tip For a slight conversion performance boost, tell PSP Video 9 to save encoded files on a different hard drive from that which holds your virtual memory swap file (oftentimes this is the boot, or C:\, drive). If you don't know which drive holds your swap file, right-click My Computer, select the Advanced tab, and then click the Performance button. When the Performance Options window comes up, click Change in the Virtual Memory box, and a list appears showing which drives have virtual memory swap files on them. Once you know, click Cancel so you don't modify anything, and now you have the information you need.

Video Compression Crash Course

So how does video compression work? How does MPEG-2 take over 100GB of raw video data and crunch it down to fit on a 4.3GB single-layer DVD? Well, you're about to find out.

The PsychoVisual Model of the Human Brain

The human eye can process only so much information. In particular, we are sensitive to different extremes the primary colors of light: red, green, and blue. We are most sensitive to green (meaning we can discern more shades of green than any of the other primary colors). Next comes red, and finally, very low on our scale, is blue.

How Video Compression Models Work

When you record *raw* (uncompressed or lossless compressed) video to a DV tape, *all* of the video information is stored on the tape, including the exact intensities of each of the primary colors and their positions in the digital frame (pixel mapping). Each frame is recorded individually (and also uncompressed), and laid down with the audio track using SMPTE time coding. Because of all this information, raw video files can grow to be huge (hundreds of gigabytes) and require lots of storage to hold them.

Lossy and Lossless Compression Techniques

There are two types of data compression techniques: *lossless* and *lossy*.

Lossless data compression (it doesn't matter what kind of data, the same terminology applies) means that when the data is compressed and then decompressed, you end up with the exact same data you started with. Some examples of lossless compression formats include ZIP, GIF, and RLE (Run Length Encoding).

Continued

Continued

Lossy compression techniques, on the other hand, mean exactly that—the data isn't the same after compressing it and decompressing it. Lossy compression techniques are often used in systems where certain data can be thrown away, such as MP3s for audio and MPEG for video. A good way to experience how loss works is to look at JPEG, which is a lossy compression algorithm. Find a high-quality JPEG photograph and recompress it in JPEG 10 times. You'll see the image get blockier and less detailed as more data is thrown away through each compression "pass."

In the case of MPEG, we take the psychovisual model I described previously and assume that, because the human eye cannot tell the difference between certain shades of certain primary colors, we can "throw out" those shades of colors from the video stream. So, if in a particular frame of video I have 100 shades of blue, and I know that, based on my psychovisual model that most people can see only 10 of those, I can just throw away 90 percent of my existing color information and make all of those shades of blue closer to the ones most people *can* see. Once I have just 10 shades of blue, that's a lot less information to track and store, and I can compress more effectively.

Of course, MPEG doesn't stop there. It does a lot more! Instead of tracking each frame of the 29.97 frames-per-second video defined in the SMPTE standard (24 frames per second for film), MPEG only tracks the *changes* in each frame. It saves only the changes in the video, with occasional "key frames" for it to restart from if the data stream changes considerably or gets corrupted. You have likely seen this before when watching streaming video on the Internet—when starting a video feed you see only parts of the video and it eventually "fills all the way in." This often happens when you start watching a video before one of the key frames has been transmitted, so all you can see are the changing pixels instead of the frame those changes were initially based on.

New Term

SMPTE—Society of Motion Picture Television Experts. These guys set the standards for the video industry—timing, formats, and so forth. Check out a SMPTE meeting and you'll learn a lot. The SMPTE Web site is www.smpte.org.

Optional: Modify Video Encoding Settings

Most of the time, the video settings PSP Video 9 uses (320 × 240 resolution, 15 frames per second, or *fps* for short) are just fine for viewing on your PSP. However, sometimes you may want to tweak the output, possibly bumping up the frame rate for movies, or slowing it down for converting "static" video such as PowerPoint presentations (more on that particular topic later in this chapter). PSP Video 9 has a wealth of options for you to choose from, as you can see in Figure 10-3.

FIGURE 10-3: PSP Video 9 encoding options

Step 4: Transfer the Video

After the video has been converted, you will likely want to transfer it to your PSP. Make sure your PSP is powered on and plugged into your PC with the USB cable and set it to host mode (if you don't know how to do this, plug the USB cable into your PC and your PSP, then go to Settings on your PSP, then USB Connection; otherwise, refer to your PSP's manual).

Once your PSP is connected, click the Copy button in PSP Video 9 and it gives you a few options. If you want move the file off your computer to the PSP (deleting it from your computer in the process), click Move Video to PSP. If you want to leave the converted video on your computer and transfer it to the PSP, click Copy Video to PSP, as shown in Figure 10-4.

Step 5: Play the Video

Once you have your converted video transferred to your PSP, just navigate to the Video section in the PSP Navigator, select the movie, and play.

Tip

To get duration, size, and other information about a video on your PSP, press the TRIANGLE button.

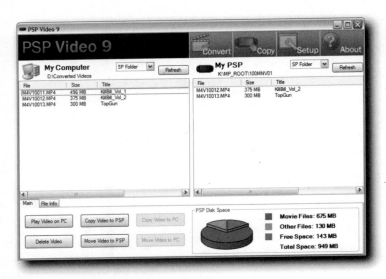

FIGURE 10-4: PSP Video 9 video transfer options

TivoToGo Video on the PSP

If you have a TiVo Series2 personal video recorder and want to take your shows and movies on the road with you, you can easily transfer your recorded shows and movies to your PSP.

Note The TiVo Desktop software and video transfer function aren't available for all TiVo models. Make sure your model is supported before starting this hack.

Here's what you need:

- At least a Series2 TiVo ($99–$399 at most stores)
- A network connector for your TiVo if you don't already have one
- A PC with Windows 2000 or Windows XP to run TiVo Desktop on (or a Mac with VirtualPC running the same; $149 from Microsoft at http://microsoft.com/mac)
- Enough disk space on your PC to hold the transferred movies
- Enough space on your PSP Memory Stick to hold converted transferred movies

Step 1: Get the Latest Version of the TiVo Service

This should happen automatically if your TiVo is connected to the Internet or has dialed-in to TiVo lately. You will need at least version 7.1 in order to do this hack.

Step 2: Connect the TiVo to Your Home Network

Make sure your TiVo is connected to your home network so video can be transferred to the PC that your PSP will be connected to. The faster the connection, the better. If you're transferring 2 hours of video to your desktop over an 11 megabit wireless connection, be prepared to wait a long time for gigabytes of data to come over. It's better to just connect to a hub or run a long cable so you can transfer the video as quickly as possible.

Step 3: Download and Install TiVo Desktop

The proxy between you and your TiVo's video is TiVo's own TiVo Desktop software. Getting this software is easy — go to http://www.tivo.com/4.9.4.1.asp and download it.

Note   You will need TiVo Desktop version 2.1 or greater to gain access to the TiVoToGo capability.

Once you've downloaded the TiVo Desktop software, install it and follow the instructions for setting it up. They're pretty straightforward.

Step 4: Transfer Video from Your TiVo

Using the TiVo Desktop software, transfer the shows you want from your TiVo to your computer. Figure 10-5 shows what it looks like when a show is being transferred.

Note   It can take a very long time to transfer shows. The TiVo desktop software will give you an estimated transfer time, which usually translates to "go get some coffee or play some games while you wait."

Tip   The TiVo Desktop software works both ways. It can also transfer audio and photos *to* your TiVo for listening to and viewing your media on any TiVo in your home.

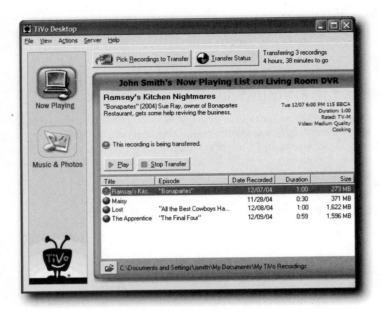

FIGURE 10-5: Shows on the TiVo being transferred to a PC.

Once the video is transferred, you may want to edit the video before moving on to the next step. When editing video, keep your source file separate from your edited movie, just in case you mess up and need to edit again. Also, because TiVo uses a lossy compression algorithm, you will lose more and more video quality as you re-encode the edited video. (See the "Video Compression Crash Course" sidebar for more information on how video compression works.) It is important to keep the video in as high a quality as possible before converting it for the PSP, or it may turn out blocky and hard to view.

Step 5: Convert the Video

Once you have the MPEG-2 video from your TiVo, bring up your video conversion program, such as PSP Video 9 or iPSP, and convert the video (and possibly go get some more coffee or play some more PSP while you wait).

Step 6: Transfer the Video to Your PSP

Once your video is converted, transfer it to the PSP in USB host mode, or just drag it to the video location on the Memory Stick (see Table 10-1 for the location).

Step 7: Play the Video

Now that the video is on your PSP, play and enjoy.

ReplayTV Video on Your PSP

If you have a ReplayTV 4000 or 5000 series personal video recorder and want to take your shows and movies on the road with you, you can easily transfer your recorded shows and movies to your PSP.

Note ReplayTV was the first commercial PVR to allow transfers of shows between PCs and other ReplayTV devices. TiVo caught on to this with its Series 2 product line.

Here's what you'll need:

- A ReplayTV Series 4000 or 5000 (earlier models don't have the networking capability you need)
- Shows to transfer from your Replay

Tip Encode shows at medium quality to get decent video results that have manageable file sizes that are easier to encode. You can set your ReplayTV to encode video at medium quality on a show-by-show basis, or go to your main settings and set the default to medium recording for all shows.

- A PC running Windows 2000, Windows XP, or greater
- WinReplayPC software for transferring video from your ReplayTV
- A network connection to get the video off your ReplayTV

Step 1: Download WinReplayPC

WinReplayTV is a very easy to use application that transfers video off any ReplayTV 4000 or 5000 on your network and places it on your PC. Even better, it's free! The official Web site and download location for WinReplayTV is `http://www.pcphotovideo.com/ReplayPage .htm`. Figure 10-6 shows the WinReplayPC interface.

Note An alternative to WinReplayPC is DVArchive, a free, Java-based program that should run on practically any operating system with the latest Java runtime installed. DVArchive is unique in that it looks like just another ReplayTV box to the other ReplayTV units on your network, and they will interact with it as such (including letting you transfer shows back and forth between your PC and the ReplayTVs in your household). DVArchive can be downloaded from `http://dvarchive.sourceforge.net/`, and Sun's Java runtime can be downloaded from `http://www.java.com`.

However, keep in mind that you want an operating system that can manage large data files, as television shows and movies tend to be hundreds of megabytes to a few gigabytes in size. Windows 98's FAT32 file system does not handle such large files very well, but Windows XP's NTFS file system does.

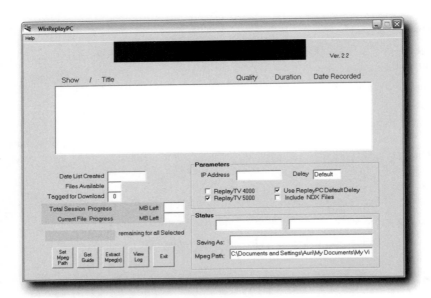

FIGURE 10-6: The WinReplayPC interface

Step 2: Set Up your ReplayTV on the Network

Follow the ReplayTV manual's instructions for setting up your ReplayTV on the network. Then write down the IP address your ReplayTV device so you can use it with WinReplayTV.

Note If you don't know where your network settings are on your ReplayTV, press Menu on your ReplayTV's remote control, then scroll to Setup, and finally scroll to Network Settings. Your ReplayTV's IP address should appear to the right of the menu.

Step 3: Transfer Videos from your ReplayTV

Once you've installed WinReplayPC, bring it up and connect to the ReplayTV you want to transfer videos from by entering the IP address of the ReplayTV on your network, as shown in Figure 10-7.

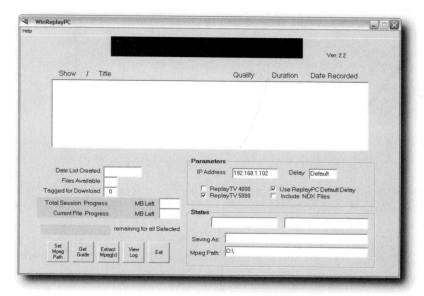

FIGURE 10-7: Selecting the ReplayTV unit to transfer videos from

Check the following boxes under Parameters:

- Check ReplayTV 4000 if you have a 4000 series, or ReplayTV 5000 if you have a 5000 series.

- Check Use ReplayPC Default Delay.

A list of shows appears in the selector box, as shown in Figure 10-8.

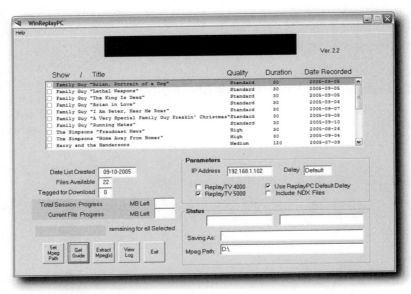

FIGURE 10-8: The list of shows appears in the WinReplayPC selector box

Note If you have trouble getting guide information from your Replay 5000 series, go back to the WinReplayTV Web site and download the GParse5K.exe updater. Your guide should come through properly.

Note If you get an Overflow error, you probably have the wrong IP address entered in the IP Address field in WinReplayTV. Verify your network settings on your ReplayTV.

Before transferring the video, set the location where you want to store the transferred video by clicking the Set Mpeg Path button. I recommend creating a directory named "ReplayTV Video" in your My Videos folder (located in your My Documents folder) or on a drive that has plenty of room for the video.

When you're ready to transfer the video, click Extract Mpeg(s), and your videos start transferring, as shown in Figure 10-9. Depending on your networking speed and the number of videos selected, this could take anywhere from a few minutes to many hours. If you have the opportunity to connect your ReplayTV and your PC to a 100 Mbit Ethernet network, please do so — it will save you a lot of time. WinReplayTV tells you how many megabytes have been transferred as well as how many megabytes are remaining in the transfer of the current file.

FIGURE 10-9: The files being siphoned off your ReplayTV

Tip To speed up the transfer process, and to prevent lockups during the transfer process, make sure the ReplayTV isn't scheduled to record any shows while you're transferring video from it. The transfer process also runs faster if the system is off (still plugged in, of course).

Step 4: Convert the Transferred Videos

Once your videos have been transferred, fire up PSP Video 9 and convert the transferred videos as described in the "Converting and Transferring Video to Your PSP" hack earlier in this chapter.

Tip For television shows or movies with lots of action, you may want to change the encoding settings in PSP Video 9 (or whatever program you use). For movies, 24 fps is excellent, and for television shows, 24 fps is ideal. These settings are shown in Figure 10-10.

FIGURE 10-10: Optimizing video encoding settings in PSP Video 9 for a movie

Tip

If you have multiple hard drives in your system, you can shorten the video conversion time by saving the converted video file on a different drive from the one containing the source video. In PSP Video 9, change the destination directory appropriately.

Step 5: Transfer the Videos to Your PSP

Once your videos are converted, transfer them to the PSP in USB host mode, or just drag them to the video location on the Memory Stick (see Table 10-1 for the location).

Step 6: Play the Videos

Now that the videos are on your PSP, play and enjoy!

Watching DVDs on Your PSP

If you've been wondering how to get those DVDs in your collection onto your PSP, there are a number of ways to do it. I don't condone video piracy, of course, but I do believe in having access to the movies I paid for on DVD without having to buy a new copy of the item every time digital formats change. In this section, I hope to give you ideas, although I'm not legally allowed to tell you exactly how to move copy-protected movies to your PSP.

In this section, I don't discuss how to convert or transfer video to your PSP. See the "Converting and Transferring Video to Your PSP" section near the beginning of this chapter to learn how to do that.

Method 1: Use a DVD Backup Program and Rip the Unprotected Movie VOB

A few years ago, there were a number of programs that would let you make a "fair use" backup of the video on your commercial DVDs. These programs, while their good intent was shaky both morally and legally, worked fairly well. The most popular company was 321 Studios, which was shut down by the legal hounds of the MPAA. Their DVDXCopy utility (see Figure 10-11) converted the popular DeCSS program into a functional, easy to use, Windows-based application that let you make "one-click" backups of your DVD collection. The result was a DVD without the CSS encryption used on DVDs to prevent unlawful copying.

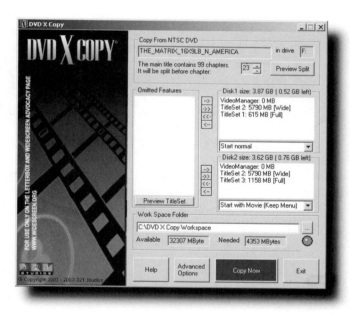

FIGURE 10-11: 321 Studios DVDXCopy utility

New Term **VOB**—Video Object. This is the file format used on DVD-Video discs (named so by its .VOB filename extension) to hold the transcoded video and audio data making up the combined media track. When a DVD is mastered, the MPEG-2 video and digital audio tracks (usually in PCM, Dolby Digital, or DTS format) are multiplexed together into a single file for playback by a DVD player.

CSS—Content Scrambling System. This is the digital content encryption algorithm used to encode the VOB files on commercial DVDs. CSS is not required on DVD-Video discs, of course, but is often employed to deter would-be video pirates from making pure digital copies of commercial DVDs and selling them for a profit. The CSS algorithm was defeated shortly after its release on publicly-available DVDs by "DVD Jon," who wrote the DeCSS program. DVD Jon is also responsible for cracking other protection algorithms, such as Apple's M4P protected AAC content algorithm. DeCSS was so elegantly simple that a version was once released that was only one line of Perl code (although it was slow, it still worked).

Macrovision—A video copy protection system, created by the Macrovision corporation (http://www.macrovision.com), originally used on VHS tapes and now used on DVDs to prevent unauthorized duplication of protected video content. Macrovision prevents simple copying of DVD Video over analog connections to analog VHS decks. However, the techniques it uses to prevent analog copying tend to be defeated by digital recording solutions.

If you can get your hands on programs like these, and they still run, get one—it's very easy to use. If you can't, there's always the DeCSS program that inspired it all. I can't tell you where to download it, but I can tell you it's a good thing that Google exists.

Method 1 is the fastest way to get a high-quality version of *your* DVD ready for conversion to your PSP. However, it's also possibly a very expensive option, as the remaining copies of DVDXCopy tend to be $150 when purchased on the Internet and are rarely found on eBay.

Even though 321 Studios was banned from selling their product after the Summer of 2004, existing copies (including those you buy now) are apparently covered by a grandfather clause that lets them still be activated over the Internet. There is an activation disk that, if you can find one, may be very useful when those activation servers eventually get turned off.

Another product exists called DVD43, available for free from www.dvd43.com. It works like a "realtime" DVDXCopy. Take a look at it and you'll see what I mean.

If you get the multiple VOB files that make up the movie (each will be no larger than 1GB in size), you can combine them using a free program like CombiMovie, available from www.bobyte.com.

Method 2: Buy the UMD Version of the Movie

This method isn't much of a hacker's approach, but it will get you a movie in very high-quality optimized for the PSP, and possibly with special features. Unfortunately, as of the writing of this book, only Sony's titles were slated for release on UMD (although they have made the format "open" for other studios to release their titles as well). For now this means you can't watch a UMD version of *Star Trek* or *Star Wars*, but who knows what will happen with the very young PSP market.

Summary

In this chapter you learned how to convert and transfer video from many popular formats and devices for playback on your PSP. As your video collection grows, your PSP can grow with you — just buy more Memory Sticks or erase old movies from those sticks and replace them with others. Now you'll never be without your favorite shows and movies again!

Audio Hacks

The PSP's audio capabilities are second to no other portable gaming platform on the market today. In this chapter, you will learn the audio formats supported by your particular PSP, the right formats to use when encoding audio, how to access your iTunes library with your PSP, and much more.

It's All in the Firmware

The music file formats your PSP can play via its Music function depend on the firmware version of your PSP. Table 11-1 lists the file formats by firmware revision.

Table 11-1   Audio file formats by firmware revision

Firmware version	Audio playback formats
1.0, 1.5, 1.51	MP3, ATRAC3
1.52	MP3, UMD-Music
2.0	MP3, UMD-Music, MPEG-4 (.m4p, .aac extension), and WAV (limited)

Of course there are homebrew audio players for the PSP, but they only run on PSP Firmware 1.0 and 1.5. Using the hack in Chapter 16, "Reverting from a 2.0 PSP to a 1.5 PSP," you can downgrade your 2.0 PSP (not 2.01) to version 1.5.

Note If you have a 1.51 or 1.52 PSP, you can update it to 2.0 (not 2.01 or higher) and then downgrade it. Of course, you can go beyond 2.0, but then you may not be able to downgrade to run homebrew software. You can find an appropriate 2.0 update file by checking on the official *Hacking the PSP* Web site at www.hackingpsp.com or other reputable PSP Web sites such as www.pspupdates.com.

Changing Sound Equalizer Settings

The PSP has a sound equalizer, with settings such as Pop, Rock, and Jazz. However, these settings are available *only* when something is plugged into the headphone port (such as headphones or external speakers). So, if you need to make a setting change, make sure a device is plugged in there.

Getting Music on Your PSP

To get music on your PSP for use by its built-in player, you need to copy the songs to your Memory Stick, either via the built-in USB connection or a Memory Stick reader on your PC. Of course, you will want to make sure your Memory Stick can hold all the songs you want on it.

Programs like iPSP and PSPWare attempt to automatically fit your music on your PSP, but those programs cost money. For the most part, your music takes up the same amount of space on your PSP as it does on your hard drive, so if you select all the files you want to copy and get properties on them, you'll be shown how much space they take up and can plan accordingly.

New Term **Encode**—The process of converting one data format to another.

New Term **Bit rate**—The amount of bits per second (bps) of audio the data is encoded at. This ultimately affects file size.

Because your PSP is generally used on-the-go and with headphones, not high-end speakers, the audio quality doesn't have to be as high as when you're playing the music through your home theater. In this case, you can actually re-encode your music at a lower bit rate so you can fit more songs on your PSP. Table 11-2 shows optimal bit rates for PSP listening.

Table 11-2 Audio bit rates	
Type of audio	*Bit rate*
Music	160kbps MP3 or 128kbps AAC or ATRAC3
Audio Books	128 kbps MP3 or 64kbps AAC or ATRAC3

Transferring Music to Your PSP

While not as small as an iPod or many of the other digital music players out there, the PSP is very capable of bringing music to your ears. Using the iPSP or PSPWare program, you can automatically convert and fill your PSP with music from your iTunes, Windows Media, and other music collections. The only gotcha is protected music — because that music is encrypted, you can't legally transfer it to your PSP. Of course, any audio CDs you have can be ripped and transferred to your PSP because they are not encrypted.

Create a "PSP shuffle" — Automatically Fill Your PSP with Music

In 2005, Apple released the iPod shuffle, a slick little device the size of a flash memory thumb drive that has an MP3 + AAC music player built-in. The approach taken by the iPod shuffle was you could queue up your iTunes playlists and automatically send one or more of them to your iPod shuffle for quick mixes on-the-fly. You can perform that same useful task with your PSP, plus add the ability to quickly take video and images with you, something the iPod shuffle doesn't even support.

Using the free program PSP shuffle, available for download at http://www.pspshuffle. com, you can shuffle music, photos and video onto your PSP using a very easy-to-use interface. First, you tell PSP shuffle where to look in your media files. Then, using simple sliders, you can set what percentage of space on your PSP you want taken up by music, video, and images, as shown in Figure 11-1. Then simply click, and media is siphoned from your PC to your PSP for a random assortment of media goodness.

FIGURE 11-1: Space percentage sliders in PSP shuffle

Determining Encoded File Sizes

When you encode a file in MP3 or AAC (MPEG-4) format, you encode it at a certain bit rate, which dictates how much storage space per second the encoded audio will use. This is often called the *bps*, or *bits per second*. Table 11-3 contains the formulas you can apply to approximate the amount of storage space you need when encoding an audio file from a standard audio CD. Keep in mind that the formulas assume a "constant bit rate," which means the data will always use 256 kilobits per second, even if an entire 256 kilobits are not needed after the one second of uncompressed audio has been processed, compressed, and encoded. There is another setting for many encoders called *variable bitrate encoding*, which varies the bps as needed up to the maximum set by the user's encoding preferences.

Table 11-3   Standard CD vs. MP3 CD data rates for 150 seconds of audio

Audio source	Data/second	Average song size
CD Audio (44.1 KHz 16-Bit Stereo Audio)	(((16 bits * 44100 Hz) / 1024 bits) / 8 bits) * 2 audio channels* 150 secs = 172 Kbytes/sec	25,800 Kbytes
128 Kb/s Stereo MP3	((128,000 bits/8 bits) / 1024 bits) * 150 secs = 15 Kbytes/sec	2,344 Kbytes

Listening to AudioBooks

Many books today are available on audio CDs, via Audible (www.audible.com), iTunes, and many other stores. The PSP is capable of reading any unprotected MP3, AAC, or ATRAC3 file, so you can easily rip any CD with audiobook content to your PSP and listen to it on the go. The ideal bit rate for audiobooks when ripping them from CD in MP3 format is mono audio at 128 kbps. For AAC or ATRAC3, use mono audio at 96 kbps.

Teach Your PSP How to Read

Using affordable, easy to use programs, you can convert any text document to an MP3 file for listening on your PSP. Cut and paste your news into text files and convert them to MP3s and listen to your news instead of reading it. The following programs, all under $30, can do the job quickly and easily:

- Visual Text-To-Speech MP3, http://www.visual-mp3.com/text-to-speech/
- Alive Text-To-Speech, http://www.alivemedia.net/textspeech.htm
- Natural Reader, http://www.naturalreaders.com/standard_version.htm

Natural Reader stands out because it's free, and it can read Adobe Acrobat (PDF) documents, Word files, Internet Explorer Web pages, and more. Using Natural Reader in conjunction with the free Audio Recorder application included in all versions of Windows (the Macintosh also ships with a similar product), an MP3 converter to convert the audio (the Mac and newer versions of Windows running Windows Media Player can record directly to MP3) such as Windows Media Player or iTunes, and an audio cable run from your computer's headphone port to your computer's microphone port lets you convert your audio to MP3 without spending more than $10 (for the audio cable). Better yet, if you invest in a dual headphone jack (about $5), you can still run your speakers while running your audio to your microphone port and actually hear what you're recording.

Here's what you need for this hack:

- Natural Reader Standard

- MP3 Audio Recording Software (see the next section, "Record the Audio")

- Text you want to convert (I chose the U.S. Constitution, located at http://www.house.gov/Constitution/Constitution.html)

- Enough free space to store the audio file on your computer (most likely no more than 1GB of space is needed)

- Enough free space on your PSP's Memory Stick to store the converted audio (depending on the length and quality of what you record)

- A PC running Windows or a Mac running Mac OS 9 or higher

- A dual-male 3.5 plug stereo audio cable (about $10, available from Radio Shack and almost any store that carries audio cables; refer to Figure 11-2)

- A mini-stereo headphone adapter (it looks like a "Y" cable) so you can listen to the audio you're recording (about $5; see Figure 11-3)

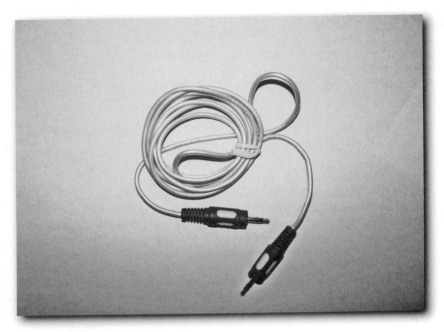

FIGURE 11-2: Dual-male 3.5 plug stereo audio cable

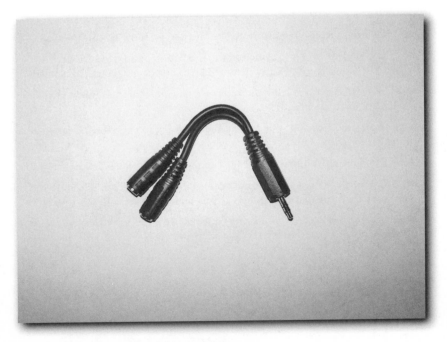

FIGURE 11-3: Mini-stereo headphone adapter

Record the Audio

Now you have to record the converted text as speech to a digital file.

If You Have a PC Running Windows

Download Audio Recorder For Free, available at `http://www.download.com` (although the official company Web site is `http://www.audioeditor.us`, the free version didn't appear to be downloadable from there). The Audio Recorder For Free program can record from any audio source directly to MP3 and has a very simple interface.

If You Have a Mac Running Mac OS 9

Use the Sound Recorder application under the Apple menu to record your audio.

If You Have a Mac running Mac OS X

Use the Sound Recorder application in the Utilities folder. To find this application, select the Go menu in Finder, and then select Utilities. In older versions of OS X, you may need to open the Applications folder first, and then the Utilities folder.

Connect the Audio Cable

Connect one end of the audio cable to your computer's audio input port (or headphone port, if an audio input port is not available), and the other end to your computer's audio input port, as shown in Figure 11-4.

FIGURE 11-4: The audio cable properly connected

Tip The default audio quality settings should be fine in all of the aforementioned applications. You can fine tune the settings as you desire. Remember the rule "garbage in, garbage out." If you aren't sure what quality you want, first record at the highest setting, and then re-encode a copy of the original recording to lower quality levels, so you always have a high-quality recording to start from.

Record the Text

Select Record in Audio Recorder for Free or Sound Recorder and then select Read in the Natural Reader program or the Natural Reader toolbar in your application, as shown in Figure 11-5.

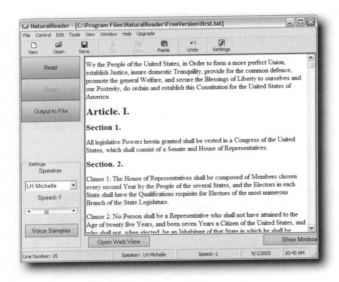

FIGURE 11-5: Natural Reader reading text

Your computer starts recording the audio. When the text has been read, press Stop in the sound recording application, such as Audio Recorder For Free, which is shown recording in Figure 11-6.

Transfer Audio to PSP

Now that you have an MP3 recording of your audio, you need to move it to your PSP. Either use the USB connection and manually transfer your audio to the PSP \ MUSIC folder, or use a program like PSPWare or iPSP to transfer the audio automatically. It is best to put the music in a folder so you can easily separate it from other audio in the MUSIC folder. Remember, you can have only one folder level in the MUSIC folder, so while you can have a folder for each music type or category, you cannot have folders within folders.

How Does Audio Compression Work?

Have you ever wondered how "normal" audio CDs you buy in the store can hold only around 12 to 14 songs, but an MP3 CD can hold dozens to hundreds? The secret lies in the audio compression used in MP3s.

Audio CDs use an audio format called AIFF, or Audio Interchange File Format. AIFF files are not compressed, so the data has no loss in quality. This type of audio encoding is called a *lossless* format. The bits that are recorded are played back, just as they are in the file, just like a record player runs over the grooves on an LP and plays them back as they're formed on the vinyl. Unfortunately, this translates to a very large file.

MP3s, on the other hand, are much more complex. MP3 compression takes into account the *human psychoacoustic model*, which dictates what sounds the human ear can discern, among many other factors (sometimes called *filters*). For example, in AIFF, all frequencies are saved in the file, whether or not you can hear them. In MP3, it can safely "throw out" the sound that is at frequencies you can't hear, thus saving quite a lot of space.

Another factor that's taken into consideration is *masking sounds*. A loud sound will muffle out a softer sound, so there's no reason to keep all the softer audio waves of music when they won't be heard anyway.

After the psychoacoustic model and masking filters are applied to the sound, other advanced digital compression technologies are applied (similar to how ZIP files work). The end result is a much smaller file than an AIFF, which doesn't apply filters or compression at all.

So how do you tune the amount of compression? You've most likely heard MP3 files that sound better than others. The key is often the *bit rate*, or the amount of bits (storage space) the audio file can consume per second of *source* (original) audio. The higher the bit rate, the less harsh the compression, and the less data that must be thrown out to achieve the bit rate, and thus the better the audio is. Tests have shown that true *audiophiles* (professional audio enthusiasts) couldn't tell the difference between a 320 kbps MP3 and a standard audio CD track that used up six times the space on a disc.

You've likely also heard of AAC (Advanced Audio Codec), RealAudio, Windows Media Audio (WMA), and ATRAC3+, among other formats. These audio encoding formats work much like MP3, but they utilize often superior psycoacoustic models and filters and more advanced compression techniques to trim audio files down to even smaller files with higher quality audio than their MP3 counterpart. The PSP supports MP3 in all firmware versions and AAC in firmware version 2.0 and beyond.

FIGURE 11-6: Audio Recorder For Free Natural Reader's output

Podcasts and PSPCasts

Podcasts, which are downloadable non-live broadcasts (often in MP3 format), have become quite the rave on the Web. Many radio stations, news stations, tech shows, and even many Web sites release daily Podcasts of their shows for download onto portable music players for listening on-the-go. (Podcast gets its name from the popularity of these files on Apple's iPod.) The PSP can play any MP3 or MPEG-4 AAC or ATRAC3 formatted Podcast — just copy it to your PSP's Memory Stick using the USB connection and drag the file into the PSP \ MUSIC folder, or use a program like PSPWare or iPSP to automatically move the file onto your PSP.

Controlling iTunes with Your PSP and a Mac

With iTunes installed on a Mac and a special application named DotTunes to communicate with its remote access features, you can access your entire iTunes library and control iTunes using your PSP's Web browser, be it the official Sony browser or the hacked Wipeout Pure browser. DotTunes requires Mac OS X 10.1 or higher and can be downloaded from http://www.dotpod.net. There is a similar application called Kung Tunes available at http://www.kung-foo.tv/itti.php. No equivalent existed for Windows or Linux at the time this book went to press, but if an equivalent appears, I will list it on the official *Hacking the PSP* Web site.

Controlling WinAmp with Your PSP

If you use the popular media player WinAmp, you can get similar functionality to the project described in "Controlling iTunes with Your PSP and a Mac" by installing a special plug-in for WinAmp called BrowseAmp, which is available as a free download at http://www .browseamp.com, shown running in Figure 11-7.

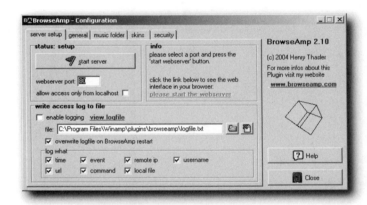

FIGURE 11-7: BrowseAmp in action

Make Your Media Available via Web NAS Devices

You don't have to install any media software to get music on your PSP. Using ADS Tech's NAS Drive Kit ($99, available at www.adstech.com) and a spare hard drive, you can copy all your MP3s and AAC files to the ADS drive and turn on its Web sharing function. Then, using the PSP's Web browser (the official Sony one), you can connect to the ADS NAS device, browse your music collection from anywhere you have a Wi-Fi Internet connection, and download your music to your Memory Stick on-the-fly. Figure 11-8 shows the Drive Kit.

New Term   **NAS**—Network Attached Storage.

FIGURE 11-8: The ADS NAS Drive Kit

Summary

In this chapter you learned how to exploit the many musical talents of your PSP, and how to get the most out of your music collection with your PSP. While most of the audio hacks in this chapter were offline hacks, meaning you couldn't buy music albums online and have them automatically downloaded to your PSP (although you could do something similar with the NAS project), it is almost certain that Sony will make commercial audio downloads available for the PSP through its own online music store, and possibly other online music retailers will follow suit so you can enjoy and purchase music anywhere in the world!

Image and Photo Hacks

The PSP has a great interface for viewing photos — it's deceptively easy to use and fairly powerful. The original PSPs (1.0 in Japan, 1.5 in the U.S., and 1.51 elsewhere), were capable of viewing only JPEGs. However, with System Update 2.0 (also known as firmware version 2.0), Sony introduced a wealth of new formats: PNG (Portable Network Graphics), BMP (Bitmap Graphics), TIFF (Tagged Image File Format), and GIF (Graphic Interchange Format).

JPEGs by themselves were fine, because most digital cameras use the JPEG format by default, but the expansion into other formats enabled the PSP to be quite a bit more to a broader audience. Of course, this doesn't accommodate PDF and eBook readers and a Macromedia (now Adobe) Flash player, among a few other esoteric formats, such as RAW. Running homebrew software can cover these bases, but it is very possible that Sony or third-parties will release additional viewers for the platform.

In this chapter, we will explore the image capabilities of the PSP and bend them to our will.

Images on the PSP

Your PSP is capable of displaying many types of images in full-color on a high-resolution, 16:9 "widescreen" form factor display (as opposed to a 4:3 "full frame," like most non-HD television sets). The PSP has a native screen resolution of 480 × 272, meaning it has more pixels than most similarly-priced PDAs in the market, which is about one-fourth the resolution of an 800 × 600 PC screen. The display is also capable of displaying more than 16.7 million colors, just like a laptop, whereas most game systems are limited to displaying between 256 and 65,536 colors. This means that most images you view will have to be scaled, but compared to other devices in the price range, the pictures will look great.

Note While Sony refuses to officially comment on it, the infrared port on the PSP has been known to be able to control Sony's Aibo Robotic Pet. Competition for Nintendogs. Who knows.

What's the Difference between 16:9 and 4:3?

16:9, or "16 by 9" or "widescreen," refers to the aspect ratio of the television set's viewing area—in this case, 16 "units" wide by 9 "units" high, more of a rectangle than a square, as shown in Figure 12-1. Most HDTV television sets sold today are 16:9 "widescreen," such as DLP, LCD, Rear-Projection, and Plasma displays. Some HDTV sets, however, are still "full frame," but have enough resolution to display 16:9 scaled in the middle of the display without distortion.

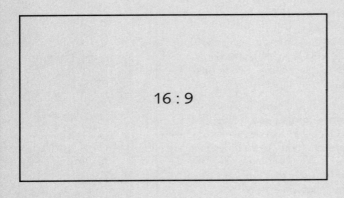

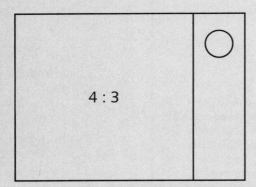

Figure 12-1: 16:9 widescreen vs. 4:3 full-frame

4:3, or "4 by 3" or "full frame," means the television's viewing area is 4 "units" wide by 3 "units" high, closer to being a square. All standard television sets are 4:3, yielding less display space, and hence they can't show as much picture unless it is manipulated, such as squeezing, which makes everyone look very tall (you'll see this in the credits on many 1980s shows shown on television), clipping (cutting the sides of a 16:9 to make it fit in a 4:3 frame), or panning the video (moving the 4:3 frame to show the "ideal" frame of the 16:9 content, often seen on television movie broadcasts).

Note 4:3 and 16:9 do *not* define the resolution of the display.

Tips and Tricks When Viewing Images

While the PSP at first appears limited to only showing the images one by one, scaled to the screen, you can indeed do much more. Firmware version 2.0 (also known as System Update 2.0) added even more capabilities. Let's go through them — I'll let you know which capabilities are only in firmware 2.0 and above.

Photo List Mode

Before you can view an image from PHOTO in the PSP Navigator, you will see a list of images and image folders. While you can scroll to an image or folder and press ⊗ to select it, you can also use △ to get additional "high-level" options for the image, including the ability to delete the image and to get information about it (including the name of the image, its size, when it was last updated, its pixel resolution, and the file format). In firmware 2.0, an additional option is available — Send — which enables you to send the selected image to another PSP via the built-in Wi-Fi, as shown in Figure 12-2.

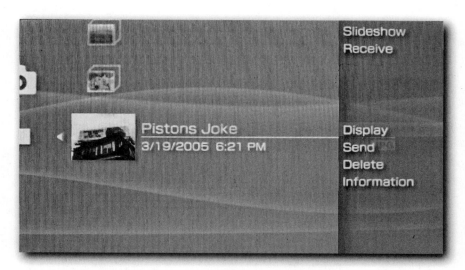

FIGURE 12-2: The picture options menu from Photo List mode

Photo List mode also automatically generates thumbnails of the first image in any folders full of images. This is dissimilar to Windows XP, which generates a custom folder icon for the first four images in the folder. You can tell an item in the list is a folder because it is displayed as a cube with a white border instead of just a square image.

By pressing ⃝ on a folder of images you are given the following options (shown in Figure 12-3):

- **Slideshow:** Shows all the images in that folder the PSP can display. For firmware versions prior to 2.0, this is limited to JPEGs. For PSPs with 2.0 or higher, PNG, TIFF, GIF, and BMP files can also be displayed. Slideshow images are shown in the order they were copied to the PSP, not alphabetically, so if you're intending to use your PSP for a slideshow, make sure you copy files over in the order you want them. You can change the Slideshow speed in the PSP Navigator by selecting the Settings menu, then Photo Settings, and then Slideshow Speed. Use the Left Trigger and Right Trigger controls to quickly skip images or go back to images, in the same order the slideshow would play them. PSP Firmware 2.0 allows you to have music playing while the slideshow runs, 1.52 and prior do not.

- **Receive:** Enables you to receive images from other PSPs over a Wi-Fi connection into the selected folder. Unfortunately, this doesn't support Infrared data sharing, so you can't (at this time, anyway) share images with wireless cameras and PDAs.

- **Delete:** Enables you to delete the entire folder of images from the Memory Stick. Only use this option if you are sure you want to delete *all* the images *and* the folder; otherwise, open the folder and delete the images you don't want.

- **Information:** Gives you the name of the folder, the total size of the files in the folder, and the total number of images the PSP recognizes in the directory.

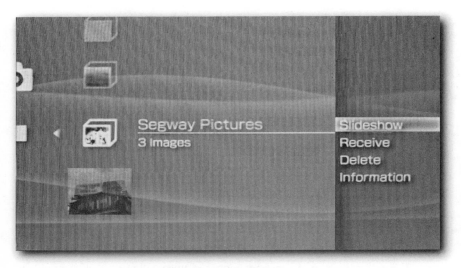

FIGURE 12-3: Folder options from Photo List mode

Tip If you accidentally delete images you need, you can use a flash media file recovery program like Photo Rescue, available from www.datarescue.com/photorescue/index.htm. You can also search on www.download.com for **file recovery software** and **Memory Stick recovery**.

Viewing an Image

When you press ⊗ to view an image, the image is displayed and you can press the following buttons to change the view:

- **Left and right triggers:** Change the image you're viewing. The left trigger goes back an image, and the right trigger goes forward. The image order is based on the time each file was copied onto the Memory Stick.

- **Analog stick:** If the image is too big for the screen, you can use the analog stick to scroll up, down, left, and right. By default, the PSP scales the image to fill the screen.

- △: Pressing this button while viewing an image brings up the View Options menu. The options on this menu are as follows:

  - **View Mode:** Toggles between scaling the image to fit and showing it full size. Note that when you press ⊗ on this option, the percentage it was scaled briefly flashes in the bottom-left corner of the PSP's screen. This can be helpful if you're writing games or applications for the PSP and you need to know how much to scale an image to make it fit properly on the display.

  - **Display:** Brings up a status bar that shows you the name of the image, the total number of images in the folder you're viewing, and the date the image was taken. Select this option again to turn it off.

  - **Set as Wallpaper (Firmware 2.0 Only):** Enables you to set the current image as the background, or "wallpaper," image for the PSP Navigator.

  - **Send (Firmware 2.0 Only):** If there is another PSP within range, you can send the current image to them by selecting this option. Make sure your Wi-Fi switch is on before sending or you'll get an error.

  - **Help:** Displays the help for the photo viewer feature.

  - **Zoom Out, Zoom In:** Self-explanatory.

  - **Clear Zoom (magnifying glass with an equal sign):** Only shows up after you've zoomed in or out. Scales the image back to the screen.

  - **Rotate Left, Rotate Right:** Self-explanatory.

  - **Up, Down, Left, Right:** Moves the image up and down, similar to scrolling with the analog stick, but this takes longer. Left and Right are only available on firmware 2.0 for some strange reason.

While you use these features, the image is *not* modified on the Memory Stick. This is different from Windows, where the built-in image viewer saves every rotation of an image to disk.

If you turn zoom on or change the display mode and press ⚠ again, you can use the analog stick to scroll the image up, down, left, and right. This is a lot faster than using the Up and Down options in the View Options menu. While you scroll an image, a thumbnail of the image appears to the left and shows your position in the overall image.

Image Conversion Programs

If you need to get a file in one format to another, such as RAW to JPEG, there are a number of free applications out there that will do it for you. One of the most popular open-source applications is The Gimp, available for download at www.download.com, a great site for finding many types of applications. The Gimp is available for Windows, Mac OS X, and Linux. In addition to The Gimp, you can also take a look at your digital camera's software package — it probably came with a photo conversion program such as Adobe Photoshop LE, Adobe Photoshop Elements, Paint Shop Pro, ArcSoft PhotoStudio, Ulead Photo Impact, or one of many other commonly bundled applications.

Viewing Any Type of Document on the PSP

Unless you're running homebrew viewers, the PSP is limited to viewing JPEGs and, with firmware 2.0, PNG, TIFF, BMP, and GIF. So how do you get all the other document types on there?

Homebrew Viewer

One option is to find a homebrew viewer. This works fine if you have a firmware 1.5 or earlier PSP and can find a viewer. Many different document and media viewers have been written and can be installed for use by copying them to a Memory Stick if you run firmware 1.0, or copied using the KXploit if you run 1.5. For more information on this approach, read Chapter 19, "Running Homebrew Applications." If you have a firmware 2.0 PSP, Chapter 16, "Reverting from a 2.0 PSP to a 1.5 PSP," explains how to downgrade to a 1.5 PSP.

Paperless Printer and Related Software

The other option is to take whatever document format you want to view and convert it into a format the PSP can display. Of course, the PSP is limited to graphic formats, so you won't be able to edit your documents, but at least you can view them. The goal is to convert each page of your documents, say Word or PDF, to a graphic format like JPEG so your PSP can view it. Luckily, there are programs out there that do this — it just depends on what operating system you're running.

For PCs running Windows, Rarefind's Paperless Printer prints from any standard Windows application (anything that supports an installed printer in Windows, which is practically all of them) to any number of different graphic formats, including JPEG, BMP, PNG, and others. You can download Paperless Printer for free from `www.rarefind.com/paperless printer`. Paperless Printer works just like a regular printer in Windows (see Figure 12-4), so you can set it to print at 5 inches by 3 inches using the Page Setup feature found in most applications and practically all of your pages will scale very nicely. You also can print full pages and the PSP will let you scroll through them using the analog stick (discussed earlier in the "Viewing an Image" section).

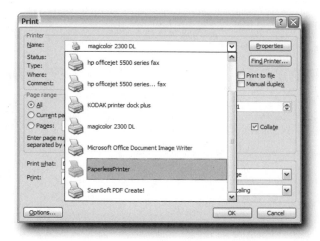

FIGURE 12-4: Paperless Printer looks just like a regular Windows printer

For Macintoshes running Mac OS X, you need to print to a PDF first (all applications can do this — just check PDF as the output format when printing, as shown in Figure 12-5), and then convert the PDF to images using a program like Port Peg, available from `www.versiontracker.com/dyn/moreinfo/macosx/24934`. Apple's own Preview tool can save any individual PDF page as a JPEG, GIF, BMP, TIFF, and many other formats, so if you don't want to pay for Port Peg, you can just use Preview, although it will take longer to convert multiple pages.

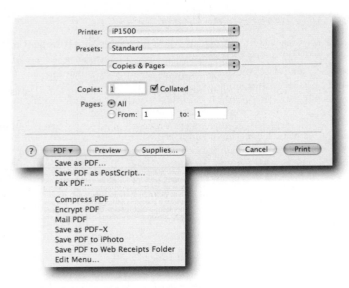

FIGURE 12-5: Printing documents to PDF in Mac OS X

Creating Custom Thumbnail Previews for Video Files

If you want to have a custom preview icon for the videos on your PSP, you need to create a THM image file. THM files have the same name as the video file, except they are 160 × 120 (width × height) JPEG images and have the file extension of THM.

Follow these steps to create a custom preview thumbnail for your video files:

1. Find the file you want to use as the thumbnail image.

2. Load the file into your favorite image editing program, such as Photoshop Elements, The Gimp, PhotoStudio, GraphicConverter, and so forth.

3. Resize the file to 160 × 120.

4. Save the file as a JPEG without any attached preview image (Macintoshes tend to save a preview image along with the file — don't let the application do that), with the same name as your video file, which is case-sensitive. Your best bet is to use the Save for Web option, or a similar Web-compatible image generating tool, to make sure the image doesn't have any "extras" attached to it. With PCs this shouldn't be a problem.

5. Close the image editing program and find where you saved your file.

6. Change the JPG or JPEG file extension to THM, so your filename has the .thm extension instead of .jpg.

7. Connect your PSP to your PC with USB Connection mode (Settings ➔ USB Connection in PSP Navigator) and copy your new THM file into the same folder as your video file.

8. Disconnect USB Connection mode and navigate to Video, then Memory Stick, and you should see your new thumbnail.

Note Programs like iPSP (http://ipsp.kaisakura.com/), PSPWare (www.nullriver.com), PSP Video 9 (www.pspvideo9.com), and Kinoma Producer (www.kinoma.com) automatically create THM files for various media types.

Using the PSP as a Digital Photo Album

You can use your PSP as a digital photo album and take your images anywhere you want to go. Of course, there are different approaches to this, appropriate for different needs, such as when you want to bring only a few photos, or if you want to bring hundreds of them.

Offline

Your PSP can store a virtually unlimited number of images on a Memory Stick Duo. All you have to do is copy all the images you want to the PSP / PHOTO directory on the Memory Stick.

To access the PSP / PHOTO directory, connect your PSP to your PC via the USB Connection mode (Settings ➔ USB Connection) and a USB cable. When your PSP's contents show up, open the PSP folder, and then the PHOTO folder. If these folders don't exist, you will have to create them. To do this, first create the PSP folder in the root (first level) of your Memory Stick, and then create the PHOTO directory, as shown in Figure 12-6.

Now, you *could* just copy all your images into the PHOTO folder. That's not very clean, though, is it? Dozens of photos can be hard to sort through. Instead, it's better to create a separate folder in the PHOTO folder for each set of images you have, as shown in Figure 12-7.

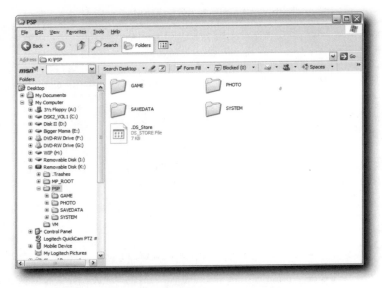

FIGURE 12-6: The PHOTO folder created in the PSP folder

FIGURE 12-7: Images separated into folders

The PSP automatically creates a thumbnail of the first image in the folder, as shown in Figure 12-8, so you can get an idea of what's in it. The name can be almost as long as you want, but the best bet is to keep the folder name under 32 characters. While your PC or Mac may let you make super long folder names, the PSP just doesn't have the screen real estate to display anything much larger than the 32 characters. The same rule goes for filenames.

FIGURE 12-8: Photos and photo folders on PSP

Online

If you need to take a lot of photos with you, you can put them all on a Memory Stick and schlep them along. Of course, a better idea may be to use a free photo site, like Flickr, and upload all your images so you can bring them up anywhere you have an Internet connection. This can save you a lot of money, because Memory Sticks are fairly expensive, especially if you're showing a lot of photos. Of course, if you're showing only a few photos, smaller Memory Sticks, including the 32MB Duo that comes with the PSP Value Pack, are fine.

Sharing Photos with Other PSP Users

Starting with firmware 2.0, Sony included a feature enabling PSP users to share photos wirelessly. No special configuration is needed.

Sender

Here is what you do to send a photo from your PSP to another PSP:

1. Open the Photo viewer and find the images you want to send. You will have to send them one at a time — the PSP does not (yet) support sending entire folders of images. We will go through the steps to send one image here, and then you can repeat the same steps to send the others.

2. Make sure your Wi-Fi switch is on (it should be in the upper position) or you'll get an error during this process.

3. On the image you want to send, press (△), highlight Send, and press (✕). Your PSP begins waiting for the other PSP to accept the image, as shown in Figure 12-9.

FIGURE 12-9: The sender's PSP waiting for a receiver

4. Your PSP asks you which PSP you want to send the photo to (see the top PSP in Figure 12-10). The PSPs that have turned on Receive (as described in the receiver's steps that follow) show up in the list. Select the one you want to send to and press (✕) on its name. After a few seconds the transferred images are shown on the receiving PSP, waiting for them to save the image, and the sending PSP returns to its list of images, as shown in Figure 12-11.

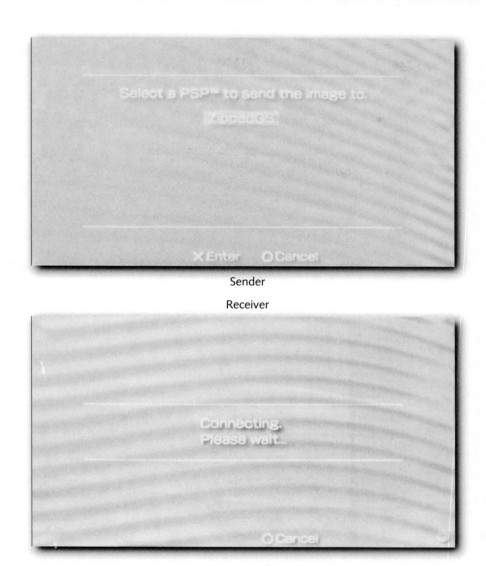

Sender

Receiver

FIGURE 12-10: The receiver waiting for the image from the sender

Sender

Receiver

FIGURE 12-11: The two PSPs after transferring the image

Receiver

Here's what you do to receive photos on your PSP:

1. Navigate to Photo in the PSP Navigator and highlight the folder you want to receive into. Do not press ⊗ to enter that folder or this won't work. If you don't have any folders, you can skip this step.

2. Press △ on the selected folder. If you don't have any folders, go back to Memory Stick and press △. A list of options appears.

3. Highlight Receive and press ⊗ and your PSP starts waiting for the sender, as previously shown at the bottom of Figure 12-10.

4. The fact that the image is showing on your screen does *not* mean that the image has been saved. You must press Ⓞ to save the image and *then* you're done.

Note It is possible for other nearby PSPs to get your image as well. Of course, they would have to be attempting to receive an image at the same time—the PSP doesn't notify you automatically when an image is being sent without your first telling it to receive.

Summary

In this chapter you learned the image capabilities of the PSP, how to make any type of document (be it Web, manga, comic strip, Word, or whatever) viewable on your PSP, how to send and receive images between PSPs, and tips and tricks for viewing images on your PSP. Other things you may want to try are creating your own animated GIFs and playing them back on your PSP, or downloading images from the Web to your PSP.

Getting More Power

Portable game systems are awesome. Especially the PSP. Unfortunately, they all require batteries. The PSP addresses the power issue quite comfortably with its included rechargeable lithium-ion battery. This provides anywhere from four to eight hours of battery life, depending on screen brightness, UMD drive use, wireless network use and processor usage. But what if you need more?

This chapter discusses the various power solutions available for the PSP. While this isn't hacking per se, it's a resource to help you find the right stuff to get the power you need when you need it.

Replacement Batteries

Sony offers replacement batteries for the PSP that are available from practically any electronics store that sells PSPs. In addition to the standard replacement battery, which is 1800 mAh and identical to the battery that comes with your PSP, Sony offers a higher capacity battery pushing out 2200 mAh.

All is not lost if you can't afford a new Sony battery (they usually run about $40). If you check your local used game store, such as GameStop or EB Games, they may have used batteries or possibly even their own, cheaper brand. eBay is also an excellent resource for both new and used batteries and PSP accessories — just watch out for those shipping costs.

Third-party batteries are also available for the PSP. Third-party batteries are usually much cheaper than OEM (Original Equipment Manufacturer) batteries from Sony. However, make sure you check on PSP forums before you buy a third-party battery and make sure it works well with the PSP. Third-party batteries that are cheaply made may explode in your PSP or damage it. At the time this book was going to press, Datel was shipping a battery that had double the output of the stock PSP battery (3600 mAh) for practically double the running time. They also shipped a similar battery with a 4GB hard drive built in that connects to the PSP's Memory Stick slot for a whopping amount of affordable storage space.

Note The fact that your PSP uses a lithium-ion battery is a great benefit to you. Many handheld systems and rechargeable batteries use NiMH, or Nickel-Metal Hidryde batteries, which have a "memory effect" after a few charges. Lithium-ion batteries, or LIon, are much more tolerant of hundreds of charges, thus lengthening your battery's life to a few years of continuous use instead of a few months. Other battery technologies you may want to learn about include nickel cadmium (the popular predecessor to NiMH batteries) and lead acid (used in car batteries).

Charging Cases

Replacement batteries can be a burden to carry, especially since the included PSP carrying sleeve doesn't hold anything but the PSP (don't stick Memory Sticks in there — those expensive suckers will likely fall out). Thankfully, Nyko (www.nyko.com) makes a sturdy metal carrying case for the PSP that has a built-in lithium-ion battery, called the Nyko ChargerCase for PSP (see Figure 13-1). When you plug your PSP in the case, it uses its own battery to power your PSP while you play, at the same time it's charging your PSP. This can yield four to six more hours of gameplay, movie watching or music listening, all without carrying any extra dongles or wires. The Nyko case is reasonable, too, running about $50, which is just above the cost of a new Sony battery, and it protects your PSP to boot. The Nyko case also uses your PSP's charger to charge itself, so if you go on a trip, you don't have to carry more than one charger.

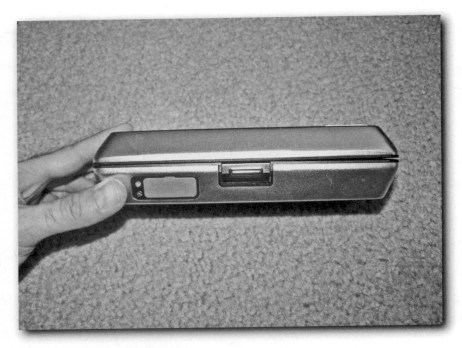

FIGURE 13-1: The Nyko PSP charging case

Pelican Products (www.pelicanperformance.com) also sells their PSP Power Brick, shown in Figure 13-2, which is about two inches square and plugs into your PSP's power outlet and charges it like the Nyko case. The benefit is about the same as the Nyko case, but at a cost of only $20. However, the PSP Power Brick is not a carrying case, so it is an extra device you have to carry (although you could carry both and get three times the original battery life).

FIGURE 13-2: The Pelican PSP Power Brick

Car Chargers and A/C Inverters

If you need to charge your PSP while on the road, you have a number of options. The first route is to buy a PSP Car Charger, which simply plugs into your cigarette-lighter adapter (called an A/C adapter in newer cars) and the other end has the same connector your PSP's power adapter uses, plugging right into your PSP and charging it while you drive. These adapters usually cost between $12 and $20 and you can pick them up at any store that sells PSPs. Many manufacturers sell these. Some examples include the Pelican PL-6003 Car Charger (www.pelicanperformance.com), the MadCatz PSP Power Solution kit (www.madcatz.com; it comes with the car power adapter, a battery pack, and UMD game cases for a scant $15; and is shown in Figure 13-3), and the Arsenal APSPM601.

FIGURE 13-3: The MadCatz PSP Power Solution kit

When you combine one of these adapters with the Nyko ChargeCase mentioned earlier, you can play your PSP and charge both your PSP and ChargeCase batteries while in the car, giving you maximum power on the road.

Your other option is to buy an A/C Power Inverter, such as those from Belkin, APC, and many others, which provides household-like power sockets in your car. A/C Power Inverters plug into your cigarette lighter adapter and usually have an On/Off switch to prevent battery drainage when the car is off or the inverter is not in use. Using an inverter is very straightforward — plug your PSP's charger into an available power socket, and then plug the other end into your PSP. An A/C inverter is pictured in Figure 13-4.

You can purchase an A/C inverter at any consumer electronics or auto parts store. For your PSP you don't need anything more than a 120W inverter with a single socket. If you get one with two sockets, you can then plug a couple of devices in. However, don't overload the inverter. You'll know if you do this, as most of them beep and stop working when that happens.

Front   Back

FIGURE 13-4: An A/C inverter

A few notes when you're using an A/C inverter or any powered device from your cigarette lighter:

- Keep the power cords off the carpet as much as possible. Wet carpet or wet or snowy feet could cause an electrical fire or shock hazard, potentially killing you. Remember, an electrical socket in your car is just as dangerous as one in your home.

- Don't plug surge strips into your A/C inverter. If you need more power than an A/C inverter provides, look into adding hot power terminals in your car. I cover this in my other book, *Geek My Ride*, also available from Wiley.

- For the most part, your charger or inverter runs off your car's gas-powered generator (called the *alternator*). If your device needs more than the alternator can provide, your charger or inverter may start drawing power from your battery. The rule is to not treat the inverter like a household electrical socket — you don't have unlimited power, so only plug low-power devices into the cigarette lighter.

- Make sure the power solution you choose has a sensor for when it's draining the battery. Most inverters have such a feature, although it's not guaranteed. Check the box and make sure you will get a warning if you're drawing too much power and/or draining your car's battery instead of just running off its gas-powered generator.

- Carry extra fuses for your car if you're going to plug in more than one device, just in case you draw too much power and blow a fuse on the road.

Warning Some cars keep the cigarette lighter adapter "hot" (powered) when the car is off. If you leave your PSP plugged in to the charger or A/C inverter, there is a slight chance you could drain your battery. It is best to unplug any powered devices or inverters from your cigarette lighter adapter to prevent draining your battery after leaving your car.

Getting Just a Little Bit More:
Build an Emergency Battery Pack

Here's a quick, cheap solution for building your own portable battery pack. You're going to spend about $25 on this solution, but it's easy to build a number of battery packs and the batteries are interchangeable and charge quickly. Unlike when you use the Pelican Power Brick, you can put the 15-minute rechargeable battery solutions available from Energizer, Rayovac, and many others, in this battery pack and have it ready to go in under 20 minutes (after it's built, of course).

Here's what you need:

- Four-battery AA battery holder with a snap connector, available at Radio Shack (about $3, model number 270-383, shown in Figure 13-5)

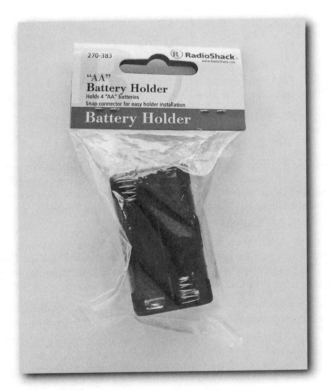

FIGURE 13-5: The battery holder from Radio Shack

- Four NiMH 1800 mAh or greater AA rechargeable batteries (such as those shown in Figure 13-6, although any rechargeable batteries will do; about $15 or about $25 with charger). I recommend the 15 minute rechargeables, such as those from Rayovac.

FIGURE 13-6: Quick-charge NiMH batteries

- The charger for the lithium ion batteries (about $10–$20)

- 9V battery snap connector (Radio shack model number 270-325; about $1.99; see Figure 13-7)

- A Radio Shack DC power plug to connect the battery pack to your PSP (Radio Shack model number 274-1532; about $2.59: usually found in their "B" bin — they'll know what that means; shown in Figure 13-8)

- A soldering iron and solder so you can connect the DC power plug to the battery snap connector

FIGURE 13-7: 9V battery snap connectors

Step 1: Charge the Batteries and Place Them in the Battery Holder

Charge the batteries with their associated charger and place them in the battery pack. This is where you will be glad you purchased the quick-charge batteries, because they can be charged right before you go to school, to work, or on a trip (no more overnight charging), as shown in Figure 13-9.

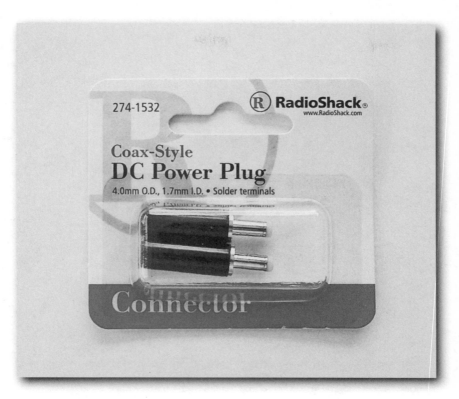

FIGURE 13-8: DC power plugs

Warning Do not charge quick-charge batteries at the same time with other non–quick-charge batteries or other quick-charge batteries of a different brand. Most chargers warn you about this, but I'm reiterating the fact. Some batteries were not made for quick-charge chargers, and the results can be anything from all batteries charging slowly, to battery leakage or battery explosions. Be careful and read the instructions that came with your charger!

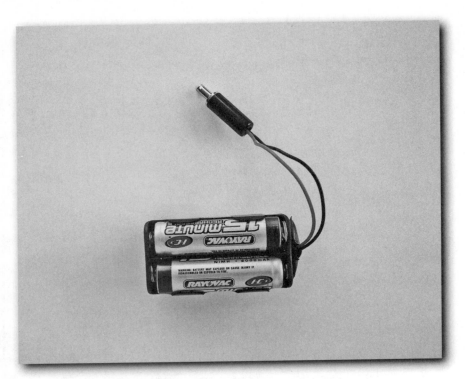

FIGURE 13-9: The batteries charged and placed in the battery pack

Step 2: Solder the Snap Connector to the DC Plug

Unscrew the power plug casing and you will see two connections—one on the outside and one on the inside. On the PSP, positive (+) is the center pin while the outside is ground (-), so you need the red wire from the snap connector soldered to the inside contact, and the black wire to the outside connector. Before you start soldering, make sure you run the wires through the DC plug's casing, as shown in Figure 13-10.

Make sure the wires and their respective solder don't touch each other or you will short your batteries and possibly damage your PSP.

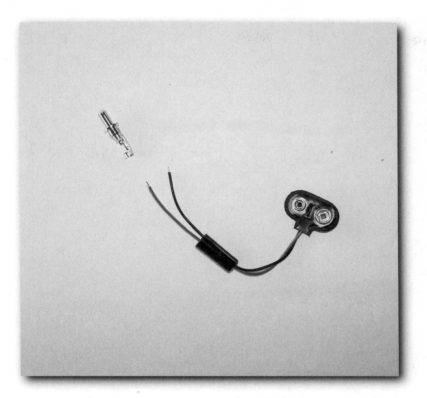

FIGURE **13-10: The snap connector wires run through the DC power plug's casing**

 Warning Apply the soldering iron to the surface you are soldering, not the solder, otherwise you may get a *cold solder joint*, which may not let enough current through and your battery pack may not work.

If you don't know how to solder, get a friend who does to help you. I used a Cold Heat soldering iron because it's clean, easy to use, and wireless (see Figure 13-11), although it's harder to use on small components like the DC power plug. If you are buying your first soldering iron, you may prefer a classic soldering iron because it's more straightforward.

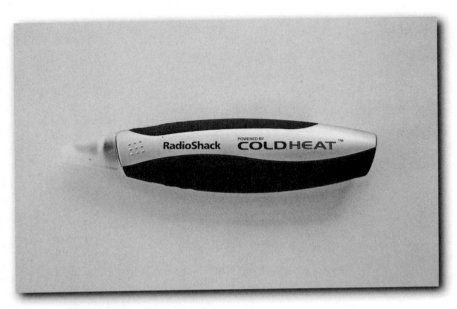

FIGURE 13-11: The Cold Heat soldering iron

Do not have the snap connector connected to the battery pack while you're putting together the power plug.

After you have soldered the wires, let everything cool for about 10 minutes. The connector should be cool to the touch after that amount of time.

After everything has cooled down, screw the DC plug casing back on and connect the snap connector to your battery pack.

Step 3: Play

Well, that's it! Plug the power cable from your battery holder into your PSP and you're good to go, as shown in Figure 13-12. Your new battery pack charges your PSP's lithium-ion battery while you play. Your PSP should automatically stop drawing power from the battery pack once it is charged. However, I suggest unplugging the external battery pack when it's not in use, or when the light on your PSP goes from orange (charging) to green (charged). You should also consider buying a battery pack cover from Radio Shack for additional protection.

FIGURE 13-12: The external battery pack in action

Summary

In this chapter you learned of the many power options available for the PSP, from replacement batteries to cases that actually have batteries in them, to car power solutions, to actually building your own battery packs. You can never have enough power when you're about to beat that level and your PSP's power meter is flashing that its power death is near. Take one of the battery packs with you or a power brick product and get the extra time you need to take that big bad boss out!

Taking Your PSP on the Road

This chapter takes a quick look at items you should bring when going on a vacation or road trip with your PSP, then gets into the must-have do-it-yourself roadtrip accessory: the car mount. Sometimes it's just not comfortable holding your PSP in your hands for hours on end, especially when you want to sit back and relax in the car on long road trips. It's also hard to share the PSP when it's playing a movie if you're holding it.

Bring Extra Power

You're not always going to have the opportunity to charge your PSP when you need power most. When you're on an airplane watching UMD video, bring extra batteries, a car charger, and possibly a charging case. Also, make sure to pack your PSP's charger. Chapter 13, "Getting More Power," covers the different power options available for your PSP, including a project on building your own battery packs.

Bring Movies

Besides (expensive) UMD-Video movies (available at practically any store that sells DVDs or PSP games), you can get a lot of value out of a 1GB Memory Stick Duo with many of your favorite shows and movies on it. At medium quality, you can store four full-length movies, or about eight hours worth of video on that 1GB stick. Take your favorite *Family Guy* episodes, *Futurama*, *Sex in the City*, whatever. Chapter 10, "Video Hacks," covers how to snag all the shows off your TiVo or ReplayTV, as well as other sources, for viewing on your PSP.

Bring Music

Your PSP with a 1GB Memory Stick can hold anywhere from 250 to 1,000 songs, depending on the audio quality you encode the music at. Transfer a lot of songs or a few audiobooks for a road trip and play them on your car stereo as discussed in Chapter 11, "Audio Hacks," or via headphones. If you're going to be in a noisy environment, such as an airplane or a bus, bring noise-canceling headphones, which can be had for under $100 and really make trips on airplanes much more enjoyable.

Pack a Sturdy Case

Your PSP is not very resistant to drops and scratches, so it is best to keep it in a sturdy case, such as those from Logitech and Nyko. Many cases are available, just check at any store that sells PSPs. Most cases are under $20 — a wise investment over replacing the PSP at $200–$249.

Also consider some cases can be propped up, such as the Logitech solution, so you can watch movies on your PSP when on a plane just by folding the case back a bit (see Figure 14-1). This comes in incredibly handy on long flights, and saves you from craning your neck to see the poorly positioned, washed out screens usually found on planes (and you can watch your own movies and videos).

FIGURE 14-1: The Logitech case easily props up for table-top or tray-top viewing

Building a Car Mount

This section covers how to build a car mount that easily fits in any cup holder. You can adjust the angle vertically and horizontally, and you can twist it. (I wrote the book *Geek My Ride*, also part of the ExtremeTech series, so this book would be remiss without at least one PSP car hack.)

Note This project will take about 12 hours to complete due to drying and curing times. Your time involved will be about 30 minutes, but be prepared to wait for your results.

The following list tells you what you need for this hack. You shouldn't spend more than $60 on this project if you don't have all the tools. If you do have the tools, you'll spend much less. The majority of these items can all be purchased by making one stop at Wal-Mart and one at Radio Shack:

- Ash Grabber cup-holder ash tray ($6 at Pep Boys; see Figure 14-2)
- Logitech PlayGear Pocket Case ($20; available from practically any store that sells PSP games and accessories; see Figure 14-3)

FIGURE **14-2:** An Ash Grabber

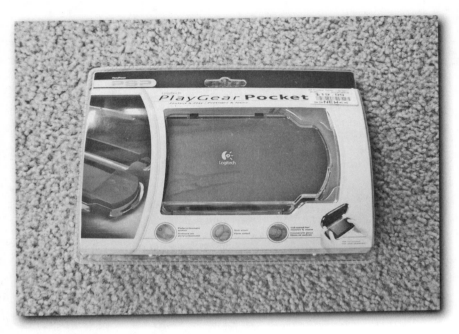

FIGURE **14-3: The Logitech case**

- Drill and Dremel, or just a Dremel
- Metal cutting bit and sanding bit if you are using a Dremel (usually included in the Dremel package; see Figure 14-4)

FIGURE **14-4: Dremel bits**

■ One package of Liquid Nails or equivalent epoxy; 2,000 lbs; 30 minute cure time ($8; see Figure 14-5)

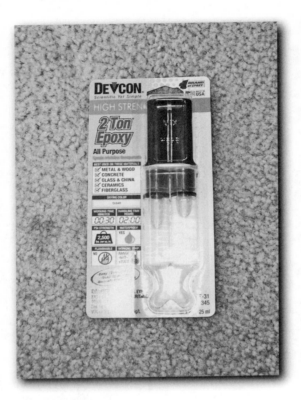

FIGURE **14-5:** Epoxy

- Two Radio Shack microphone extensions (Model No. 33-330; $12.99 each; see Figure 14-6)

- Hot glue gun and superglue for hot glue gun to seal hole in cup holder ($12; superglue usually comes with the hot glue gun)

- Workbench vice grip (see Figure 14-7)

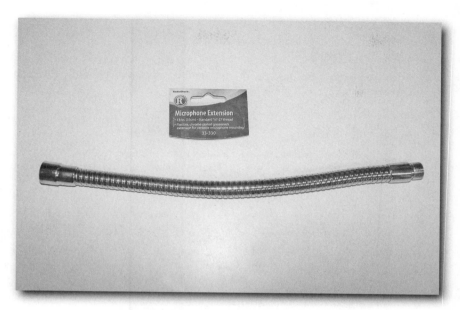

FIGURE 14-6: Microphone extension

FIGURE 14-7: Vice grip

- A flat, heavy book

- A mask, protective eyewear, and a long shirt to protect from metal filings hitting your skin (see Figure 14-8)

- Velcro, to fine-tune the fit of the ash grabber — buy a small roll from a hardware store or fabric store ($9; see Figure 14-9)

- Black Sharpie

- Box cutter or scissors

- Cardboard, non-porous, flat disposable surface to mix epoxy on (you can use the non-greasy part of a pizza box cover, or just some random box you don't care about getting glue on)

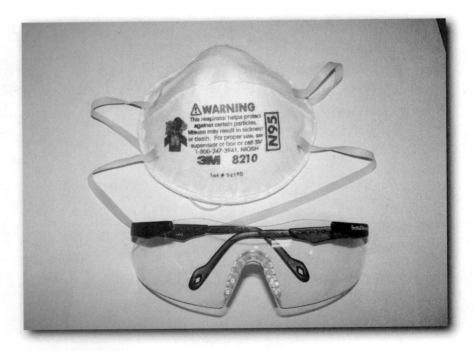

Figure 14-8: Protection

FIGURE 14-9: Velcro roll

Drill Holes in the Ash Grabber

The first step is to place the holes in the lid of the Ash Grabber, which the microphone extensions will slightly protrude through and be mounted to.

Warning Sparks will fly as you work with the Ash Grabber's metal lid. Make sure you don't have anything flammable near you as you work.

Using a Sharpie, mark holes on either side of the Ash Grabber lid, as shown in Figure 14-10. The holes should be a couple millimeters larger than the diameter of the protruding threaded end of the microphone extension, which is pointed out in Figure 14-11. Make sure the holes are the right size by placing the threaded end of the microphone extension over the black Sharpie area and making sure you can see a few millimeters of the black markings. Another approach is to try placing the Dremel sanding bit over the hole and see a couple millimeters of Sharpie marking, too.

FIGURE 14-10: The holes marked on the Ash Grabber lid

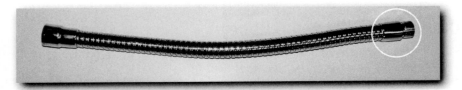

FIGURE 14-11: The threaded end of the microphone extension

Once you've got the holes marked, secure the Ash Grabber in the vice with the hole markings in a vertical position. This ensures you can safely drill without hitting the metal of the vice.

If you're using a drill, attach the appropriate metal drill bit. If you're using a Dremel, attach the metal cutting bit, shown earlier in Figure 14-4.

Now you're ready to cut the holes in the lid.

Warning

Make sure you have your safety eyewear, mask, and long sleeve shirt. The metal flakes and shards that will fly off the lid as you cut will *hurt* if you aren't wearing a long sleeve shirt. If there are other people or pets in the room, get them out of there — you don't want the lid to fly off and hit somebody by accident, or have metal shavings and shards hitting your loved ones.

Using the drill or Dremel, cut a round hole where the black Sharpie marking is. If you're using the Dremel, it's easier to just punch holes through the metal ash grabber lid. Then rotate the ash grabber lid in the vice and drill the other hole. The result should be similar to Figure 14-12.

FIGURE 14-12: The holes cut in the Ash Grabber lid

Smooth Holes in the Ash Grabber

Now that the holes have been cut, it's a good idea to smooth the metal so you don't cut yourself working with the metal. Smoothing the metal also gets rid of any pointy edges that may prevent the microphone extension from getting through the hole.

Using the Dremel sanding bit, gently sand the edges of the hole to smooth it out. You should be able to easily place the sanding bit through the hole with no more than a couple millimeters of space between it and the edge of your hole.

Insert the Extensions into the Cup Holder Holes

Now that the holes are ready, remove the Ash Grabber lid from the vice. Place the non-threaded ends of the two microphone extensions into the vice, align them vertically, and secure them so they don't budge. With the microphone extensions properly aligned, push the threaded ends through the cupholder lid, making sure the extensions protrude through evenly, as shown in Figure 14-13. If the extensions aren't even, you will have trouble aligning the case later.

FIGURE 14-13: The microphone extensions in the vice grip

Mount the Extensions in the Cup Holder Holes

Now is the time to heat up the hot glue gun. It may take about 5 or 10 minutes before it's hot enough. Once it's ready (the glue should easily flow through), use the superglue to fill in the holes where the extensions are protruding, as shown in Figure 14-14. This keeps the extensions from coming loose. Make sure to connect the two glued areas, which should be apparent in the figure.

FIGURE **14-14: The applied glue**

 Tip Make sure the glue doesn't get on anything you value, like your carpet. Once this stuff dries on fabric it can be difficult to get off.

Let the Glue Dry for Four Hours

Once you've applied the glue, it's time to let it cure. Leave the extensions and Ash Grabber lid in the vice and just let it dry. Go get dinner or some coffee, or play some golf on your PSP. These types of projects take time.

Score the Logitech Case

Using the box cutter or scissors, score the back of the Logitech case as shown in Figure 14-15. Make sure you score the area shown, not just random areas on the back of the case. (Remember this from seventh grade science class? Scoring edges helps adhesive stick better.)

FIGURE 14-15: Scoring locations on the Logitech case

Align the Extensions on the Case

If you have not done so already, remove the Ash Grabber lid with the mounted extensions from the vice. Align the ends of the extensions with the back of the case, making sure they are even on both sides, as shown in Figure 14-16.

Note   So why are you using microphone extensions? Microphone extensions use *gooseneck cable*, which is very flexible and sturdy, so you can bend it to a certain position and it will stay in that position. The Radio Shack microphone extensions happen to be the perfect length, and you don't have to cut any wires, so that's why you're using them.

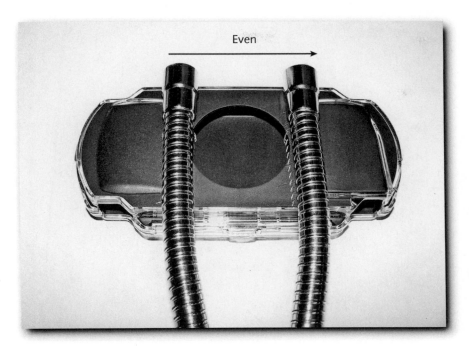

FIGURE 14-16: Aligning the extensions

Verify the Case Position before Affixing the Extensions

Before applying the epoxy, make sure the case opener is facing you, as shown in Figure 14-17. If you apply the extensions to the back of the case and the case is facing the wrong way, the case will open backwards after it's mounted. While it would still work, it would look really, really bad.

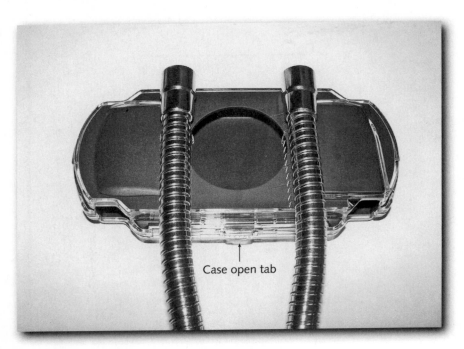

FIGURE **14-17: Make sure the case opening tab is facing you**

Mix the Epoxy

Now you need to apply the epoxy to the case. First, you must mix the epoxy. The instructions included with the particular epoxy you purchased should be very clear. Generally, you find a surface you don't care about (the pizza box), and squirt even amounts of both chemical tubes onto that surface (see Figure 14-18), and then mix it with the included mixing stick. If a mixing stick wasn't included, you can use a straw or some other clean plastic tab you don't mind throwing away.

Note After you are done mixing the epoxy, either throw away the box you mixed it on in a place where other people can't touch it for at least four hours, or put it away where nobody can touch it until the remaining epoxy dries. You can wipe off the epoxy you don't use and throw that away, too—just use a paper towel. If you get any epoxy on your hands, *wash it off*. Epoxy is not fun to remove from skin after it has cured. (That's why I had you buy the 30 minute stuff.)

FIGURE **14-18:** Mixing the epoxy

You are likely not going to use all the epoxy in the two chemical tubes. When you are done with the tubes, place the protective cap back on the tubes and place the tubes in a plastic Ziploc bag. Never leave epoxy out in the open.

Apply Epoxy to the Logitech Case

Now that you have the epoxy out, you have only 30 minutes before it cures, so time is of the essence. Using the mixing stick, scoop up the epoxy and apply it liberally to the scored area on the case, as shown in Figure 14-19. Make sure not to get any epoxy on the joints of the case. If you do drip some epoxy accidentally, simply wipe it up with a paper towel and throw that towel away. After you have applied the epoxy, *wash your hands thoroughly*!

FIGURE **14-19:** Applying the epoxy

Apply the Extensions to the Case

Now align the extensions so they're even over the epoxy and place them into the epoxy and don't let them move, as shown in Figure 14-20.

Place the heavy book or heavy flat object on top of the extensions to keep them from moving and then wait. It takes about 12 hours for the epoxy to completely cure.

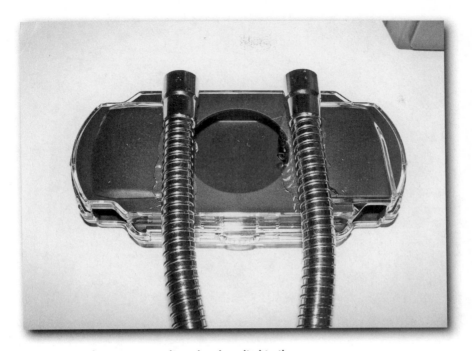

FIGURE 14-20: The extensions aligned and applied to the epoxy

Reattach the Lid to the Ash Grabber

After the epoxy has cured, put the lid back on the Ash Grabber and you should have the car mount shown in Figure 14-21, ready for installation.

Warning When adjusting the gooseneck cable, be gentle and don't pull on the case. The case *will* come loose from the epoxy if you're not careful. Of course, you can always reattach it using epoxy or some other type of glue, but the clear epoxy looks much better.

FIGURE **14-21:** The finished PSP car mount

Install the Mount in the Car

Now it's time to install the mount in your car. Simply find a cupholder to place your mount in and put it in there. Make sure it fits snugly — you don't want the mount falling on your lap while you drive. To make the mount fit snugly and not move, use the fuzzy Velcro (not the hard plastic side) to pad the sides of the mount to make it a tight fit. Another good option is to take a bunch of pennies you don't use and fill the Ash Grabber with them to add counterweight to the metal extensions and PSP as you drive.

The installed mount is shown in Figure 14-22.

FIGURE 14-22: The installed mount

Summary

In this chapter you learned what to consider when taking your PSP on a trip. I refined these needs after taking my PSP on a number of trips and realizing what I needed wasn't there when I arrived at my destination. I hope I've saved you some time and grief now that you've read this chapter.

You also learned how to build a car mount for your PSP. The car mount can be used to entertain passengers, keep maps near you while you drive, and make your friends drool with envy. Enjoy!

Running Linux and Windows on the PSP

So the PSP can do games, movies, video, music, photos, and the Internet. Well, that's not enough — it should be able to run software you enjoy on your home PCs. By using an open source x86 emulator called Bochs, which emulates the hardware usually found in PCs, and creating a few hard disk images with the software you want, you can run Linux and even Windows on your PSP!

Here is what you need:

➤ A hackable PSP that can run homebrew applications

➤ A Memory Stick with enough space for Bochs files and a virtual hard drive image (a 512MB stick is probably plenty, but a 1GB stick is better so you still have plenty of space for other stuff)

➤ Virtual PC or VMWare, if you're going to create your own disk images ($99+ depending on what version, but there are free trials available that will suffice for this project)

➤ Virtual DriveCreation Software, such as R-Drive Image (www.r-tt.com; about $49, and there's a free trial), if you're going to create your own disk images

➤ Windows 95 or Windows 98 disks or disc if you're going to install Windows

Note The American PSP has only 32MB of available RAM, and the emulator uses a little of that, so that's why we're sticking to Linux and lightweight versions of Windows like Windows 95 and 98.

Note There is also a Macintosh emulator called Basilisk II, available for download from http://forums.ps2dev.org/viewtopic.php?t=3741. Basilisk can run Mac OS 7.5 through 7.6.1, and cannot run Mac OS X, but that's not bad!

Download Bochs for PSP

Bochs is an open-source x86 PC emulator. Files included with this highly configurable emulation solution enable different VGA emulation, serial port, and other IO port emulation, and the use of disk images to act as hard drives and the like. Matan Gillon ported the emulator to the PSP, complete with full-screen image scaling. You can download Bochs for the PSP from Matan's Web site at www.hacker.co.il/psp/bochs.

To learn more about Bochs, which is a SourceForge project, go to `http://bochs.sourceforge.net`.

Create or Download a Hard Drive Image

The next item you need after Bochs is a drive image to boot from. You can either use one of the sample Linux images provided on the Sourceforge Web site, or you can create your own.

This example uses the Linux distribution from the Sourceforge Web site at `http://bochs.sourceforge.net/diskimages.html`. If you are going to run Windows 95, you need to use a program like Virtual PC (`www.microsoft.com/virtualpc`) or VMWare (`www.vmware.com`) to create a virtual machine running Windows 95 and then Norton Ghost to image the resulting hard drive.

Configure Bochs

Bochs relies on a configuration file to tell it what ports it supports, where its hard drive images are, what video type to support, and so forth. After you have decompressed your Bochs PSP file, find the bochsrc.txt file (which you can also download from `http://www.hacker.co.il/psp/bochs/bochsrc.txt`) and open it in Notepad or a similar text editor and make sure its settings are as follows:

```
###############################################################
# bochsrc.txt file for DLX Linux disk image.
###############################################################

# how much memory the emulated machine will have
megs: 8

# filename of ROM images
romimage: file=ms0:/VM/BIOS-bochs-latest, address=0xf0000
vgaromimage: file=ms0:/VM/VGABIOS-lgpl-latest

# hard disk
ata0: enabled=1, ioaddr1=0x1f0, ioaddr2=0x3f0, irq=14
```

```
ata0-master: type=disk, path="ms0:/VM/hd10meg.img", cylinders=306,
heads=4, spt=17

# choose the boot disk.
boot: c

# where do we send log messages?
log: ms0:/VM/bochsout.txt

# disable the mouse, since DLX is text only
mouse: enabled=0
```

Copy Bochs Files to Your PSP

Put your PSP in USB Connection mode by going to Settings ➔ USB Connection. In the root directory (the topmost directory) of your Memory Stick, create a folder named **VM** (all capital letters). Then, rename your Bochs configuration file, which you created earlier as bochsrc.txt, to **bochsrc.bxrc**.

If You Have a 1.0 Firmware PSP

Follow these steps:

1. Open the PSP folder, then the GAMES folder, and create a new directory named **BOCHS**.

2. Copy the Bochs EBOOT.PBP file to the BOCHS folder.

3. Copy the hard disk image file and the BIOS file to that same directory.

If You Have a 1.5 Firmware PSP

Follow these steps:

1. If you have a 1.5 firmware PSP, use the KXploit hack, outlined in Chapter 19, "Running Homebrew Applications," to convert the EBOOT.PBP to run on your PSP.

2. Use the tool as directed in Chapter 19 and name the "game" **BOCHS**. This creates two directories in your PSP \ GAME folder, BOCHS and %BOCHS.

3. After your EBOOT.PBP has been converted and transferred, open your PSP and open the PSP folder.

4. Open the GAMES folder, and open the BOCHS directory.

5. Copy the Bochs EBOOT.PBP file to the BOCHS folder.

6. Copy the hard disk image file and the BIOS file to that same directory.

Boot Up Your PC on Your PSP

Now you have all the necessary files on your PSP, so disconnect from USB mode and use the PSP Navigator and select your Game menu. Then select Memory Stick and you should see your new application somewhere in the list, as shown in Figure 15-1.

FIGURE 15-1: Bochs on your PSP as a runnable application

Now all you have to do is press X to launch Bochs, just like launching a game. Bochs loads and you can see Linux start up on your PSP (see Figure 15-2). Of course, there really isn't much you can do with it right now, but it's a cool hack nonetheless.

Bochs was originally presented as a portable Windows 95 emulator. If you create a Windows 95 disk image, you can use the on-screen keyboard for data entry, which is located in Windows 95, located under Start ➜ Programs ➜ Accessories ➜ Accessibility ➜ On-Screen Keyboard. You also can use the buttons shown in Table 15-1 on your PSP to simulate different mouse functionality:

FIGURE 15-2: Bochs loading Linux on the PSP

Table 15-1   Button functions in Bochs for the PSP

PSP Button	Function
◁	Move the virtual mouse
▷	
△	
▽	
□	Simulates the left mouse button

Continued

Table 15-1 *(continued)*

PSP Button	Function
	Simulates the right mouse button
	Simulates the middle mouse button
	Start key
	Quits the Bochs emulator
	Quits the Bochs emulator

Summary

In this chapter you learned how to run Linux (and pretty much any other operating system that runs on an x86 PC). While not all emulators are complete, they get better all the time and let you do amazing things with your PSP.

Reverting from a 2.0 PSP to a 1.5 PSP

I n this chapter you will use an exploit called a "buffer overflow," discovered by toc2rta (http://toc2rta.com) and well exploited by MPH (http://www.chez.com/mph) to trick a firmware version 2.0 PSP (not 2.01 or higher, at least at the time this book went to press) into running the original PSP 1.5 "updater" from Sony, basically making a 2.0 firmware PSP a 1.5. You'll also take a look at the handy WAB version changer, which tricks a firmware 1.5 PSP into thinking it's a 1.51, 1.52, or 2.0 PSP, and thus tricking games that require later firmware versions into running.

Buffer Overflows

Buffer overflows have been the bain of users' existences for many years now. Practically every Windows, Linux, MacOS, and other operating system or application exploit has been due to these types of issues. A buffer overflow occurs when a system accepts input from another source, such as server software accepting a malicious packet of data from a hacker, and then doesn't properly work with the data.

For example, if a server application is designed to accept 256 characters of input from a data stream, such as a form request from the Internet, but instead accepts as much as it can take, assuming the sender will only send 256 characters, a buffer overflow condition can exist. If the application does not trim the data stream to 256 characters, but instead just tries to cram what it received into a 256 character buffer, the rest of the characters received "overflow" out of the data container and very possibly into executable space (or into other data variables), such as the application heap or system heap, enabling the code to run in the context of the application, which on many consumer machines is administrator-level (basically, the application can do anything).

So, if a malicious user sends 256 Xs, because they know that fills up the 256 character buffer, and then sends code after the string of buffer-filling characters, that code may very well execute, or at least affect other variables in the program. This is what happened with the Code Red vulnerability, Slammer, Nimda, and many, many others — holes in code that wasn't checking constraints on data. Figure 16-1 illustrates a buffer overflow attack.

Buffer Overflow

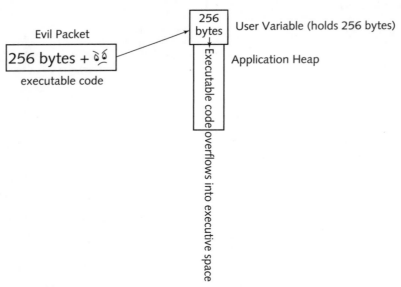

FIGURE **16-1: Memory overflowing onto the system heap**

For all you programmers out there, you may be thinking this is only for those who code in "unmanaged" languages, like C. Actually other languages can have secure coding issues, such as array bounds issues. Some managed languages also let you run unmanaged code if you flip the right compiler switch — so be careful, and be a safe programmer.

The exploit that enables you to downgrade 2.0 PSPs to 1.5 takes advantage of a known buffer overflow in the TIFF image viewing library that the 2.0 PSP software uses in its photo viewer. TIFF viewing was a new feature introduced in firmware 2.0, so 1.0–1.52 users cannot take advantage of this hack.

Note Windows XP Service Pack 2 supports detection of buffer overflows, making sure user data doesn't invade the system heap. Even processor manufacturers such as AMD and Intel are building in capabilities in their processors to mark data as "No Execute," so under no circumstances will the processor execute "NOX" data, even if a buffer overflow occurs.

Here's what you need for this hack:

- A fully-charged PSP running firmware 2.0 (also known as System Update 2.0). This hack will *not* work on a 1.51 or 1.52 PSP, and may very well not work on anything beyond 2.0.

- At least a 32MB Memory Stick with at least 20MB available (usually comes with the PSP)

- Your PSP power supply
- Patience — firmware updates, hacks or not, are serious business — always pay close attention to what you're doing when modifying the stuff that makes your PSP tick!

Step 1: Make Sure the PSP Is Fully Charged and Eject Any UMD Disc

Before you run this hack, it is imperative that your PSP be fully charged (the charge light will turn off when it's done charging). Keep it plugged into the wall during this entire process. Failure to have your PSP charged or not keeping your PSP plugged into the wall could prevent this hack from working, or possibly "brick" your PSP, making it entirely unusable.

You also must remove any UMD disc you have in your drive.

Step 2: Download the Needed Files

You need the following files, available from the official *Hacking the PSP* Web site, or via other PSP hacking sites, such as www.PSPUpdates.com. The following files are necessary:

- frame_buffer.png — This file contains the code to enable the update code to run.
- Sony 1.5 firmware updater EBOOT.PBP — This file contains the firmware 1.5 updater, which you will run to "update" your PSP to firmware 1.5.
- overflow.tif — This file has the code that executes the code hidden in the frame_buffer.png file by exploiting a buffer overflow contained in Sony's TIFF viewer, enabling exploit code to run.
- index.dat and h.bin — These are other necessary files to enable the downgrading process to work.

Step 3: Create the Updater Directory

Connect your PSP to your PC with a USB cable and enable USB Connection mode on your PSP by using the PSP Navigator and scrolling all the way left to Settings, then USB Connection and pressing ⊗ (see Figure 16-2).

Open the PSP from My Computer (or select Open the Device to View Files in Windows XP). Open the PSP folder, and then the GAME folder. If these folders don't already exist, create the PSP folder, and then create the GAME directory in the PSP directory. Finally, create an UPDATE folder inside the GAME directory, as shown in Figure 16-3. Make sure you keep the folder names in all capital letters — everything in this chapter is case-sensitive.

FIGURE 16-2: The USB Connection mode option under Settings

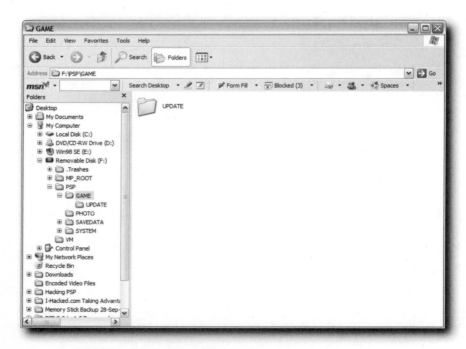

FIGURE 16-3: Creating the UPDATE folder in Windows

Now that you've created the UPDATE folder, you need to copy the 1.5 firmware updater application, EBOOT.PBP (.PBPs are similar to .EXEs on PCs and .apps on Macintoshes), into the UPDATE directory, as shown in Figure 16-4.

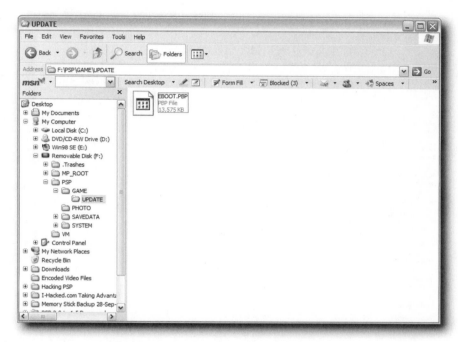

FIGURE 16-4: The EBOOT.PBP application in the UPDATE folder

Back Up

Because you're about to make a major change to your PSP, now would be a good time to back up everything that's on your Memory Stick, just in case things go awry. You should also write down the nickname you use on your PSP just in case you've forgotten it. You can find this in the PSP Navigator by scrolling to Settings, then System Information, and then looking at the name next to Nickname. Downgrading your PSP removes all your settings except your clock settings, so write down any particular configuration settings you want to save. This, by the way, is standard operating procedure whenever you're running a firmware update on *any* device.

Step 4: Copy the Exploit Background Image

The next file you need is frame_buffer.png, a small file that has code hidden inside it that will be exploited by the buffer overflow initiated by the overflow.tif file that you will be copying over later. It is imperative that you *do not copy the overflow.tif file to the PSP* until the proper step or the process won't work and you could damage your PSP!

Copy the frame_buffer.png file to your PSP's PHOTO folder, located in the PSP folder, and then open the PHOTO folder, as shown in Figure 16-5. Again, if these folders don't exist, you will need to create them.

FIGURE 16-5: The frame_buffer.png file copied into the PHOTO folder

Step 5: Disconnect and Set Your Background Image

Now that you've copied the frame_buffer.png file, you need to set it as the wallpaper for your PSP. Disconnect from USB mode by pressing ⊚ on your PSP. Then, navigate over to PHOTO in the PSP Navigator and select Memory Stick. Your frame_buffer.png file should be listed. Select it and press ⊗ to view it (Figure 16-6).

Now that you're viewing the image, press △ to bring up the View Options menu. Scroll to Set as Wallpaper and press ⊗. Confirm that you want to replace your existing wallpaper by pressing ⊗, as shown in Figure 16-7.

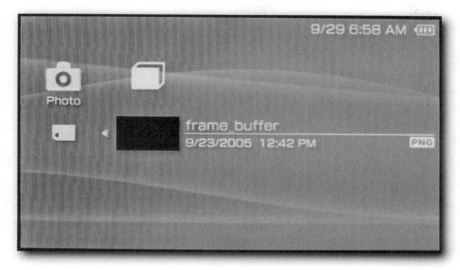

FIGURE 16-6: The frame_buffer.png file in the list of photos

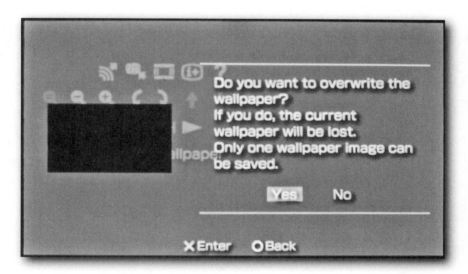

FIGURE 16-7: Confirming your wallpaper selection

Press ⊗ again after your PSP tells you the wallpaper has been saved, as shown in Figure 16-8.

FIGURE 16-8: The wallpaper has been set

Your PSP's background image changes to a mostly black image (there will be some coloration on the bottom right—this is normal).

Step 6: Reconnect Your PSP via the USB and Copy the Remaining Files

Now that your PSP's background has been set to the proper "image," press until you get back to the PSP Navigator. Plug your PSP back into your PC and then scroll back to Settings and select USB Connection again. Your PSP should reappear on your desktop.

> **Note** There may be other files in these directories when you view them in Windows or in Mac OS X, such as .DS_Store or thumbs.db. Don't worry about these files—they won't affect the down-grading process.

Now you need to copy the remaining files you grabbed earlier as follows:

- Copy index.dat and h.bin into the root directory of your Memory Stick, as shown in Figure 16-9.

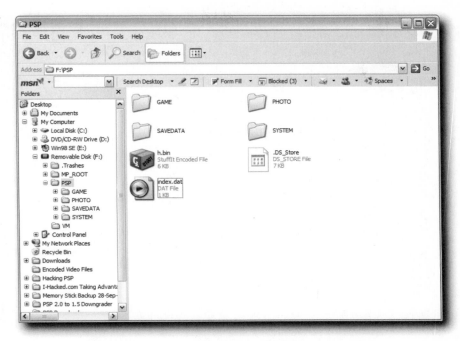

Figure 16-9: index.dat and h.bin copied into memory stick's root directory

- Copy overflow.tif into your PSP's PHOTO directory, the same place you copied frame_buffer.png, as shown in Figure 16-10. Do not delete frame_buffer.png — it needs to stay in that folder until your updates are complete.

Note You don't need to leave the overflow.tif and frame_buffer.png files in your PHOTO directory after updating. You should delete them just to make sure they don't cause problems when using homebrew PNG and TIFF viewers. (Only firmware 2.0 supports PNG and TIF files.)

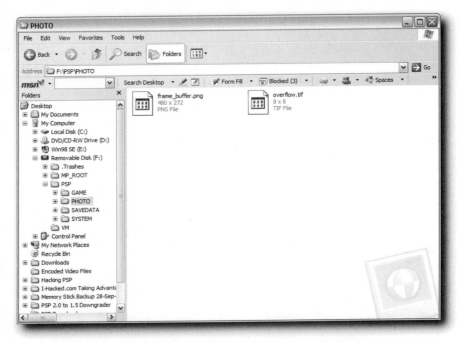

FIGURE 16-10: The overflow.tif file copied into the PSP's PHOTO directory

Step 7: Double-Check that Your PSP Is Fully Charged and Plugged Into the Wall

Now that all the files are in place, make sure your PSP is plugged into the wall. I made this a separate step for a reason—because it's very important!

Step 8: Disconnect USB Cable and Run the Exploit

It's time to run the exploit that enables the downgrader to work. Disconnect from USB Connection mode by pressing ⊙ and then disconnecting the USB cable from your PSP. Don't disconnect the A/C adapter!

Once everything's disconnected, scroll over to PHOTO in the PSP Navigator and select Memory Stick from the list. Your PSP's screen almost immediately goes blank. After a moment, a few rows of letters and numbers appear on your screen, as shown in Figure 16-11.

Count off about 40 seconds once you see those numbers. If instead, your PSP simply turns off after a few seconds, run steps 6 and 7 again.

Note What's happening here is code hidden in the overflow.tif image uses the code in the frame_buffer.png, which executes the code that prepares your PSP for downgrading, giving it the ability to run the Sony 1.5 Firmware "Updater." Buffer overflows are a fascinating topic, and you can learn a lot about them by picking up any good security book. One excellent book on securing programming practices is *Writing Secure Code 2*, by Michael Howard and David LeBlanc, available from Microsoft Press.

FIGURE 16-11: The running exploit

After 40 seconds has elapsed, you need to turn off your PSP. This does NOT mean removing the battery or unplugging the PSP. Hold the power switch in the up position for about 10 seconds, turning the device off completely. Don't just slide it up and let go — that only puts it to sleep.

After your PSP has been off for a few seconds, turn it back on as you normally would. You should see the Sony Computer Entertainment banner appear, and then you should be brought immediately to the GAME menu, with Saved Data Utility highlighted.

Scroll to Memory Stick and press ⊗, which is where you would normally find games or, eventually, homebrew applications, on your PSP. You should see the PSP Update program you installed into the UPDATE folder in step 2 (see Figure 16-12).

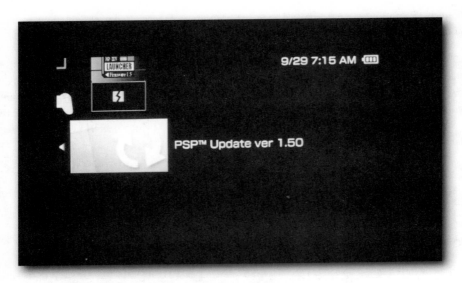

FIGURE 16-12: PSP Update appears as a program you can run

Press ⊗ on the PSP Update program and it should launch, as shown in Figure 16-13.

FIGURE 16-13: The first screen of the PSP Update.

If you get an error saying your PSP is already at version 2.0 and does not need to be updated, you will need to run through all the steps again, making sure your power supply is plugged in this entire time and that your USB cable is disconnected when you run the exploit.

Step 9: Run the Firmware 1.5 Update Program

Once the 1.5 Update program comes up, it will look like any PSP Update. It asks you to confirm you want to "upgrade." Laugh for a moment at the text that says "Once the update is started you cannot go back to the previous version of the system software," as shown in Figure 16-14.

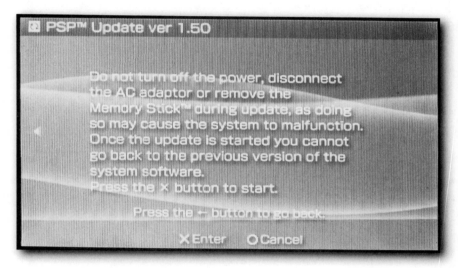

FIGURE **16-14:** The screen you should laugh at

Follow the prompts to update your PSP. Your PSP "updates" itself to firmware 1.5, as shown in Figure 16-15. Keep a close eye as the bar approaches 99% — you will get an error that the update failed with an error of FFFFFFFF and to contact Sony Support, which is okay — don't panic!

When you receive the "blue screen" error that the update failed, as shown in Figure 16-16, completely turn off your PSP (again, *do not remove the battery or the A/C adapter*), holding the power switch up for 10 seconds or until your PSP turns off. Then wait a second and turn it back on.

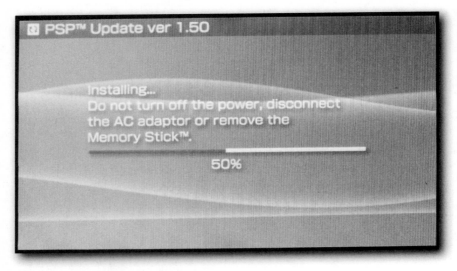

FIGURE 16-15: The PSP "updating" itself

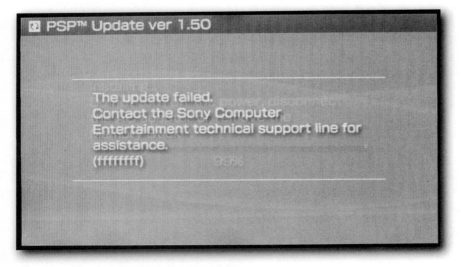

FIGURE 16-16: The "update failed" error message

Step 10: "Repair" Your PSP

After you turn on your PSP, you'll see the Sony Computer Entertainment banner again, and then a blue error screen appears telling you to repair your PSP, as shown in Figure 16-17, and possibly freaking you out. Again, don't panic.

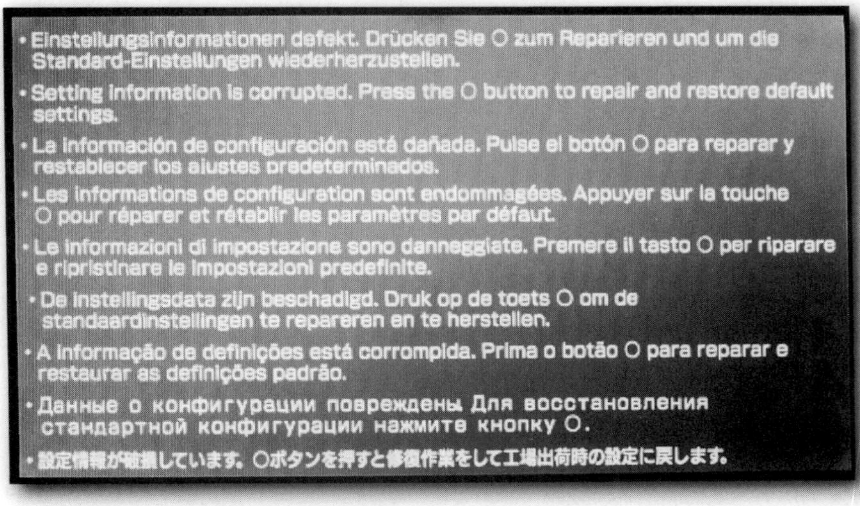

FIGURE **16-17:** Another blue screen on a PSP

Simply press ⊚ to have your PSP "repair" itself.

Step 11: Configure Your PSP

After you let your PSP "repair" itself, you'll be back to firmware 1.5. Your PSP starts acting like it's a new machine, so you'll have to select your preferred language and also confirm your clock settings. Then that's it—you're all set! *Now* you can unplug your power supply and go get on the Web on your PC and start downloading all those cool homebrew applications!

To verify you are indeed running firmware version 1.5, use your PSP Navigator to select Settings, then System Settings, and finally System Information. You should see System Software and Version 1.50 (as shown in Figure 16-18).

FIGURE 16-18: Yep, it's running 1.5

To learn how to run homebrew applications, see Chapter 19, "Running Homebrew Applications."

To learn how to write your own programs, see Chapter 17, "Programming the PSP: Setting Up the Development Environment," and Chapter 18, "Programming the PSP: Hello World."

Note   If any of your games require a firmware 2.0 PSP, simply use the WAB Version Changer application and your games should work. The WAB Version Changer is downloadable from the official *Hacking the PSP* Web site and many other great Web sites, including www.PSPUpdates.com.

Can I Flash Back to 2.0?

Yes, you can! However, it is likely that by the time you pick up this book Sony will have either released an update to prevent this hack. Look around on some of the hacking Web sites to find an official "non-tainted" EBOOT.PBP containing the 2.0 firmware update. A rule of thumb: It is always a good idea to keep a backup copy of firmware update EBOOT.PBP files, just in case you need them at some point in the future. That's how I reverted mine back to 2.0 (which I subsequently downgraded to 1.5).

Note I did not exhaustively test how many times the PSP's firmware can be flashed. While I don't anticipate you changing your firmware between 1.5 and 2.0 often, nor do I believe Sony will release PSP updates all too often, I wouldn't go nuts flashing your system all the time. This does not apply to Memory Stick use, however. Memory Sticks can be written to thousands of times before they go bad.

Warning Please keep in mind that downgrading to firmware 1.5 and having the ability to run homebrew applications is not an open invitation to piracy. Please don't pirate software. You're not an "elite hacker" if you engage in piracy. Pirates only hurt the software industry and make an even better case for device manufacturers to lock down their systems to prevent good people from enjoying their systems' capabilities.

WAB Version Changer

Sometimes you may find that you need a newer version of the PSP's firmware to run a new game or UMD, but you don't want to update your PSP to 1.51 or higher and lose the ability to run homebrew applications. A utility written by Yoshihiro of Team WAB named WAB Version Changer is your answer. Using this homebrew utility, you can trick your firmware 1.0 or 1.5 PSP into thinking it's a firmware 1.51, 1.52, or 2.0 device.

Getting WAB Version Changer

WAB Version Changer is available at http://pspupdates.com in their Files section. You install the application on your Memory Stick. If you have a firmware 1.0 PSP, simply place it in your PSP \ GAMES folder. If you have a firmware 1.5 PSP, use the KXploit program to place it on the Memory Stick.

Running WAB Version Changer

Once you've installed the application on your PSP, launch it from the Games → Memory Stick menu in the PSP's Navigator.

You can then use the keys described in Table 16-1 to trick your PSP into thinking it has a different firmware version:

Table 16-1	Version trick buttons
Use This Button	**To Do This**
⬛	Trick PSP into thinking it's running Firmware 1.0

Continued

Table 16-1 *(continued)*

Use This Button	To Do This
⊗	Trick PSP into thinking it's running Firmware 1.52
△	Trick PSP into thinking it's running Firmware 2.0
○	Go back to Firmware 1.5
START	Quit without changing anything

After you have made your changes, you can go to the PSP's Navigator and select the System Settings menu, then System Information, and you'll see the "new" firmware version. Now you can run your games!

Summary

In this chapter you did what many thought impossible to do after Sony released firmware versions 1.51, 1.52, and 2.0. Using this exploit, you can finally downgrade your 2.0 PSP to run homebrew applications, which are both fun and useful. Appendix A, "Additional Resources," will help you find homebrew software.

Programming the PSP: Setting Up the Development Environment

This is the chapter I've most been looking forward to writing. Programming any computer has always struck a special chord with me, and the PSP is by far no exception. Such a powerful machine is destined to be exploited and made to do awesome things. Unfortunately, Sony doesn't feel the same way unless you're a big time software development and publishing firm with millions of dollars. Luckily there are hackers like us who figure ways to get what we want.

Note Microsoft's Xbox team has expressed interest in opening the Xbox 360 to "Indie" software developers. Considering how great their development tools are, this would be awesome!

If you haven't programmed before, never fear. You can still go through the motions in these chapters and type in the code and it should work fine. However, if you are a developer, specifically a C++ developer, you'll find you can really go places from these humble beginnings in PSP development. Note that the instructions in these next few chapters are not for a development environment blessed by Sony. Quite the contrary — you'll be using hacking tools to get your application running on your PSP, and you'll be using text editors and a Linux shell (don't worry if you have Windows, this will all work fine, you'll see). What I promise is that, at the end of the first chapter, you won't be able to find enough people to show your Hello World application to (and when was the last time *that* happened?).

Running Your Applications

In version 1.0 of the Japanese PSP's firmware, "homebrew applications" ran like a champ. Unfortunately, Sony saw how pirates and warez-mongers could take advantage of this capability and attempted to lock it on out in the U.S. version, which only shipped with firmware version 1.5. Clever hackers found a few different methods around this called the Swapsploit and the KXploit, both of which are discussed in more detail in the next chapter, including how to run your applications.

As of the writing of this book, the latest firmware revision is 2.0, but most PSPs in the U.S. are still at version 1.5. As long as you haven't updated your firmware past version 1.5, you're probably in good shape. However, if you are running 1.51, 1.52, 2.0 or greater, you may not be able to run your applications. New hacks around this limitation are coming out all the time, and I will keep a running list on the official *Hacking the PSP* Web site, www.hackingpsp.com.

Tip Don't have a 1.5 Firmware PSP? Try your local GameStop and see if their used PSPs are still firmware 1.5. If you're looking for a Japanese PSP, look on eBay.

Checking Your Firmware Version

To check your firmware version, simply go to the PSP Navigator and select Settings, then System Settings, and press ⓧ. Select System Information, and press ⓧ again. The firmware revision is the number next to System Software, as shown in Figure 17-1.

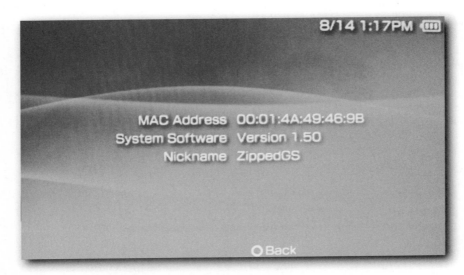

FIGURE 17-1: Determining your PSP's firmware version

Basic Terms

Software development isn't difficult. In fact, it's quite fun. If you have never developed before, especially if you haven't developed in C or C++, you need to learn a few basic terms so you're familiar with what your fellow PSP developers are talking about:

- **Source Code:** As the name implies, this is source of all the code for the programs you are going to write. Source code can comprise many files, linked together with Include Files, and ultimately compiled into a single program, called an EBOOT.PBP.

- **Compiler:** A compiler takes the C source code you are going to write and converts it into the binary representation the PSP will execute. (Years ago there were no compilers and people had to do this work by hand.)

- **Include files:** Include files contain the precompiled routines necessary to perform certain operations from within your code. You are not likely to redo all the code that has already been written that lets you draw images, write text, play sound, and so forth on the PSP. Instead, you simply add Include files to the top of your code that needs those routines, and then you can call them at will.

- **SDK:** Stands for Software Development Kit. SDKs contain all the files you need to write and compile programs for certain environments — in this case, the PSP.

- **EBOOT.PBP files:** These are the equivalent of executable files on the PC, where an executable is denoted by an extension of .EXE. The PSP generally only launches an application named EBOOT.PBP, although there are exceptions. When you use your PSP to search for Games in Navigator, the games listed are the EBOOT.PBPs it finds. Of course, without appropriate tools, those games will say "Corrupted Data" because Sony doesn't want you to run them, but we'll attempt to get around that later.

- **PSP SDK Toolchain:** The well-written script file that sets up the PSP SDK environment for you. It downloads all the include files you need, compiles them, and makes it possible for you to create EBOOT.PBP files without having to know all the gory inner details.

- **MakeFile:** The file you create that contains references to all your source code, tells the compiler how you want the EBOOT.PBP created, and then instructs the compiler to build your EBOOT.PBP file. On a fast computer, your EBOOT.PBP can be created in a few seconds.

Getting Started

Now that you know the lingo, let's set up the development environment. If you don't already have Linux, never fear — we're going to install an application called Cygwin, available from www.cygwin.com, that emulates Linux on top of Windows. It's a very handy tool, incredibly easy to set up, and is required to go forward from here.

Note

The files you are about to download are very small, but those files in turn download very large files. A broadband connection is a great thing to have at this stage. If you don't have broadband, see if a friend that does will let you bring your computer to their place to do this download, as it takes about two to four hours to download and compile.

Here's what you need:

- Windows 2000, XP or greater
- Cygwin (downloadable from www.cygin.com)

Note

If you already have Linux or Mac OS X, you don't need Cygwin and you can skip the Cygwin step because a Unix shell is already available in your operating system. In Mac OS X the shell is accessed via the Terminal application, while in Linux and Unix you likely will know how to open a "new shell window," which varies based on the Linux/Unix distribution you are using.

- 500MB of free hard disk space
- Preferably a broadband Internet connection (dial-up will take *forever*)
- The PSP Toolchain SDK file (get the latest version at www.ooponet.net/ consoledev under Playstation Portable - Toolchain Files)

Setting Up the Development Environment

To set up our development environment, you need to configure three items: Cygwin, PSP SDK Toolchain, and the Cygwin batch file.

Installing Cygwin

Now that you've downloaded Cygwin, you need to install it. Launch the Cygwin setup.exe file and click Next to get to the Download Source screen. Select Install from Internet, as shown in Figure 17-2.

Now set your install directory to the default of C:\cygwin (although elsewhere will work fine — just make sure the directory is called *cygwin* so you can easily find it), set it so All Users have access to Cygwin, and set the Default Text File Type to Unix (as shown in Figure 17-3). Then click Next.

Cywin asks where you want to deliver your local packages. Just keep the default, and then click Next.

You are then asked how you are connected to the Internet (see Figure 17-4). For most people, Direct Connection is fine. If you have to use a different option, you probably already know that you do and you will likely know the details, or you should ask your system administrator.

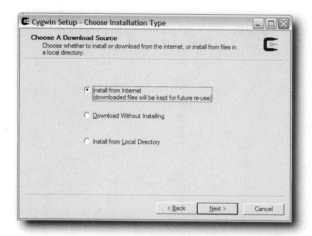

FIGURE 17-2: Selecting the Install from Internet option in Cygwin

FIGURE 17-3: Setting the Cygwin environment defaults

Cygwin now downloads the list of available sites you can get its files from. I tend to choose only sites that end with .edu, as they usually have fast connections. I also choose http connections instead of ftp — I've found the ftp sites often have problems while the Web-served files tend to come across flawlessly. In Figure 17-5, you can see I chose http://mirror.calvin.edu, a reputable school that likely keeps its servers running well.

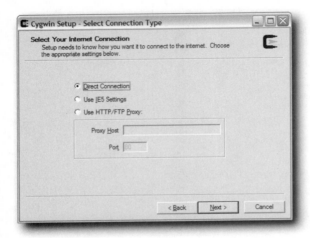

FIGURE 17-4: Choosing your Internet connection type

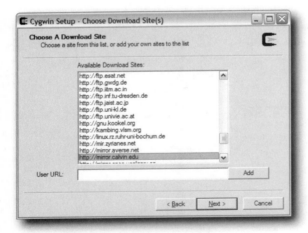

FIGURE 17-5: Choosing where to download
the additional Cygwin setup files

Cygwin now presents you with a list of packages you want to install. Click the View button
on the top-right so it changes to Full and you can easily choose the packages. You need to
choose the following:

- autoconf2.1
- automake1.9

- gcc
- gcc-g++
- make
- nano
- patchutils
- subversion
- wget

Note Cygwin supports practically all of the packages available for Linux. If there are any others you want to get, such as irc, ncftp, and many others, you can choose them for installation as well. Of course, you may not want them now. If that's the case, simply run the Cygwin installer again and it will remember what you have installed and only install the new packages you select.

Figure 17-6 shows what it looks like when items are selected. When you've checked what you need, click Next. Cygwin starts downloading and installing all the necessary files. When it's done, it does the usual dance of asking you if you want an icon on your desktop and so forth. I just keep the boxes checked because it's useful to have on the desktop, but do whatever suits your fancy.

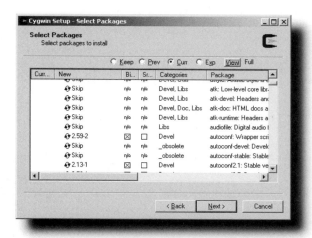

FIGURE 17-6: Selecting Cygwin packages to install

Now that Cygwin is installed, you need to create a few directories. Launch Cygwin and you are greeted with a (possibly familiar) Linux $ command prompt, as shown in Figure 17-7.

Note The $ in the command prompt means you're logged in as a regular user. The powerful Linux root account is defined by a ! (sometimes called a *bang*) character.

FIGURE 17-7: Running Cygwin for the first time

Warning The first time you run Cygwin, it sets up all the files it needs to run, so running Cygwin once before you work with its directories is very important. Don't just dive into its install directory and mess around until you've run it once!

Now that you're at the command prompt, and Cygwin is set up, you need to create a few folders using the Linux `mkdir` command, which stands for "make directory" and is practically identical to the DOS `md` command.

At the command prompt, type the following commands, pressing Enter after each one:

```
mkdir projects
mkdir psptoolchain
```

After you have done this, type **ls**, which means "list subdirectory." You should see your new folders, as shown in Figure 17-8.

Now, minimize Cygwin—you'll get back to it in a moment.

Installing the PSP SDK Toolchain

The PSP SDK Toolchain takes all the work out of creating the PSP development environment. You just have to run it within Cygwin, then sit back and relax (well, better yet, go get some dinner and watch a movie, because it *will* take a long time, up to 5 hours on a slow machine).

The first thing you need to do is locate the PSP SDK Toolchain file you downloaded and decompress it. The file is likely a TAR file, so you need a program like WinZip or Stuffit Expander (both available from www.download.com) to decompress it. (I assume that because you have purchased a book with "hacking" in the title, you know how to decompress files.)

FIGURE 17-8: Your newly created working directories

Once the files are decompressed, open the directory you installed Cygwin into. In this directory there should be a directory named *home*. Open this directory and you should see your user directory, which you can open to find the psptoolchain folder you created earlier. Copy all the PSP Toolchain files into this directory, and then open the Cygwin window again.

Once you're back in Cygwin, type **cd psptoolchain** to change into the PSP toolchain's directory. Your command prompt should have the text *username@computername ~/psptoolchain* above it.

Now type the following and press Enter and go get some food or watch a movie (see Figure 17-9 for an idea of what your screen will look like):

```
./toolchain.sh
```

The ./ command means "execute," which forces Linux (in this case, Cygwin), to execute the toolchain shell script (denoted by .sh, although .sh will not always trail a shell script file).

Your Cygwin springs to life, downloading files and building all the programs it needs to make PSP programs. Let it do its job. Figure 17-10 is a snapshot of what you will see as things get going.

FIGURE 17-9: Entering the ./toolchain.sh command

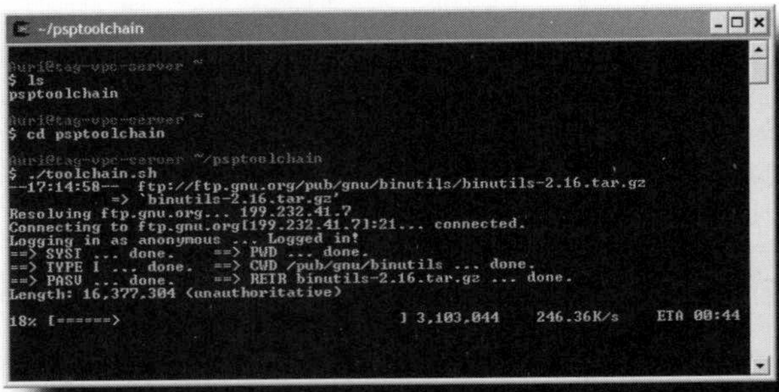

FIGURE 17-10: The PSP SDK Toolchain starting up

When the toolchain is done working its magic, you'll be brought back to the command prompt. At this point you can just type **logout** and press Enter and move to the next step.

Making the Final Cygwin Settings

Now that the SDK is installed, we need to make some small changes to the Cygwin configuration file so it knows where to find all the stuff the toolchain just installed.

Open up your Cygwin directory again and you should see the cygwin.bat file, as shown in Figure 17-11.

FIGURE 17-11: The cygwin.bat configuration file

Right-click the cygwin.bat file and select Edit. Notepad appears. Change the contents of the file to read as follows:

```
@echo off

C:
chdir c:\cygwin\bin

set path=%path%;c:/cygwin/usr/local/pspdev/bin
set PSPSDK=c:/cygwin/usr/local/pspdev

bash --login-i
```

Then go to the *File* menu and click *Save* and close Notepad.

Next Stop: Hello World!

That's it — you're all set up to start building PSP applications! If you want to learn how to load your applications, turn to the next chapter. If you want to start coding right away, skip over the next chapter and read how to write Hello World in Chapter 19.

Summary

In this chapter, you learned the basic terms for PSP software development, installed Linux on your Windows machine, installed the PSP SDK, and readied the environment for your use. Now you're all set for building PSP applications — let's get going!

Programming the PSP: Hello World

The classic first program to write for any new device or language is Hello World. This simple program functionally only writes the words "Hello World" on the screen, but educationally teaches you the structure of the development environment, introduces a few gotchas, and lets you get your feet wet without actually hurting anything.

All software development for the PSP, is written in C or C++, with the exception of Web pages that you view and scripts run with the Lua Player discussed in Chapter 21, "Alternative Development Languages." The SDK you installed in Chapter 17, "Programming the PSP," gave you the fundamental functions and tools you need to write and compile your own programs. This chapter builds on that environment.

My approach is to have you type in the entire program *source code* first, then go through what each section does. You can enter the program in any text editor you desire, even a code editor if you have one. What's important is where you save the files and what you name them. If you've never programmed before, don't worry, I'll be gentle. If you have programmed before, you'll already know what parts of my educational thread you can spare.

Getting to Know C

If you don't know already, C is a programming language. It was invented many years ago in Bell Laboratories, with predecessors named, oddly enough, A and B. C is a powerful programming language, as close as you can get to *assembly* (another type of programming language) and still write in something that resembles English. C++ is the object-oriented version of C.

If you don't know C or C++, there are many good books you can read. Knowing C is important if you want to go beyond this Hello World program and really take advantage of what the PSP is capable of in your own programs. The SDK you installed in Chapter 17 has a multitude of examples ranging from simple text display to audio waveform generation to all-out 3D graphics, shading, and lighting effects. It even supports USB and Infrared port communications, wireless networking, and other neat capabilities of the PSP. However, without knowing C, it will probably all look like gobbledygook to you. While you're at it, learn C++, too, and put your résumé out because C and C++ developers are in hot demand.

A note to Microsoft C# (pronounced *C Sharp*) and Sun Java developers: you will likely pick up on C very quickly because the syntax is very similar. I would still pick up a *For Dummies* book to go over the basics of the language (don't feel bad, I use *For Dummies* books to learn the basics of new languages, and they're great) and you can likely just skim over those books, too.

I'm a big fan of the *For Dummies* series — they go through learning any topic in a very straight-forward, methodical way.

A Few Gotchas When Entering Code

For those of you who can program but don't know C, and for those of you who have never programmed before, here are some gotchas when writing in C (don't worry if you don't know all the terms I use just yet — I'll go over them when we walk through the code):

- C (and C++) is case-sensitive. This means if you name a variable with a lowercase *j*, you cannot reference that variable later as a capital *J*.

- Use good variable naming conventions. If you have an integer or string variable, start the variable with *int* or *str* respectively. Most developers don't use proper variable naming conventions, and then they're dumbfounded when they come back to their code a couple months later and can't figure out what the variables are for.

- Use comments throughout your code. Comments prevent you from forgetting what your code does, similar to proper variable naming. For the unwary, this is called *documenting your code*.

Create Your Project Folder

It's always good to organize the programming projects you're working on. You should always keep your source code and all other related program files in the same directory. In Chapter 17 you created a directory named *projects* to contain your individual programming projects' folders. You need to add a new directory named *helloworld* (all lowercase) to that folder. You can do this in Cygwin or Windows Explorer, or in Finder on Mac OS.

I prefer to do this in Cygwin, just because it's convenient and that's where I do a lot of my coding. Open Cygwin and type **cd projects** at the command prompt. When the projects directory comes up, type **mkdir helloworld** and press Enter and your project directory will be created. Then type **ls** to make sure your directory has been created, as shown in Figure 18-1. This is where you will store all of your program's files.

FIGURE 18-1: Creating the helloworld project folder

The Hello World Source Code

Now here's the difficult part — entering all the following code without making a typo! I honestly suggest typing it in yourself. Make sure you enter the text exactly as it appears here. Where there appears to be a long space, that's usually a tab or two (pressing the tab key). If you don't want to type all of this, you can just download it from the official *Hacking the PSP* Web site, www.hackingpsp.com.

When you enter the code, you'll notice lines that begin with // marks followed by text, and text in between /* and */ marks. These are *comments*, which tell you what is being done on that particular line or section of code.

Tip

Comment as much as possible. It is better to document your code while you write than to come back later and try to remember what a particular section of code was used for. You can even use comments to write what you *want* to do, then fill in the steps between the comments to "code your logic" based on the comments you've written (in school they call this *pseudocode*). Comments do not slow down your program. They are actually automatically omitted from the compilation process.

To enter this code, I suggest using Notepad, a built-in text editor in Windows. It has actually shipped with Windows since Windows 1.0 (back in 1985). To open Notepad, select Start→ Run, and then type **notepad**.

Make sure Word Wrap is off before you enter the code. You can do this by opening the Format menu in Notepad and making sure there is no check mark next to Word Wrap. If there is a check mark, simply select the menu item and Word Wrap will be disabled.

Okay, ready? Enter the following code:

```
// Hello World - My First App for the PSP!!!

#include <pspkernel.h>  // PSP kernel functions include file.
#include <pspdebug.h>   // PSP debug functions include file.

/* Set the application information. */
PSP_MODULE_INFO("Hello World", 0, 1, 1);

/* Define debug parameters. */
/* Replace standard C printf() function with PSP printf()
function. */
#define printf pspDebugScreenPrintf

/* Exit callback */
int exit_callback(int arg1, int arg2, void *common)
{
    sceKernelExitGame(); // Exit the application.
    return 0;
}

/* Callback thread */
int CallbackThread(SceSize args, void *argp)
{
    // Local vars.
    int cbid;

    // Create the exit callback in for the PSP shell.
    cbid = sceKernelCreateCallback("Exit Callback", exit_callback,
NULL);
    sceKernelRegisterExitCallback(cbid);


    // Sleep the kernel until we tell it to exit.
    sceKernelRegisterExitCallback(cbid);

    // Return success.
    return 0;
}

/* Set up the callback thread and return the thread ID */
int SetupCallbacks(void)
{
    // Local vars.
    int thid = 0; /* Thread ID */
```

```
    // Create the thread.
    thid = sceKernelCreateThread("update_thread", CallbackThread,
0x11, 0xFA0, 0, 0);
    if (thid >= 0)
    {
            sceKernelStartThread(thid, 0, 0);
    }
}

/* Main Function */

int main()
{
    pspDebugScreenInit();
    SetupCallbacks();
    printf("Hello World!");
    sceKernelSleepThread();

    // Return success.
    return 0;
}
```

After you have entered this code, navigate to your helloworld directory in Cygwin (by default, it's c:\cygwin\home\projects\helloworld) and save it as **main.c** (make sure you enter the filename in all lowercase letters — the compiler is case-sensitive).

So What Does This Code Do?

Now that you've entered the code, let's go through each line and see what it does. Here's the first one:

```
// Hello World - My First App for the PSP!!!
```

This part is just a comment. It tells you what your program does. The // characters denote the beginning of a comment. If your comment is going to span more than one line, you instead enclose the text in between a /* and a */, similar to how HTML has beginning and ending tags.

On to the next two lines:

```
#include <pspkernel.h>   // PSP kernel functions include file.
#include <pspdebug.h>    // PSP debug functions include file.
```

The #include statement is what tells C to include the source code files necessary to make your code work on the PSP. Include files are pre-written pieces of code with functionality you need. There's no reason to write your own routines to print text to your PSP's screen or render 3D graphics — you just need to have access to those functions so you can pass the parameters you need (draw a circle at x and y coordinates, and so forth) and get the results you expect.

I have added comments to the right of the include directives to tell you what they do. You can leave these out if you want, but I recommend you keep them so you get into the habit of commenting and that if you come back to this code later, you'll understand what it does.

New Term   **Directive**—An instruction for the compiler when it is building your application's executable file. #include files direct the compiler to include certain files. Other compiler directives include #IF statements that tell the compiler to include or exclude pieces of your code depending on settings you made, such as code for debugging when you set a debug flag. C programming books explain directives in much more detail.

Here are the next two lines:

```
/* Set the application information. */
PSP_MODULE_INFO("Hello World", 0, 1, 1);
```

This code enables the compiler to build in the name of the program into your compiled program. You would generally replace this with the name of the program you were writing if it was different from Hello World. Because you're actually writing "Hello World" it's okay to leave this alone.

In the following lines, you rename a function from one of the Include files you brought in earlier:

```
/* Define debug parameters. */
/* Replace standard C printf() function with PSP printf()
function. */
#define printf pspDebugScreenPrintf
```

To print text to the screen on the PSP you have to use a function called pspDebug ScreenPrintf(). That's a lot to type, and most C programs use the printf() function to do practically the same thing. Of course, printf() doesn't work with the PSP, but by using a compiler directive of #define, you can force the compiler to replace every instance of printf with the longer function name, hence saving you time and getting you the results you need.

The next block of code is a *function*, which you can call from other code to make something happen. This code executes only when you call it from another function (everything in C runs from functions, unlike some other programming languages that are less structured and more ad-hoc). In particular, this piece of code enables you to actually exit the program when you're done with it, such as when you press the HOME button on the PSP to go back to the Navigator.

This function is named exit_callback and takes three arguments — arg1, arg2, and common — although those arguments aren't used in this case. The function returns an integer (numeric) value of 0, indicating to the calling function that it did its work successfully:

```
/* Exit callback */
int exit_callback(int arg1, int arg2, void *common)
{
    sceKernelExitGame(); // Exit the application.
    return 0;
}
```

The next several lines are more functions you need to interact with the PSP's operating system while your program runs:

```
/* Callback thread */
int CallbackThread(SceSize args, void *argp)
{
```

```c
    // Local vars.
    int cbid;

    // Create the exit callback in for the PSP shell.
    cbid = sceKernelCreateCallback("Exit Callback", exit_callback,
NULL);
    sceKernelRegisterExitCallback(cbid);


    // Sleep the kernel until we tell it to exit.
    sceKernelRegisterExitCallback(cbid);

    // Return success.
    return 0;
}

/* Set up the callback thread and return the thread ID */
int SetupCallbacks(void)
{
    // Local vars.
    int thid = 0; /* Thread ID */

    // Create the thread.
    thid = sceKernelCreateThread("update_thread", CallbackThread,
0x11, 0xFA0, 0, 0);
    if (thid >= 0)
    {
        sceKernelStartThread(thid, 0, 0);
    }
}
```

The use of these functions isn't very important to this lesson other than that they're required. For you programming types, here are some highlights of what the preceding code does:

- An execution thread is created in the kernel.
- The thread ID is returned from the kernel.
- A callback event handler is created to handle returning to the PSP's Navigator.

Next, there's the meat of our code — what you've spent all this time trying to get to:

```c
/* Main Function */

int main()
{
    pspDebugScreenInit();
    SetupCallbacks();
    printf("Hello World!");
    sceKernelSleepThread();

    // Return success.
    return 0;
}
```

Every C program starts from its main() function. The main() function should always return an integer value of 0 to signify that it has run to completion successfully. This is defined when you put the word int in front of main(), which means your function will return an integer (numeric) value back to the PSP's operating system when it's done running.

Next comes a few function calls. These calls invoke the functions you entered earlier. After each function call, the code continues from where you left off. So first you call pspDebug ScreenInit() to initialize the PSP's screen for displaying text. Then you call Setup Callbacks() so the PSP's operating system knows what you're doing (this is important).

Finally, you call printf("Hello World"), which passes the text (called a *string*) you want to "print" to the screen. You can replace Hello World with whatever you want. However, if you want a quote, you have to enter it as \" and if you want a \ you have to enter \\ instead. The \ has a special meaning in C, which you will learn in a C tutorial book.

 Note See all of those semicolons after each statement of code? Make sure you enter those! If you don't, your code won't compile. The most common code entry error is forgetting to add the semicolon at the end of the line of code. If you get compiler errors, you probably missed one of those darn semicolons!

Creating the Make File

You're almost done! Now that the code is entered, you have to give the compiler a few details in order to make the file into a runnable PSP program. Create a new file in Notepad (or whatever editor you used) and enter the following text, again making sure you type everything just like it's written here (don't swap uppercase and lowercase, and so forth):

```
TARGET = hello
OBJS = main.o

CFLAGS = -O2 -G0 -Wall
CXXFLAGS = $(CFLAGS) -fno-exceptions -fno-rtti
ASFLAGS = $(CFLAGS)

EXTRA_TARGETS = EBOOT.PBP
PSP_EBOOT_TITLE = Hello World
PSPSDK = $(shell psp-config --pspsdk-path)
include $(PSPSDK)/lib/build.mak
```

When you're done, save it as Makefile (again, the filename is case-sensitive).

Running Your Program

Now that you've entered all your code, do the following:

1. If you are using Cygwin to emulate Linux (as discussed in Chapter 17), launch it. Or, if you have Linux, open up a shell prompt. If you have a Mac, open a Terminal window (go to Applications → Utilities, and then double-click Terminal).

2. Once you're at the command line, type **cd projects** to change to your projects directory.

3. Type **cd helloworld** to change to your Hello World program directory.

4. Now you need to make the PSP program. Simply type **make** and your PSP compiler will come to life, compile the program, and you should be fine. If you see warning messages, that's OK. However, if you see ERROR messages, you made a mistake in your code. Re-open your code and make sure you entered everything properly, and then recompile until you get no errors.

Your screen will look similar to Figure 18-2.

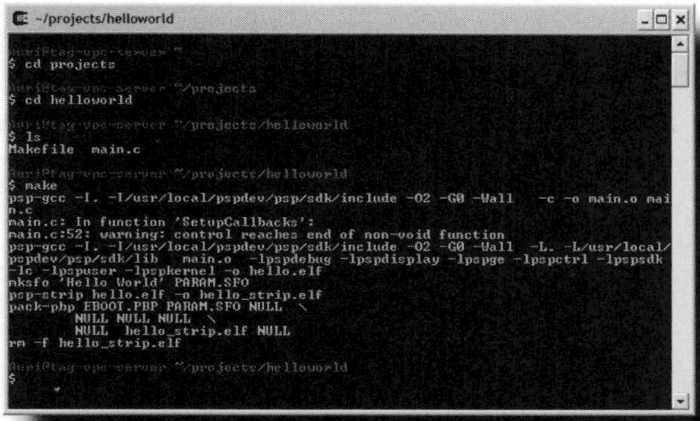

FIGURE 18-2: Compiling your source code in Cygwin

Now if you type **ls** you should see your EBOOT.PBP file, which is your PSP program. If you have a U.S. PSP, copy the EBOOT.PBP file over to your PSP using the KXploit method or the KXploit program (discussed in Chapter 19). If you have a Japanese PSP that's still running firmware 1.0 you can just copy it into your PSP / GAMES / HelloWorld directory.

Summary

In this chapter, you wrote, compiled, and ran your first PSP program. Congratulations! The next couple of chapters, discuss how to run Homebrew PSP applications and what the PSP SDK (Software Developer Kit) gives you, and how you can move forward now that you're past the hardest part — writing your first program!

Running Homebrew Applications

While the original Japanese PSP could run applications written by any developer, called "homebrew applications," Sony disabled such a feature in the U.S. release with their version 1.5 firmware (the original Japanese unit came with firmware version 1.0). Uber-smart hackers figured out how to get around this limitation with a number of "exploits," which took advantage of holes in Sony's application security architecture to enable users to run their applications. Sony once again patched these holes in their 1.51 firmware and beyond, and application developers and hackers continue to try to break their protections. (Chapter 16 discussed how to downgrade a 2.0, not 2.01 or higher, PSP back to firmware version 1.5.)

Unlike most game systems, where a hack can work forever, the PSP was made to be upgradeable. Sony can add new features at will to keep the unit competitive in the marketplace (such as adding video-on-demand services, music download and Web browser capabilities, and more), but they can also thwart hackers' attempts at feigning their security.

Considering the rampant piracy present in the computer industry, Sony obviously doesn't want a malicious developer to come out with a program that lets you run UMD disc images you have downloaded off the Internet — that hurts Sony's bottom line and ultimately disuades well-known and respected software houses from writing software for their product. Unfortunately, because of this piracy and distrust of software developers, Sony has come out with new protections to prevent our applications from being run. The latest is code-signing, which affixes a digital signature to each application that is allowed to run on the PSP, and unfortunately only Sony and its game-authoring partners have the software to generate these signatures.

But what if you want to run homebrew applications, which range from neat games to Nintendo and Sega Genesis emulators to actual server software that utilizes the PSP's wireless connection? As long as you have a PSP with firmware version 1.5 or lower, you can. New hacks that enable homebrew applications to run come out all the time, and Sony's underlying code still appears to exist, so as new hacks come out you should still be able to run all the homebrew applications out there. This chapter introduces you to the tools you need to run homebrew applications on firmware revisions that allow or can be modified for homebrew applications to be run.

Keep in mind that authorized Sony PSP applications may end up being distributed by Sony (and thus you may eventually be able to buy non-UMD programs for your PSP that you can download off the Internet). There is also a possibility, albeit a small one, that Sony will release a development kit for the PSP. It has its plusses and minuses for Sony, so only time will tell if they figure a way to profit from authorizing homebrew application development.

The Swapsploit and K-XPloit

The first exploit that enabled running homebrew applications on U.S. PSPs was the Swap Exploit, also known as the "Swapsploit." This method involved two Memory Sticks, and you would load a dummy application on your PSP, then quickly swap out the Memory Stick that had the actual homebrew application on it, and it would run. However, this was a dangerous solution, as removing a Memory Stick while it's still in use can damage the Memory Stick, an expensive loss.

Obviously there had to be a better, easier method to run homebrew applications. Less than a month after the Swapsploit was released, the K-Xploit came out, from some leet hackers called the PSP-Dev Team. The K-Xploit builds two folders, both with identical names, but one folder with a % in the title. The dummy folder is located in one folder, while the actual EBOOT.PBP is in the other, and it executes. You can perform this hack on a PC or Mac using the utility programs described in this chapter.

K-Xploit Software for PC

You can download the K-Xploit software from http://www.psp-hacks.com/psp-kxploit-howto.php, or from the official *Hacking the PSP* Web site (www.hackingpsp.com).

Once you've downloaded the software, and found the homebrew applications you want to install, install the K-Xploit software. Plug in your PSP and put it in USB Connection mode ("host mode"), so the program can automatically install the software on your PSP.

Once your PSP is in host mode, launch the K-Xploit software. You will be greeted with a screen similar to the one in Figure 19-1.

Tip If your software comes up in Spanish, select the *Idioma* menu at the top of the window and change the language to English.

FIGURE 19-1: The K-Xploit software

In the Name field, enter what you want your application's name to appear as on your PSP. For example, if you have a Hello World application, you would type **HELLOWORLD** in the Name box, as shown in Figure 19-2.

FIGURE 19-2: Naming your PSP application

Next, show the software where your EBOOT.PBP is located by clicking the button with the three dots (...) on it and navigating to your EBOOT.PBP file.

Finally, select your PSP from the list of drives, so the software knows where to copy the file.

When you're done, select Generate Files, and wait while the EBOOT is converted and transferred to the PSP. Keep in mind that if there were any supporting files other than the EBOOT.PBP (such as sound and text files), these are not transferred by the program, and you will have to manually copy them into the directory on your Memory Stick that contains the modified EBOOT.PBP (just look for the folder with the same name as your application, *not* the one with the % symbol in the title). The program will tell you all of this as well, as shown in Figure 19-3.

FIGURE 19-3: The application has been successfully transferred to the PSP

K-Xploit Software for Mac

Those with Macs aren't out of luck. You can get the same basic functionality using an application from RnSK Softronics called HomebrewPSP Converter, available at http://ipsp .kaisakura.com/homebrew.php or from the official *Hacking the PSP* Web site (www .hackingpsp.com).

Running the Software

Once the software is on your PSP, exit host mode and you will be brought back to the PSP Navigator. Remove any UMD disc you have in the drive at this point as well.

Now, navigate to Game, and then select Memory Stick. After a few moments, all the home-brew applications you've installed on your PSP appear, as shown in Figure 19-4. Select the one you want, such as Hello World, and it will run!

<small>FIGURE **19-4:** Selecting a homebrew application to run on your PSP</small>

Figure 19-5 shows an early build of an x86 processor emulator named Bochs running Linux on the PSP.

<small>FIGURE **19-5:** Linux running on the PSP</small>

Summary

In this chapter you learned the history of homebrew software on the PSP. You also learned how to run your own homebrew applications. Of course, with this knowledge you can now launch your own PSP applications, as well as search the Web for other homebrew applications, such as cool new games and old gaming system emulators (there are even ways to run Windows 95 and Linux!). Have fun!

Navigating the Unofficial PSP SDK

Now that you've written and run your first program on your PSP, you're probably salivating to do more. It's got to be capable of doing more than just displaying black-and-white text on the screen, right? The PSP SDK you installed in Chapter 17, "Programming the PSP," has a *plethora* of examples to get you on your way to writing 3D games, musical applications, and much more.

Note that the PSP SDK you installed is *not* the official SDK from Sony. Sony doesn't make its official PSP available to mere mortal developers, but the unofficial PSP SDK is awesome and quite capable — just look at all the homebrew applications that have already been written using it!

If you haven't already downloaded and installed the PSP SDK, follow the instructions in Chapter 17.

in this chapter

☑ Getting around the unofficial PSP SDK

☑ SDK sample programs and what they're used for

Getting to the SDK Files

The PSP SDK files are installed in the following directory:

```
C:\Cygwin\usr\local\pspdev\psp\sdk
```

Note that C:\Cygwin is a placeholder for whatever drive letter and directory you installed Cygwin into. On a Macintosh or Linux machine it will just be the following:

```
/usr/local/pspdev/psp/sdk
```

In this directory is a *samples* directory, which contains samples of all the capabilities of the PSP SDK. We will go over what each of these sample programs do, so you know which ones to play around with. In addition to the samples here, many PSP applications also have source code available so you can see how those developers did their magic on their PSPs.

Compiling the Sample Files

You can compile the sample files just like your Hello World application. Just navigate to the directory with the sample you want to build and type the **make** command to get the associated EBOOT.PBP file. Each folder contains a main.c file that contains the sample's source code. The better option is to make a new folder in your projects directory and copy the sample files into there so you can play with the sample code without messing up the original should you need to go back.

Audio Library

The audio library handles all functions related to sound generation and playback. The PSP supports both polyphonic tones (like a cell phone) and waveform generation of tones (playing sounds waves of different types and frequencies):

- **Polyphonic:** This sample code shows you how to use multiple instruments to play music on your PSP, similar to MIDI file playback.

- **Wavegen:** This sample code shows you how to create soundwaves of different frequencies using the PSP's built-in sound synthesizer. It lets you use the analog stick to turn the frequency up or down. Don't play with the super-high pitches this program creates near pets, animals, or glass, please!

Controller Library

The controller samples enable you to interact with the game controller buttons on your PSP, such as the analog stick, the arrow keys, the shape keys, and the other buttons on your PSP.

For example, the Basic demo reads from the controller pad and tells you the basic keypresses.

Debugging Library

The debugging library is crucial for any developer. It helps you handle the testing and debugging of your code, such as handling exceptions, profiling your code, and more. The debug sample files include the following:

- **Exception:** This sample shows you how to build a basic exception handler. Exception handlers are pieces of code that gracefully handle errors when they are encountered during program execution. If you've ever programmed in Java or .NET, you're probably familiar with Try, Catch, and Finally statements. This enables similar functionality on the PSP.

- **KprintF:** Handles printing errors to the screen from the kernel.

- **Profiler:** Enables code profiling during execution.

- **PRXDecrypt:** Decrypts PSP PRX files, and also demonstrates File IO.

Graphics Unit (GU) Library

The real meat of the PSP is its extensive graphics capability. The sample items here are cool enough just to compile and run, and monkeying with them is even more fun. Just as with any powerful PC graphics card, the PSP supports many advanced graphics and image processing capabilities, including the following (and there is a sample for each of these):

- **Blend:** Combines two graphics using two or more colors for transparency.
- **Clut:** Handles Color Lookup Tables (CLUT).
- **Cube:** Draws a cube (three-dimensional square) with an applied texture.
- **Lights:** Creates light sources that highlight objects.
- **Logic:** Image logic.
- **Reflection:** Handles light reflection off an object from a given light source.
- **Skinning:** Places an image over a skeleton three-dimensional image.
- **Sprite:** A pre-rendered two-dimensional figure, sometimes with transparency, often used in two-dimensional games. For example, in Pac Man, the ghosts and Pac Man are sprites moving around the screen.
- **Blit:** Combines two bitmap patterns into one.
- **Copy:** Copies bitmap images.
- **EnvMap:** Applies a 2D image to the surface of a 3D object.
- **Lines:** Draws lines.
- **Morph:** Morphs images from one form to another.
- **RenderTarget:** Uses off-screen textures as render targets.
- **Spharm:** Spherical harmonics.

Infrared (IR) Library

The infrared library enables you to utilize the PSP's built-in infrared port for both IrDA- and SiRCS-compatible communications with other compatible devices, such as other PSPs and remote controls. A sample exists for each standard.

Kernel Library

The *kernel* is the base process that handles everything going on in the PSP, including file operations (*I/O*, or *input/output*), memory management, thread control, processor speed, and so forth. The kernel samples include the following:

- **Cwd:** A simple demo of working with directories on a Memory Stick Duo inserted into the PSP's Memory Stick Duo reader slot.

- **FileIO:** Demonstrates how to use file input/output functions such as reading and writing files from Memory Sticks.

- **Kdumper:** Demonstrates how to enter kernel mode, including reading and dumping register values, regions of memory, and more.

- **LoadModule:** Demonstrates how to enter kernel mode, and load modules into both kernel and user memory spaces. At the time of this book's writing, there appeared to be a bug in the PSP kernel that would cause this code to crash.

- **ThreadStatus:** Demonstrates how to get a list of program threads and get information on them, such as the name thread address, stack address, stack size, and more.

Power Library

There was only one sample power library project in the SDK as of the writing of this book. The demo shows checking for the power switch position, sleep mode, and power off mode, checking battery information, as well as changing the processor speed (between 1 and 333 megahertz, also listed as MHz) on-the-fly.

USB Library

The USB library enables you to work with the USB 2.0 port on your PSP, which is also backwards-compatible with USB 1.1.

 Constant use of the USB port uses more processor and battery than in normal operation, so be aware of this issue if you're doing any intensive work with the USB port (such as running a server application or doing a lot of I/O).

The storage sample demonstrates USB mass storage functionality, including activating and deactivating the USB port, and mounting the PSP as a mass storage device.

Utility Library

The utility library samples enable you to see how to work with PSP system parameters, such as your preferences, network settings, and so forth. Two of the utility samples are as follows:

- **SystemParam:** Demonstrates how to read your system parameters, such as the nickname, time format, time zone, daylight savings time, system language settings, and so forth.

- **NetConf:** A good demonstration on how to access system parameters. This sample loads the list of network configurations saved on your PSP.

Wireless Networking (WLAN) Library

There's only one sample for this portion of the SDK, and it shows you how to check if your WiFi (wireless) switch is in the on or off position, and how to get your WiFi interface's MAC Address. The MAC, or *Media Access Control*, address is the unique identifier of your PSP on a network (in this case, any wireless network).

Summary

This chapter discussed the various SDK samples that are included with the unofficial PSP SDK you installed in Chapter 17. Experimenting with these samples will help you learn to write your own applications on your PSP, which you can then share with your friends who also can run homebrew applications. The next chapter discusses how to distribute your homebrew applications.

Alternative Development Languages

In addition to the die-hard C/C++ development approach, there are many alternative ways to develop for your PSP. Some work only on programmable PSPs, such as Lua, while others utiltize UMDs and the Web to provide "official" PSP development routes, such as AdventureWorks and Adventure Player PSP. This chapter introduces the most popular non-C PSP development solutions.

Lua

While C and C++ have a very steep learning curve, Lua, another free development environment, uses a simple scripting language similar to Microsoft's C# (pronouced *C Sharp*) to make programming the PSP incredibly easy. All of the setup for working with graphics, text, controller inputs, and so forth is handled for you — all you do is make the calls you need to make things work. This easy coding capability has lead to dozens of great Lua games that run on any programmable PSP (firmware 1.0 and 1.5) and has turned the PSP into a great beginner's game programming platform.

Unlike the fairly complex C-version of Hello World shown in Chapter 18, the Hello World program for Lua can be written in under 20 lines of code, as follows:

```
-- create a new Color object
green = Color.new(0, 255, 0)

-- show some text on offscreen
screen:print(200, 100, "Hello World!", green)

-- flip visible and offscreen
screen.flip()

-- wait forever (or until they press "home" to
exit)
while true do
    screen.waitVblankStart()
end
```

Talk about easy! Lua also makes it simple to work with sprites (animated objects on the screen), perform collision detection (when one object or spite hits another), and much more.

Lua has spawned quite a following. There is a dedicated Lua users Web site at www.lua-users.org, and now there's even an integrated development environment called *LuaIDE* for programming and bugging Lua scripts in an environment similar to many professional development tools, like Microsoft's Visual Studio or Eclipse. You can find LuaIDE at www.gorlice.net.pl/~rybak/luaide/.

Running a Lua-based game requires the use of the Lua Player, similar in function to the Flash player used in Web browsers, or the Java runtime on desktops. The Lua Player runs the script and makes the game work. Installing the Lua Player is easy. Install it like you would any other homebrew application (see Chapter 19, "Running Homebrew Applications," for information about how to install homebrew applications on a programmable PSP), and then copy the script you want to run to the Lua Player's directory on your PSP (it has the Lua Player EBOOT.PBP file in it). The script must be named **script.lua** or it will not run (you can safely rename your script without damaging it or your PSP).

You can download Lua and Lua games from the official Lua Player Web site, www.lua player.org. There are a number of excellent beginner and advanced tutorials available online as well at the Lua users Web site, www.lua-users.org/wiki/Tutorial Directory. You can find beginner tutorials at the Lua Player Web site, www.luaplayer.org/tutorial/index.html. The full Lua function reference is available at www.luaplayer.org/functions.txt.

Of course, if you want to do hardcore PSP development and access all of the capabilities of the PSP, such as USB, full graphics and processor control, networking, and so forth, you will have to code (for now) in C/C++ using the unofficial PSP SDK described in previous chapters.

Adventure Maker

While not exactly a PSP programming tool, Adventure Maker, a free game and multimedia software development toolkit, lets you create Windows-based applications and then port the simpler versions of those creations to the Web for your PSP using still images and Javascript and the Web browser built-in to PSP Firmware 2.0. Adventure Maker doesn't require any programming or scripting skills, which is a boon for those who want to create applications for the PSP but don't want to learn how to code. You can download Adventure Maker from www.adventuremaker.com. There is also a "full" version of Adventure Maker, but it doesn't provide any additional benefit for PSP developers.

Obviously there are caveats to limiting the scope of games to only still images and Javascript, but for adventure games, simple animations, and Kiosk-type and slide-show applications, the exported applications may work very well for you. Plus, the games should be somewhat playable on other handhelds, such as the PocketPC and Treo line of PDA phones, as well as on PCs and Macs.

You can find information on exporting Adventure Maker games to "portable gaming systems," as their Web site says, at www.adventuremaker.com/help/portable.htm. Sample Adventure Player games to try can be found at www.adventuremaker.com/games_for_portable.htm.

AdventurePlayer PSP

Available only in Japanese for now, AdventurePlayer by From Software is the only official third-party PSP development solution that actually lets you create and share PSP games. While the game is limited to creating adventure games, you can create the games on a PC and just move them to any PSP that has the AdventurePlayer game inserted and play your games, similar to how the Lua Player runs Lua scripts. The games can also be shared among other AdventurePlayer users, building a network of available games for you to choose from and contribute to.

You can find AdventurePlayer at www.adventureplayer.net, and you can usually find a copy for sale on eBay (unless, of course, you're in Japan, where you can just buy it at a store that sells PSP games). Even though the game is in Japanese, it runs on any PSP.

Summary

In this chapter you learned of the alternatives to writing PSP games and applications in C and C++. I'm not a big fan of C/C++, so any excuse I have to write something that looks more "human" as I code, the more I'm for it. Either way you go, choose your programming fancy and have a great time writing great applications for your PSP!

Distributing Your Applications

Now that you've written your killer PSP application, how do you get it out there? This chapter gives you some tips and pointers to get your product out there, and how to package it so the most people can benefit from it.

Test Fully

Test your application and make sure it doesn't break anything. Let your PSP-toting friends test it, too, because developers usually don't see all the bugs as their applications get more complex. The last thing you want to do is get sued for writing an application that blew up someone's PSP because you didn't fully test your I/O functions.

Package Hacked Versions

Some versions of the PSP firmware require a "hacked" version of the EBOOT.PBP (such as 1.5, which needs the KXploit tool to run EBOOTs), while others only require your original EBOOT.PBP (as in the original 1.0 PSP firmware, which didn't disable homebrew applications by default). While tools exist that create the needed files to make the application run on individual firmware versions, you shouldn't make your user do that, especially since your user may not know how to use those tools or may be afraid of tools marked "exploits" or "hacker tool." Build each version of the EBOOT.PBP on your machine and distribute it in a format ready to be copied to your user's memory stick.

Furthermore, if there are any special installation instructions, such as certain files that must be created or included or directories that need to be created, make sure you mention that in your installation instructions.

Include a Manual and EULA

At the very least, include a Read Me that explains how to use your program in some detail. You spent all that time writing your application, but if you're the only one who knows how to use it, that won't do your popularity much good.

Some hackers hate EULAs, or End User License Agreements. I'm perfectly content with Open Source groupies, but don't be ignorant of today's litigation-happy environment. Include a EULA that disclaims you from responsibility by the user when they use your product, even if you don't charge for it. This applies not only to PSP applications, but any application you write and distribute to others.

A EULA can be found on practically any software package. Include it in your Read Me file and say something in the download description similar to "Your use of this software is contingent upon the acceptance of the terms of the End User License Agreement."

Upload to Multiple PSP Sites

Don't just upload to one site. Post your application on the many PSP software sites out there. Many of these are listed in Appendix A.

And don't forget to discuss your application in discussion forums and blogs. If you don't get the word out, who will? Don't count on users to get the word out — you wrote it, so you should promote it. As you promote it, your users will follow through (provided your application is worth talking about). So don't write it and forget it — be famous!

Get Reviews

Once you've put your application out there, get your friends to post positive reviews, further enticing people to download it. Submit your program to the various PSP magazines out there, and maybe you'll be featured. Your word only means so much to the downloader, so make your application speak for itself, through other people.

Please Don't Be a Pirate

If you've written a utility that hacks the PSP in a way that will negatively affect the PSP industry, such as UMD game "rippers" (you're likely not doing it for backups), or ways to get around music and video copy protections, please don't distribute it. Not only could it land you a fine or prison time, it hurts all of us trying to enjoy the PSP and all of its features. If you illegally copy software and distribute it, software developers may not write more games or applications for the platform. So *please*, don't be a pirate!

Summary

In this chapter I gave you some pointers on distributing your applications. You work hard on creating a great product — make sure it gets noticed!

Synchronization and Utility Software

Utility software is a required tool to go with any advanced computing platform. There are a number of utilities to make sure your PSP lasts long enough to fulfill all your gaming needs. Even though Sony has a reputation for building solid products, things can still go wrong. Synchronization software is required to make it easy to move you media back and forth between your PC or Mac and your PSP. This chapter discusses the utilities and synchronization software and how-tos that will help you back up your games, and scan for and fix dead pixels, among other cool utilities.

As you use your PSP more and more, you may find you need more than just games to get the most out of it. You may want to put your computer's music, video, and photos on your PSP, or backup and restore your games. This chapter discusses just how to do that with a great utility for Mac and PC called iPSP.

Software for Your PSP

The following is a list of PSP utility and synchronization software available online for free or purchase:

- **PSP Sync:** Downloadable from `http://samurai.pose.jp/ryn/products.php`. It's free and there are many sync product to choose from. However, everything except the menus is in Japanese!

- **Sony's own image converter:** Purchase at `http://www.jp.sonystyle.com/Nws/Software_dl/Pc/Software/Haa/2105710294200.html?referer=PSP411.com` for 1500 Yen (approximately $15 U.S.). It has a built in MPEG-4 converter and image transfer, but it is feature-limited (no saved game or data sync). Again, it is all in Japanese.

- **PocketMac for PSP:** Downloadable from `http://www.pocketmac.net/products/pmpsp/psp.html` for $9.95. It synchronizes Entourage Contacts, Mac OS X Address Book, iTunes music playlists, and iPhoto images, and works with iSync (see Figure 23-1). This is for Mac OS X only.

---

# chapter 23

in this chapter

- ☑ Syncing your PSP with your computer
- ☑ Backing up saved games
- ☑ Backing up Memory Sticks
- ☑ Checking for dead pixels
- ☑ Fixing stuck pixels
- ☑ Repairing corrupted Memory Sticks

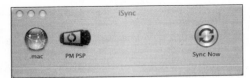

FIGURE 23-1: Pocket Mac for PSP works with iSync

- **PSP Multimedia Extender:** Downloadable from `http://sonypsp.sourceforge.net/?referer=PSP411.com` for free. It automatically converts files it transfers, but it has a dull interface (it's not "tidied up" yet).

- **Nullriver PSPWare:** Download from `http://www.nullriver.com/index/products/pspware` for $10–$15. It's a very slick, clean interface that works on both Mac and PC (see Figure 23-2 to see PSPWare in action).

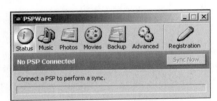

FIGURE 23-2: Nullriver's PSPWare

- **iPSP:** Download from `http://ipsp.kaisakura.com` for $19.99. This software automatically attempts to scale media to fit on your PSP, and is easy to use (see Figure 23-3 to see iPSP in action).

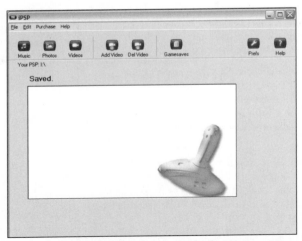

FIGURE 23-3: iPSP after it has backed up all PSP game data

Synchronizing Tips and Caveats

Here are some tips and tricks for getting the most out of your PSP synchronization experience.

Memory Sticks

Not all Sony Memory Sticks are the same. With the PSP, Sony honors Digital Rights Management, or DRM for short. This means that content that is protected can't be copied from one Memory Stick to another, or off your Memory Stick. You also can't copy protected music from a MagicGate Memory Stick to a non-MagicGate one. The PSP works with Sony's own DRM solution, MagicGate, so make sure you buy Memory Sticks that have the MagicGate logo on them, as shown in Figure 23-4.

FIGURE 23-4: A Sony MagicGate Memory Stick

Audio

When moving music in MP3 format over to your PSP, use lower bit rates, like 128 or 160 Kbps. This keeps the music at a very acceptable quality without taking up lots of space. Using Memory Sticks for music storage is expensive, as Memory Sticks are one of the most expensive flash media solutions on the market, usually commanding a 10 to 30 percent premium over competing formats.

Instead of using MP3, use Sony's ATRAC compression format. This format yields better audio quality at lower bit rates that sounds perceptibly the same as MP3 at much higher bit rates. For example, an ATRAC3 compressed music file at 96 Kbps may sound perceptibly as good as a 128 to 160 Kbps MP3 and uses 30% less space on the Memory Stick!

The PSP does not support playback or recording of ATRAC3 on Memory Stick Pro media prior to System Update (firmware version) 2.0. The manual states that, should you want to use ATRAC3, you must use a standard Memory Stick or standard MagicGate Memory Sticks.

Photos

When you're looking at an image, use the analog thumbstick to scroll around the image. If the image doesn't fill the whole screen, simply press (△) to open a host of options, listed in Table 23-1.

Table 23-1   Photo options

Option	Function
🔍	Toggles stretching the image to fill the screen.
(i+)	Displays information about the image.
‖ ‖	Brings the image back to normal size.
🔍	Decreases the zoom level.
🔍	Increases the zoom level.
↺	Rotates the image counter-clockwise.
↻	Rotates the image clockwise.
↓	Goes to the previous image in the image folder.
↑	Goes to the next image in the image folder.
▶	Plays the images in sequence, in a slideshow, by the date they were added to the camera.

Other shortcut keys when viewing images are listed in Table 23-2.

Table 23-2   Other image viewing options

Option	Function
Left trigger	Goes to the previous image in the image folder.
Right trigger	Goes to the next image in the image folder.
(○)	Exits image viewing mode.
(START)	Starts and pauses a slideshow. Once the slideshow has begun, you can use the left and right triggers to "slide" between images (a pretty cool effect).

During a slideshow, you have many other options:

■ When the slideshow is paused, press (□) once to bring up the picture time information.

■ Press (□) again and an image selector appears. Use the left and right triggers to change images from the preview-icon selector.

When you are copying images to your camera, place the images in folders. These folders will show up on your PSP, and then you can just go directly to the set of folders you want instead of paging through all of your images.

When you copy images to your PSP for a slideshow, make sure you copy them over in the order you want them. The PSP timestamps the images and then plays slideshows based on those timestamps, so if you copy them out of sequence (say, when you're copying over PowerPoint slides), your images will be out of order.

Carrying Cases

When you carry multiple Memory Sticks, consider buying a Memory Stick carrying case from your local CompUSA, Best Buy, Fry's, and so forth. Memory Sticks are small and expensive, so don't risk losing them!

Similarly, you should pick up a carrying case for your UMDs. The cases they come in tend to be too big (about half the width of a DVD case, and just as tall) for carrying around with you all the time.

Backing Up Your Games

You don't need any special software to back up your games, even though iPSP will do it for you automatically.

Backing Up Games to Your Computer

Follow these steps to back up your games to your computer (and then possibly to a CD or any other media you desire):

1. Connect the USB cable to your PSP and PC and put the PSP in USB Connection mode.

2. Open the PSP folder and copy the entire SAVEDATA folder to your computer's hard drive (see Figure 23-5). Optionally, you can back up the entire Memory Stick by just copying the entire PSP folder to your computer.

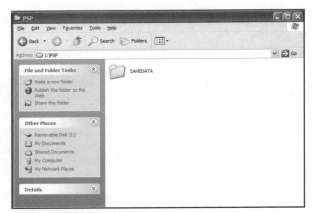

FIGURE 23-5: The SAVEDATA folder on the PSP's Memory Stick

That's it — your games are now backed up to your computer.

Note You may wonder why the game save data is so big (hundreds of kilobytes, which may seem a bit odd). Well, the saved game data may include a small movie so you can see a cool little game preview when looking at saved data. While this really doesn't do anything but provide a coolness factor, it's done nevertheless and uses space on your Memory Stick.

The PSP's Saved Data Utility

The PSP itself has a pseudo-backup function, where you can copy games to another Memory Stick in case you accidentally die in your saved game and can't get it back. Here's how:

1. In the PSP Navigator, go to Game, then Saved Data Utility.

2. Find the game you want to back up data for and press ⌂.

3. Select *Info* from the menu that pops up and press ⊗. Make note of the amount of space the saved games uses on the Memory Stick and make sure the Memory Stick you're backing up to has at least that much space left. Then press ◎ to back out.

4. Now select Copy from that same menu and press ⊗, as shown in Figure 23-6.

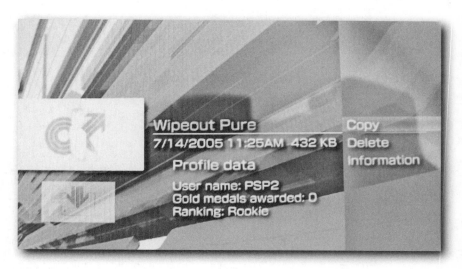

FIGURE 23-6: The Saved Data Utility menu

5. The PSP tells you how many times you will have to swap out the two Memory Sticks (see Figure 23-7). Follow the prompts and your data will be backed up.

Tip A good gamer knows to save and save often, so you can go back in time to when you had all the good stuff before you died.

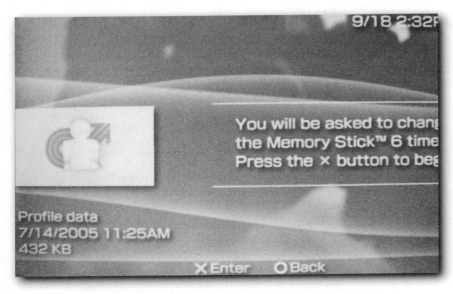

FIGURE 23-7: The PSP Saved Data Utility ready to back up a saved game

PSP Dead Pixel Checker

When the PSP was first released in Japan, and continuing with the U.S. release, there were a lot of complaints of "dead pixels" on the LCD screen. Dead pixels are defective areas of the LCD panel that show up as "dead" (meaning they never light and appear as black dots on the display when it's working) or glow just a single color regardless of what the display matrix tells them to be.

This is a common problem on laptop screens and is often the subject of fierce debate as to how many dead pixels need be present before a manufacturer will replace the display. I myself believe that if there's even a single dead pixel, the screen should be replaced, but the laptop manufacturers (including Sony) tend to disagree and require three, four, five, six, or more dead pixels before they'll replace the screen in your unit.

Sony's stance has eased quite a bit and they tend to just replace the PSP displays (or the entire unit, so be careful because your firmware may come back upgraded), but there's no guarantee that Sony will fix your PSP. Luckily for you, the dead pixels should show up within the first 24 hours of use (this doesn't mean one day—I really mean 24 hours of actual non-continuous use).

If you want to be proactive, there is a utility out there to help you determine if you have dead pixels. Well, it's not really a utility—it's four image files, three representing each primary color and one that's all white. You load the images onto your PSP and look at each one. If a pixel stays lit, or a black (dead) pixel appears when the PSP is displaying any of the colors, you have a dead pixel problem and may want to approach Sony or the store you purchased the unit from and seek a replacement. Of course, your warranty is a year, so you could wait a few weeks if the system is playable and send it off when you finish that game—it's your call—just make sure your warranty hasn't run out.

To get the images, go to http://psp.ign.com/articles/599/599236p1.html or simply log on to the *Hacking the PSP* Web site (www.hackingpsp.com).

Tip You can reach Sony's repair hotline at 1-800-345-7669. If you decide to send your PSP in for repair, make sure you remove any Memory Stick you have in the slot (it may not come back!), that you have only Sony parts installed (such as the battery), and that you haven't taken the PSP apart or damaged that sticker under the battery, or your warranty will be void and you'll be out postage *and* still be stuck with a damaged PSP.

PSP Stuck Pixel "Fixer"

If you think the dead pixel checker isn't enough and actually want to try fixing dead pixels yourself, there's an MPEG-4 movie that cycles through all the colors, hoping to eventually get the dead pixels working again. Technically, pixels may not always be "dead"—they can be "stuck" and just need a little tender loving care to get them to work properly again. Some owners have reported success, while others think it's a hoax. Either way, it doesn't hurt to try it (it's just a movie file, not an executable), and if you've had too much to drink, you might actually be entertained.

You can download the PSP stuck pixel "fixer" movie from http://www.psp-vault.com/Article168.psp or from the *Hacking the PSP* Web site (www.hackingpsp.com).

Recovering Data from Memory Sticks

While you probably have your images and music backed up on your computer, you may not have games backed up. Unfortunately, it really sucks when a Memory Stick goes kaput and you don't have a backup. This section goes over some techniques to save the data (although you should have backed up in the first place!).

Here are a few things to try before running recovery utility software:

- Try the Memory Stick in a different memory card reader, different PSP, and so forth. Sometimes it's the reader that's gone bad, not necessarily the media itself.

- Try using a pencil eraser on the gold connectors. Rub the pencil eraser (*not the pencil!*) for a few seconds on the gold connectors, then wipe it off with a paper towel (make sure it doesn't have lotion or any fragrance), and then try reading the Memory Stick again.

- Try inserting the media a few different times. It may not be completely dead, so you may be able to get data off it.

- If you have errors on the media, but it still comes up, try taking files off one at a time, not all at once. This way you can get whatever you can between "working insertions."

If these tips don't work, you can try Memory Stick utility software, such as DataRescue's PhotoRescue (`http://www.datarescue.com/photorescue/`). Note that you will *not* be able to recover the media using recovery software if you can't at least mount the Memory Stick. Chances are at that point the media is lost, and you need to revert to a backup if you have one. It's likely not worth expending the time and money sending the media to a recovery firm to attempt to restore it (if it is, why didn't you have a backup, huh?).

Summary

This chapter went over synchronization software written specifically for the PSP. Unfortunately, Sony didn't include any such software with the PSP, so getting music, movies, and so forth onto your PSP was left up to you. Thanks to dedicated developers, the PSP now has those solutions.

You also learned about the utility software available for the PSP. Just like a computer, utility software is a must for anything that holds your important data. Be it games, music, movies, applications, or something else, it's always good to have a set of tools to prevent or mitigate disaster.

Additional Resources

L ooking for more information about the PSP? Need to find homebrew software? Want cool gadgets and accessories to extend your PSP? This appendix is all about helping you go beyond this book and get everything else you need for your PSP — from news to hardware to programming advice. As I find more resources I will post them on the official *Hacking the PSP* Web site at www.hackingpsp.com.

Enthusiast and News Web Sites

- **Engadget PSP Articles**, www.engadget.com/search/?q=psp&submit=Go
- **GameSpot PSP Site**, www.gamespot.com/psp
- *Gamer's Heaven PSP Magazine*, www.gamersheavenmag.com, a downloadable magazine made specifically for the PSP
- *Hacking the PSP*, www.hackingpsp.com, the official Web site for this book
- **Matt Fazzer**, http://mattfazzer.bl.am, originally a Web site for a PSP emulator, but Sony nixed that project and now it's a PSP news and information site
- **Portagame PSP News Site**, www.portagame.com/psp
- **PSP 411**, www.psp411.com
- *PSP eMag*, http://pspemag.com, a downloadable magazine made specifically for the PSP
- **PSP Hacks**, www.psp-hacks.net
- **PSP Hacks Blog**, psphacks.blogspot.com
- **PSP Home**, www.psphome.com
- **PSP Rumors**, www.psprumors.com
- **PSP Updates**, www.pspupdates.com

Hacker and Software Development Web Sites

- **Lua Player PSP Development Environment**, `www.luaplayer.org`
- **Lua Users Web Site**, `www.lua-users.org`, a community forum and resource site for Lua developers
- **PS2Dev**, `www.ps2dev.org`
- **PS2Dev Programmers Reference**, `http://ps2dev.org/ps2/Technical_ Documentation`
- **PSPBrew**, `http://pspbrew.com`
- **PSP Emulation News**, `http://psp-news.dcemu.co.uk`
- **PSP Hacks**, `www.psp-hacks.net`
- **PSP Newz**, `www.pspnewz.net`
- **PSP Programming Frequently Asked Questions**, `http://wiki.ps2dev.org/ psp:programming_faq`
- **Seamonkey 420**, `http://seamonkey420.tech-recipes.com`

PSP Software Web Sites

- **Browser 2 PSP**, `www.hackingpsp.com`, converts your Firefox or Internet Explorer bookmarks to PSP Web browser bookmarks (written by yours truly)
- **Homebrew PSP Converter** by RnSK Softronics, `http://ipsp.kaisakura.com/ homebrew.php`, converts homebrew applications so they run on the 1.5 firmware PSP using the KXploit method
- **Lua IDE**, `www.gorlice.net.pl/~rybak/luaide`, an IDE (Integrated Development Environment), like Visual Studio and Eclipse, for writing applications in the Lua scripting language
- **MooPS**, `http://seamonkey420.tech-recipes.com/psp/Wipeout_moops .html`, A Wipeout Pure Web browser hack turnkey solution that handles the DNS and Web spoofing automatically
- **iPSP** by RnSK Softronics, `http://ipsp.kaisakura.com`, synchronizes your photos, music, bookmarks, movies, and saved game data between your PSP and your PC or Mac
- **iPSP Movie Link** by RnSK Softronics, `http://ipsp.kaisakura.com/ ipspmovie.php`, enables on-click transfer of Web site movies to your PSP
- **PSP Saved Data Viewer**, `http://samurai.pose.jp/ryn/products.php`, lets you view your saved game data
- **PSP Sync**, `http://samurai.pose.jp/ryn/products.php`, synchronizes your iTunes music collection with your PSP

- **PSP Video 9**, www.pspvideo9.com, video encoding and transfer software

- **PSPWare** by Nullriver Software, http://www.nullriver.com/index/
products/pspware, synchronizes your photos, music, bookmarks, movies, and
saved game data between your PSP and your PC or Mac

- **PSP X Studio**, www.pspxstudio.com, transfers DVDs to the PSP, and emulates
console game systems

PSP Hardware Web Sites

- **Brando**, http://shop.brando.com.hk/solarchargerforpspnds.php, sells a
solar charger for PSP

- **Controlling Your Home With Your PSP**,
www.engadget.com/entry/1234000400040802, a neat project on how to control
your home with your PSP using the PSP Web browser

- **Digital Innovations**, www.digitalinnovations.com, sells UMD cartridge cleaners, glare shields, PSP locking devices (for securing your PSP to a table and so forth),
and UMD drive laser lens cleaners as part of their GameDR series of products

- **Hobby Engineering**, www.hobbyengineering.com/SectionFS.html, sells many
types of solar panels

- **InformIT Article on Adding an External Wireless Antenna**, www.informit.com/
articles/article.asp?p=383849

- **Lik Sang**, www.lik-sang.com, a great online store to find many hard-to-find
accessories for any platform, including the PSP

- **PSP Hardware**, www.psp-hardware.com, sells Memory Stick–to–Memory Stick
Duo adapters

- **PSX Repair**, www.psxrepair.com, sells many products, such as replacement LCD
screens, for PSPs and other Sony game consoles

- **UK Console Repairs**, www.console-repairs.co.uk, also sells replacement
LCD screens

- **Xbox Repair Guide**, www.xboxrepairguide.com, sells replacement PSP motherboards and replacement buttons

PSP Miscellaneous Sites

- **PSP Designer Skins**, http://designerskins.com/Merchant2/merchant
.mvc?page=D/CTGY/PSP, sells "skins" that overlay your PSP to create unique PSP
designs

PSP Game System Emulators

Emulators let you run software for one device on another normally incompatible device. One popular type of emulator is the game system emulator, which lets you run software for one console on another. This has been quite the rage in Xbox hacking circles. Of course, there are other types of emulators, such as Virtual PC (which lets you run PC software on a Macintosh), Bernie to the Rescue (to run Apple IIgs software on a Mac), among many, many others.

If you're looking for game emulators for your PSP, you can check out Table A-1. I won't tell you how to get ROMs, games, or anything illegal, but if you have your own games there are many sites that will tell you have to rip them to files usable in these emulators.

Table A-1   Game emulator sites

System	Emulator	Web Site
Amiga 500	PSP UAE	www.kaillera.com/pspuae/
Apple II, II+, and IIe	Apple II Portable for PSP	www.xboxopensource.com/psp/modules.php?name=News&file=article&sid=7
Atari ST	CaSTaway for PSP	www.codejedi.com
Commodore 64	C64 PSP	http://files.pspupdates.qj.net/cgi-bin/cfiles.cgi?0,0,0,0,60,1510
Chip8	SCHIP8	http://files.pspupdates.com/cgi-bin/cfiles.cgi?0,0,0,0,50,918
Game Boy / Game Boy Color	RIN	http://mirakichi.hp.infoseek.co.jp/software/RIN.html
Original Nintendo Entertainment System (NES)	NesterJ	http://rukapsp.hp.infoseek.co.jp/
Neo Geo	Neo Geo Pocket Emulator	http://www.dcemu.co.uk/vbulletin/showthread.php?t=6077
PC9801-E	Neko Project 2 for PSP	http://sakahi.hp.infoseek.co.jp/
Playstation (original)	PSPSONE	http://files.pspupdates.com/cgi-bin/cfiles.cgi?0,0,0,0,48,807

System	Emulator	Web Site

SCUMM VM	SCUMM-PSP	`http://files.pspupdates.com/`
		`cgi-bin/cfiles`
		`.cgi?0,0,0,0,47,1260`

Sega Master System (the original Sega)	SMS PSP	`http://psp-news.dcemu.co.uk/` `smspsp.shtml`
Super Nintendo (16-bit Nintendo, precursor to Nintendo 64)	SNES9 PSP	`http://psp-news.dcemu.co.uk/` `unofficialsnes9xpsp.shtml`
Wonderswan	pSwan	`http://www.geocities.jp/` `kmg00010/`

ZX Spectrum	PSPectrum	`http://files.pspupdates.com/`
		`cgi-bin/cfiles`
		`.cgi?0,0,0,0,59,1247`

Sony's PSP Web Sites

- **Official Sony PSP Web Site**, `www.yourpsp.com/psp/locale.html`
- **Official Sony PSP Product Web Site**, `www.sony.com/psp`
- **Official Sony PSP Software Update Web Site**, `www.us.playstation.com/psp`
  `.aspx?id=SoftwareUpdate`
- **PSP Connect**, `psp.connect.com`, to get movies and other downloads for the PSP from Sony's official Connect content download service

Sony's PSP Technical Support and Repair

Sony's hotline phone number in the U.S. is 800-345-7669.

PSP Maintenance and Frequently Asked Questions

in this appendix

- ☑ Resolving common PSP problems
- ☑ Dealing with spills
- ☑ Finding out where to store files on a Memory Stick
- ☑ Media playback tips
- ☑ Lots of Q&A

You've got questions, I've got answers. This chapter goes over almost everything you need to know about maintaining your PSP, and gives you answers to common questions. Think of this appendix as your go-to reference when you have an issue with your PSP, or aren't sure about something. Chances are, the questions and the answers are here, including references to any related chapters that will help you in more detail. If you have a question that isn't answered here, please post it to the official *Hacking the PSP* Web site at www.hackingpsp.com and I'll quickly post the answer.

UMD Eject Latch Is Stuck or Stops Working

If your UMD latch is stuck or has stopped working, try jiggling it loose again. If that doesn't work, see if you can get the door open and then move the spring back into place by turning the PSP upside down and using a small precision screwdriver just under the eject latch. If that doesn't work, and you don't mind voiding your warranty, remove the cover to your PSP and move the spring back into place. Otherwise, send the PSP in for repair.

PSP Won't Power On

If your PSP won't turn on, check to make sure your battery is charged. Next, try removing the battery for 10 seconds and then replacing it. If that doesn't work, try removing the battery and plugging in the power supply. If that works, check the battery for a short, making sure no wires are bent on the battery, and that no wires are bent on the connector the battery plugs into. If no wires are bent, place the battery in and let it charge.

Power supplies do go bad over time, so check one of your friends' PSP power supplies, or go to a store and try theirs. Many Sony power supplies will work with your PSP — get one that takes 5V and has the positive pole on the inside. Most chargers are like this — look at the circular dot on the power supply with the + and -, and make sure the + is on the inside circle, as shown in Figure B-1.

FIGURE B-1: Determining the polarity of a power supply

If none of this works, try removing the battery for a day and let your PSP sit. Then, try powering the unit on with just the power supply and see if it turns on. If it turns on, place the battery in and charge it. If the battery won't charge or the unit immediately shuts off, you'll have to replace your battery. If none of these options work, it's likely that you need to send your PSP in for repair (again, those extended warranties really come in handy here).

Stuck or Dead Pixels

Dead pixels and stuck pixels have consistently plagued the PSP. In the Japanese, then the U.S. launch, and even the European launch, there have been issues. Dead pixels are elements on your PSP's screen that just won't light up — they're black, lifeless dots on your screen. Stuck pixels, on the other hand, are elements on the PSP screen that won't change color, are slow to change color, or intermittently work. There isn't much you can do about dead pixels other than send the unit back to Sony. You can try taking the unit apart and coaxing the screen a bit, but that likely won't help. Stuck pixels are something you can actually try to do something about. In Chapter 23, "Synchronization and Utility Software," I discuss a *Stuck Pixel Fixer*, a video that cycles through primary colors over and over again, hoping to coax stuck pixels out of their sticky state. Many PSP owners have reported success, so see how it works for you.

Lost Files on Your Memory Stick

While you probably aren't storing anything on your Memory Stick you don't already have on your computer, there's a possibility you are. So, what happens if the Memory Stick starts to go bad? Never fear, not all is lost. Many programs are available on the Internet that recover files from media that's gone bad. Go to www.download.com and search for **memory stick recovery** and a plethora of options appear. Before running these programs, and before inserting a bad Memory Stick into a Memory Stick reader, or sharing it over your PSP's USB connection, it's best to enable the write-protect switch on the Memory Stick. The first rule of recovery — don't mess with the data until you've recovered it — is very important!

Note As Sony offers more Internet-based media capabilities to the PSP, such as music and video you can purchase over any Internet connection, or you download documents from home via the PSP's Web browser to edit on your PC, you very well may have documents you need. It's always a good idea to back these documents up if you can. It is possible that Sony would prevent you from copying the files back from your Memory Stick, but it's unlikely they wouldn't offer a utility to back up the media. Another rule of thumb: if you're going to work on a file on a Memory Stick, it's best to copy the file to your computer first, edit it, then copy it back. Then you don't have to worry about your Memory Stick going bad after many rewrites, or accidentally losing data if you pull the Memory Stick out before you save.

Can't See Other PSPs When Playing Multiplayer

If you can't see other PSPs when you attempt to join a multiplayer game, make sure all your PSPs are using Ad Hoc Mode for wireless networking. Obviously, you should also make sure your wireless switch is in the On position. If you're still having trouble, it's possible your PSP's wireless daughtercard has come loose from the motherboard. If you're using over-the-Internet gaming (discussed on the official *Hacking the PSP* Web site), make sure the connection is properly configured and connected.

Can't Play Audio or Music Files

First and foremost, make sure your music files are MP3, ATRAC3+, WAV, or MPEG-4 audio files. MPEG-4 audio files only play on PSPs with firmware version 2.0 (a.k.a. System Update 2.0) or higher. iTunes Music Store purchased MPEG-4 files, which end with .m4p, will not play on the PSP, nor will Windows Media Audio (.wma) files.

Table B-1 lists the file extensions you should use for audio files on the PSP.

Table B-1	File extensions for audio
Audio Format	File Extension
MP3	.mp3 (the PSP can handle MP3s up to 1500 kilobits/second)
MPEG-4	.mp4 (you can safely rename iTunes .m4a files to .mp4)
ATRAC3+	.at3
WAV	.wav (not all WAV formats will play — MP3 is the most universal of the playback formats compatible with the PSP)

Removing Screen Scratches

There are solutions out there to remove scratches from your PSPs display cover. One to try is Displex Display Polish, which you can use with a silver polishing towel to remove the scratches from your screen. Another product is Plexus Plastic Cleaner and Polish. While I haven't had a lot of scratches on my PSP because I keep it in its case when not in use, I've heard about successes with even deep scratches with the Displex product. There also are other screen cleaners on the market that are simple wipes that may work just fine in removing light scratches. Your best bet, however, is to have a case and a screen protector, such as the Pelikan Screen Guards, so the scratches never get there in the first place.

UMDs Won't Play Anymore

If your UMDs won't play anymore, there are a few items to check. The first item is to make sure your UMDs are spinning. You should hear the UMD spin up when you turn on the PSP from an off state (not sleep mode). If you can't hear it, then your motor may be bad. Make sure your power supply is plugged in when you try this. If your power supply is plugged in, try using a friend's power supply — yours may have gone bad, or may not be providing enough amperage to start the drive motor. If your drive is spinning up, your lens may have gunk on it. There may be UMD lens cleaning utilities out there for a few bucks, or you can find a VHS head cleaning kit at Radio Shack with the small plastic sticks and chamois heads, and pick up some 92%+ isopropyl rubbing alcohol (make sure it's only rubbing alcohol— no moisturizers). Dip the tip of the cleaning stick into the rubbing alcohol and push the head against the sides of the plastic container to remove excess alcohol. Then *gently* slide the tip against your optical lens to clean it. Only do this a couple, maybe three times, back and forth, then let it dry thoroughly, about 10 minutes or so, and try your UMD again. If that doesn't work, you may need to take the unit in for repair.

Another product to try is the GameDR Motorized UMD Cartridge Cleaner from Digital Innovations, available at www.digitalinnovations.com. I have seen their products at Fry's, but nowhere else as of yet. Note that their Web site makes it hard to find the GameDR products, but they're there!

Spilled Water on Your PSP

If you happen to spill water on your PSP, all is not lost. Immediately remove the battery to help prevent shorting the electronics. Also, remove any UMD you have in there, as well as any Memory Sticks. Using a towel, sop up all the water on the device— dabbing the water to absorb it, not swishing it around where it can get into more nooks and crannies.

Now put the towel on a flat surface. If it has a rough and a smooth side, put the rough side up. Place your PSP on a dry section of the towel and let it sit there for an hour, absorbing any moisture that drips out. After the hour has elapsed, place the PSP face-up on a dry section of the towel. Let it sit for a couple of days, letting the water evaporate. Don't let it sit in a bathroom where you take showers, as the moisture in the air will counteract your work. After a few days, your PSP's circuit board should be dry enough to start up again. Test this by using your battery and see if the unit turns on— don't use the power supply. If it still doesn't turn on, give it a few more days and try again. If it still doesn't start, you can try your power supply (maybe your battery was dead or close to dead). If that doesn't work, contact Sony to schedule a warranty repair or replacement— just tell them it doesn't work anymore (don't tell them you dumped water on it). By the way, this is where those extended warranties you can buy at stores really come in handy.

Spilled Sticky Stuff on Your PSP

If you happen to spill sticky stuff on your PSP, like Red Bull or cola, all is not lost. Immediately remove the battery to help prevent shorting the electronics. Also, remove any UMD you have in there, as well as any Memory Sticks. Using a towel, sop up all the liquid on the device— dabbing the water to absorb it, not swishing it around where it can get into more nooks and crannies. Also, get that gook off your UMD, Memory Stick, and battery if it's on them, too.

Now put the towel on a flat surface. If it has a rough and a smooth side, put the rough side up. Place your PSP on a dry section of the towel. Get some isopropyl rubbing alcohol — the kind without any moisturizers or added ingredients other than water as a buffer — and dab a cotton swab into the rubbing alcohol. Rub the swab against your PSP — this breaks apart the goo. You're going to need a few cotton balls.

Get *everything* with the rubbing alcohol. Hopefully, none of the goo got inside your PSP, or you'll have to take apart your PSP to get it out. If you moved fast enough, the goo should not have gotten into any nooks or crannies.

After you've rubbed everything down, turn your PSP upside down for an hour, so any sugary stuff can fall out. If any got in your PSP, it's better that it get sticky on the inside of the buttons, rather than on the motherboard or over the metal and plastic contacts your buttons use. Then, after an hour, flip the PSP over and place it on a dry section of the towel and use the cotton swab again to get any excess goo that came through. Then, leave the PSP there to dry for a few days — around two to three should do it.

After the drying period has elapsed, your PSP's circuit board should be dry enough to start up again. Test this by using your battery and see if the unit turns on — don't use the power supply. If it still doesn't turn on, give it a few more days and try again. If it still doesn't start, you can try your power supply (maybe your battery was dead or close to dead). If any of your buttons stick, you may need to press the buttons repeatedly for a while to unstick them. You can also take the cover of the PSP off and, with the battery out and power supply unplugged, use the rubbing alcohol, a Q-tip, and gentleness to remove gooey stuff from the buttons. (Chapter 4 goes over how to take apart your PSP.) I do not suggest going beyond removing the cover, as the PSP's electronic connections aren't terribly flexible.

If none of the aforementioned options succeeds, contact Sony to schedule a warranty repair or replacement — just tell them it doesn't work anymore (don't tell them you dumped goo on it). This is another instance where those extended warranties you can buy at stores really come in handy.

Where Can I Find Replacement Parts?

Other than Sony, who might not sell you all the parts you need in the first place, www .XBoxRepairGuide.com sells replacement LCD screens, motherboards, and laser optical units for the PSP. See Appendix A for additional hardware sites.

Can't Beam Pictures between PSPs

If you're trying to beam pictures or content between two DVDs and the two units aren't seeing each other, make sure there are no items in the way of the PSPs. Infrared is a line-of-sight technology, so if there is *anything* in the way of the beam, it won't work. The PSP's infrared port is located on the top of the device next to the left trigger button. The beam also will not work very well outside in bright sunlight, so make sure you are in a shaded area or indoors to guarantee transmission.

Can't Find the Web Browser

If you are looking for the built-in PSP Web browser, press ⬤ to open the PSP Navigator, and then scroll all the way to the right to INTERNET. You should see the Browser option. If that's not there, check your firmware version — you need System Version 2.0 (firmware version 2.0) or later to use the built-in Web browser. Chapter 6 discusses how to access and use the official Sony PSP Web browser, as well as a hack using the game Wipeout Pure and its built-in Web browser for those who don't want to update to firmware 2.0.

Can't Turn Screen Back On

If you can't see what's on your screen, it's possible you have turned it off. Hold down the display button on the bottom of the PSP screen for a few seconds and the screen should come back on. If not, try plugging in your power supply — your battery may be too low. You may also need to power off your PSP and reset it due to a software glitch — hold the power button up for five seconds and your PSP will turn off. Then press up one more time to turn it back on and you should see the PSP logo.

If you hear the sound and still don't see the PSP logo or anything on your screen, your backlight may have gone bad, or your PSP display cable may have come loose. If your PSP is still under warranty, it's best to send it to Sony for repair. Of course, if you have a 1.5 or 1.0 firmware PSP, the unit will probably come back as a firmware 2.0 or higher PSP, disabling your ability to run homebrew applications. Of course, if it's out of warranty or you want to double-check the connectors and likely void your warranty in the process, follow the instructions in Chapter 4 to take apart your PSP and double-check your connectors.

Can't Turn the Sound Back On

If your sound isn't playing, make sure it isn't muted. Hold down the sound button for 5 seconds. Then press the volume up button until the bars go all the way to the right. If that doesn't work, something else is wrong with your PSP. Double-check the headphone jack to make sure none of its connectors are shorted and that there are no metal filings or bent wires in there. If any wires are bent, try to bend them back into place and see if that fixes the problem. If none of that works, try turning the PSP completely off by removing the battery for 10 seconds, then placing the battery back in and trying the volume controls again. Your PSP makes a startup sound — you should be able to hear it when it boots.

Can't Change the Sound Equalizer Settings

The PSP *does* have various sound settings, like Jazz, Rock, and so forth. However, these settings are only available when something is plugged into the headphone port, such as, well, headphones, speakers, and the like. There is no other way to access these settings. Of course, the PSP's speakers are so small that the equalizer settings likely wouldn't make a difference in their quality.

Memory Stick Door Won't Close

If your Memory Stick door won't close, don't push hard or you'll break the tab, if it isn't broken already. The door's plastic is poorly constructed, so it's common for the door to break. The PSP will still work with the door open, or if it's gone for that matter. You may want to contact Sony for a replacement door, which they will likely send you. Don't send your PSP in just for the door, though—it's not worth the shipping costs, and it's easier just to put some black electrical tape on there if you simply can't live without the door.

Restarting the PSP

The easiest way to restart your PSP is to hold the power button up for 5 seconds, and then let go. Then turn your PSP on again and it will start up anew. No, you won't lose any settings. If the power switch doesn't kill the power, then remove the battery for 10 seconds and insert it again. Turn your PSP on and it should start normally. Note that with PSP firmware 2.0, if a UMD is in the drive when you turn on the device, that UMD will start. If you don't want the UMD to start when you turn on the PSP, eject it until your PSP gets to the PSP Navigator menu.

Losing Your Place in the Game
When You Turn the PSP Off

This usually happens because you're holding the power button up for a few seconds instead of just pushing it up and letting go. Pushing up and letting go puts the PSP in "sleep" mode, enabling you to resume your game from where you left off. Holding the button up turns the PSP all the way off, hence you lose your place. Note that sleep mode uses your battery more quickly, so if you keep the device in sleep mode for too long, eventually the battery will deplete and you'll lose your place anyway—so get it to a charger if you're going to leave it sleeping for a long time!

Can't Install Firmware Update over Wireless

If you can't update your firmware over a wireless Internet connection (you don't have one, it isn't working, and so forth), you can download the update from Sony's Web site at http://sony.com/PSP and copy it to a Memory Stick through USB mode or via a Memory Stick reader in your PC. Copy the file to the PSP \ GAME \ UPDATE directory and launch it by opening the PSP Navigator and selecting the Game menu, then Memory Stick, then the Update program. If those folders don't exist, create the PSP folder, then open it and create the GAME folder, then open that and create the UPDATE folder.

How Do I Protect My UMDs?

Sony leaves a window open on UMDs for the laser to read the disc. Unfortunately, it's easy to get your fingerprints on the UMD disc surface because the opening is so big. Almost any game store will sell you UMD covers, which are simple cases you can easily slide your UMDs into, and they protect your UMDs while they're stored. Please keep in mind that it's best to hold UMDs by the edges, just like CDs, to minimize the possibility of getting fingerprints on them when they're out of their cases or out of the PSP.

How Do I Protect My PSP?

The easiest way to protect your PSP is to get a case. I recommend Logitech's Playgear Pocket because it's lightweight, looks great, and has openings for everything except the USB port (although you can use a Dremel to make a hole in the case to take care of that little issue).

How Do I Change My Nickname?

Your PSP nickname identifies your PSP to other PSPs, so you may at times want to change it when playing multiplayer games. To change your nickname, open the PSP Navigator (press HOME if you're in a game, and Yes to quit the game), then scroll left to Settings, then System Settings, and then press ⊗ on Nickname. Change your nickname, then select Enter, and your new nickname will be saved.

Where Do I Check the Firmware Version?

To check your firmware, or system software, version, use your PSP Navigator (press HOME if you're in a game, and Yes to quit the game) and scroll left to Settings. Then select System Settings, then System Information and press ⊗. Your firmware version is listed to the right of System Software. You can check battery information from the same menu, too. Just select Battery Information instead of System Information.

Should I Update My Firmware?

Firmware upgrades can provide a number of benefits, such as new features, better performance, and so forth. However, the first update from Sony, version 1.5, simply disabled the ability to run homebrew applications. Versions 1.51 and 1.52 further locked-down the device from homebrew applications. It wasn't until Version 2.0 that Sony introduced new features: a Web browser, PNG, GIF, BMP, and TIFF picture support, MPEG-4 and WAV audio support, and a few operating system changes. Of course, 2.0 also locked the device down even further. So 2.0 was the first useful update, but also disabled one of the hottest features in Japan: the ability to run applications written by those who love the machine. So, if you have a firmware 1.0 or 1.5 PSP, you only use your PSP for games, and you want to run homebrew applications, stay with the 1.0 or 1.5 PSP. You can use the WAB Version Changer program (see Appendix A for the download location) to trick your PSP into running UMDs that "require" firmware 2.0. However, if you have 1.51 or greater, you can't run homebrew anyway, and you might as well upgrade to 2.0. Future versions, however, may not be worth the upgrade. It's really a personal decision, depending on what kind of gamer and hacker you are.

What Firmware Versions Support Which Features?

Chapter 1, "Introduction," goes over the different firmware features.

Do Any Games Require Certain Firmware Versions?

Some games require firmware 1.5 or higher, while some require 1.51, 1.52, or 2.0. If you have a 1.0 or 1.5 PSP, you can use the WAB Firmware Changer (see Appendix A for the download location) to trick your PSP into thinking it's running a later firmware version so the games will run. It is likely that Sony's own titles will require newer firmware versions, because Sony (unfortunately) wants to lock-down the PSP as much as it can. However, other game manufacturers likely won't require the updating, as requiring certain firmware updates limits the sales market scope. As long as you have WAB Version Changer, or a firmware 2.0 PSP, you likely won't need to update your PSP to run any games, unless they require features of newer firmware revisions.

How Do I Back Up My Games?

Use a program like iPSP or PSPWare to automatically back up your games. You also can simply copy the PSP / SAVEDATA folder on your Memory Stick to a folder on your hard drive.

How Do I Restore My Games?

Simply copy the game-save data from the appropriate folder in the SAVEDATA directory you've backed up back to your PSP. iPSP and PSPWare make this process easier.

When Videos Copied Over Don't Show Up

Make sure your videos are encoded in MPEG-4. The free program, PSP Video 9, can take care of the encoding and follow-up transfer to your PSP. PSP Video 9's author gladly accepts donations to his cause, so please give him some money if you find the product useful (which you will). If you have encoded the video files yourself and they're not showing up after placing them in the MP_ROOT \ 100MNV01 folder, make sure they have been named using the following naming convention: M4VXXXXX.mp4, where XXXXX is any number, such as 00000 or 42424. Also, make sure you don't put more than one folder level in the 100MNV01 folder, such as a Family Guy folder in a TV Shows folder. Your PSP supports only one folder level for any media type, even though your PC or Mac allows you to create virtually unlimited subfolders.

What Do the Lights on My PSP Mean?

Table B-2 will help you understand what the lights on your PSP mean.

Table B-2	PSP Lights	
Light	**Color**	**What It Means**
Power	Green, solid	Your PSP is powered on and running.
Power	Orange, solid	Your battery is charging.
Power	Orange, blinking	If the PSP is on, it means your battery is running low. If your PSP isn't turning on, it's because you're not providing enough power to turn on the device.
Memory Stick	Orange, flashing	The Memory Stick is being accessed.
Wireless	Green, flashing	The wireless network is being accessed.
Wireless	Green, solid	The wireless network is being scanned.

How Do I Get PSP Games Cheap?

If you haven't done so already, get a Game Stop club membership at a Game Stop store near you. They give you a 10% discount on used games and accessories, including PSP games and accessories, which can be quite a savings. You can also find great deals on eBay. If there is a computer user group in town, check to see if they have discount programs for local stores, netting you even more savings. Some online stores may sell games for less or have game clubs similar to Game Stop that offer similar benefits. Just *please*, don't pirate games.

Where Can I Find Import Games?

eBay is the best place to look for these, but Fry's Electronics sometimes carries imported PSP games (for a premium, of course). Game Stop may be able to special order any games you like. The online route is often the best choice.

Where Should Files Be Stored on the Memory Stick?

Table B-3 shows where files are stored on the PSP.

Table B-3   File storage

Media Type	Location
Video	MP_ROOT \ 100MNV01
Audio	PSP \ MUSIC
Photos	PSP \ PHOTO
Games	PSP \ GAME
Saved games	PSP \ SAVEDATA
Web browser data and bookmarks	PSP \ SYSTEM \ BROWSER

Note I have placed spaces between the slashes in the table for readability purposes only. You should remove the spaces when entering any of the above folder paths.

How Large of a Memory Stick Will the PSP Accept?

The last I checked, the PSP was capable of supporting at least 4GB Memory Sticks. However, this may change as new firmware versions come out. Because there was nothing larger than 2GB available at the time I wrote this book, I didn't have a chance to buy and test the 4GB models coming out.

Datel sells a 3600 mAh battery (twice the PSP's standard battery capacity) with a 4GB micro hard drive built-in, so you can get extended playtime *and* incredible storage capacity. Check it out at www.lik-sang.com/info.php?products_id=7825.

How Do I Reduce Glare from My PSP Screen?

The easiest method is to play indoors or at night. All kidding aside, get a case — it will block the sun. Also, get a Screen Guard from Pelikan Products — their screen guards protect the PSP screen from scratches and reduce glare at the same time. Make sure your PSP screen is clean before applying the protective film.

How Do I Clean My PSP Screen?

The right way to clean the screen is to spray some Windex or similar glass cleaner on a paper towel and then wipe the screen clean. Repeat that again and then make sure the display is dry. This same method applies to laptop screens, television screens, and more. It's generally not a good idea to mist the screen directly, as the solution can get into crevices and short circuits, which is never a good thing.

Can I Get the Equivalent of a Dual Shock Controller on My PSP?

If you are looking for comfortable hand-grips for the PSP, a Hong-Kong company makes a product called Portable Grip for PSP. You can find the product on eBay — simply search for **handy joypad grip PSP**, **portable grip psp**, or **dual shock psp**.

There was also a Dual Shock hack on the PSP Updates Web site, www.pspupdates.com, that involved using the D-Pad from an old Nintendo controller, and placing it over the shape buttons on the PSP, but the article appears to have fallen off their Web site. If I can find it, I will post it to the official *Hacking the PSP* Web site.

What Kind of USB Port Do I Need to Connect My Computer to My PSP?

You need at least a USB 1.1 port to use your PSP. However, it's better to have a USB 2.0 (also called "High Speed USB") port, as it transfers data at up to 480 megabits/second, whereas USB 1.1 has a maximum of 11 megabits/second. USB 2.0 ports can also charge your PSP while it's connected, albeit slowly.

Are There Any Viruses for the PSP?

While I was writing this book, only one "virus" was discovered for the PSP. Apparently, a malicious programmer wrote a malware masquerading as a PSP downgrading utility that took advantage of a buffer overflow and then wiped out critical system files on the PSP. The programmer called the malware the PSP Team Downgrader, but it wasn't really from the PSP Team that made the *working* PSP downgrading hack. As with any computer, make sure that you only run software from trusted sources and that you verify items are really what they seem.

Index

Continued

How to take it to the Extreme.

If you enjoyed this book, there are many others like it for you. From *Podcasting* to *Hacking Firefox*, ExtremeTech books can fulfill your urge to hack, tweak and modify, providing the tech tips and tricks readers need to get the most out of their hi-tech lives.